Reinventing the Alliance:
U.S.-Japan Security Partnership in an Era of Change

REINVENTING THE ALLIANCE: U.S.–JAPAN SECURITY PARTNERSHIP IN AN ERA OF CHANGE

EDITED BY
G. JOHN IKENBERRY
AND
TAKASHI INOGUCHI

palgrave
macmillan

REINVENTING THE ALLIANCE
© G. John Ikenberry and Takashi Inoguchi, 2003

First published 2003 by
PALGRAVE MACMILLAN™
175 Fifth Avenue, New York, N.Y. 10010 and
Houndmills, Basingstoke, Hampshire, England RG21 6XS
Companies and representatives throughout the world

PALGRAVE MACMILLAN is the global academic imprint of the Palgrave Macmillan division of St. Martin's Press, LLC and of Palgrave Macmillan Ltd. Macmillan® is a registered trademark in the United States, United Kingdom and other countries. Palgrave is a registered trademark in the European Union and other countries.

ISBN 1–4039–6315–0 hardback

Library of Congress Cataloging-in-Publication Data
    Reinventing the alliance: U.S.–Japan security partnership in an era of change/edited by G. John Ikenberry and Takashi Inoguchi.
        p. cm.
    ISBN 1–4039–6315–0
        1. United States—Foreign relations—Japan,
2. Japan—Foreign relations—United States. 3. United
States—Foreign relations—1989– 4. National security–United
States. 5. National security—Japan. 6. United States—Military
relations—Japan. 7. Japan—Military relations—United States.
8. National security–Asia. I. Ikenberry, G. John II. Inoguchi, Takashi.

E183.8.J3R386 2003
355'.031'09730952—dc21   2003049788

A catalogue record for this book is available from the British Library.

Design by Newgen Imaging Systems (P) Ltd., Chennai, India.

First edition: December, 2003
10 9 8 7 6 5 4 3 2 1

Printed in the United States of America.

Dedicated to our Paulista partners, Lidia Reiko and Kuniko

Contents

Acknowledgments

In an era when a series of breathtaking events are taking place, sharing risks has become an important element of social life. In this regard we would like to express our deep gratitude to the United States–Japan Foundation, which shared with us our norms and risks and supported the project from which this volume has emerged. George Packard, its President; Takeo Takuma, its Tokyo office director, and James Schoff, its New York office director; and all including those on the governing board, especially Yotaro Kobayashi, Shinji Fukukawa, Gerald Curtis, and Yusuke Saraye, have been unfailingly helpful to us. The University of Tokyo and its Institute of Oriental Culture have been quite generous in processing all the necessary documents and transactions in the process of carrying out the project. Special thanks go to Ms. Kimiko Goko and Mr. Ken Firmalino. Georgetown University has been no less helpful in making its facilities available. We would like also to acknowledge our gratitude to those who gave us luncheon speeches in our conferences on the United States–Japan alliance as seen from inside: Hitoshi Tanaka, then at the North American Bureau, Ministry of Foreign Affairs, now Director-General of the Asia-Pacific Bureau, Ministry of Foreign Affairs, and Michael Green, Director of the Japan Office at the National Security Council.

LIST OF CONTRIBUTORS

Thomas Berger received his Ph.D. at MIT and is an Associate Professor in the Department of International Relations at Boston University.

Victor Cha, with his Ph.D. from Columbia University, is Associate Professor of Government and D.S. Song-Korea Chair in Korean Studies in the Edmund Walsh School of Foreign Service at Georgetown University.

Akiko Fukushima, with her Ph.D. from Osaka University, is a director of policy studies and senior fellow of the National Institute of Research Advancement, Tokyo, with her recent books being *Japanese Foreign Policy: A Logic of Multilateralism* and *Lexicon of Asia-Pacific Security Discourse.*

G. John Ikenberry received his Ph.D. from the University of Chicago and is the Peter F. Krogh Professor of Geopolitics and Global Justice at Georgetown University.

Takashi Inoguchi, with Ph.D. from MIT, and former Assistant Secretary General of the United Nations, is professor of political science at the Institute of Oriental Culture, University of Tokyo, with his latest publications including *Japan's Asian Policy, American Democracy Promotion,* and *Japanese Foreign Policy.*

Matake Kamiya, a graduate of Tokyo and Columbia Universities, is associate professor of international relations at the National Defense Academy of Japan, with his latest publication including "Nuclear Japan: Oxymoron or Coming Soon?" *The Western Quarterly,* 26:1 (Winter 2002–03).

Michael Mastanduno, with his Ph.D. from Princeton University, is Nelson A. Rockefeller Professor of Government at Dartmouth College.

Michael O'Hanlon received his Ph.D. from Princeton University and is a Senior Fellow at the Brookings Institution.

Stephen John Stedman is Senior Fellow and Acting Co-Director of the Center for International Security and Cooperation at Stanford University.

Jitsuo Tsuchiyama, with his Ph.D. from the University of Maryland, is professor of international relations at Aoyama Gakuin University, Tokyo, with his latest publications being *Global Governance*.

Umemoto Tetsuya, with his Ph.D. from Princeton University, is professor of international relations at Shizuoka Kenritsu University, with his latest publication being *Defense Policy of the Bush Administration* (2002), for which he was a coeditor.

LIST OF ABBREVIATIONS

ABM: Anti-Ballistic Missile
ACSA: Acquisition and Cross-Servicing Agreement
ANZUS: Australia, New Zealand and United States Treaty
ARF: ASEAN Regional Forum
ASEAN PMC: ASEAN Post Ministerial Conference
ASEAN: Association of Southeast Asian Nations
CSCAP: Council for Security Cooperation in the Asia Pacific
CSCE: Conference for Security and Cooperation in Europe
CTBT: Comprehensive Test Ban Treaty
DPRK: Democratic People's Republic of Korea
EASI: East Asian Strategic Initiatives
EASR: East Asian Strategic Review
EU: European Union
HNS: Host Nation Support
MSDS: Multilateral Security Dialogues
NATO: North Atlantic Treaty Organization
NDPO: National Defense Program Outline
NEACD: Northeast Asia Cooperation Dialogue
NMD: National Missile Defense
NTW: Navy Theater Wide
OSCE: Organization for Security and Cooperation in Europe
PACOM: Pacific Command
PKO: Peacekeeping Operations
POMUS: Pre-positioning of Oversea Material Configurated to Unit Sets
PRC: People's Republic of China
RMA: Revolution in Military Affairs
ROK: Republic of Korea
SACO: Special Action Committee on Okinawa
SDF: Self Defense Forces
SEATO: Southeast Asia Treaty Organization
TCOG: Trilateral Coordination and Oversight Groups
UN: United Nations
WMD: Weapons of Mass Destruction

CHAPTER 1

INTRODUCTION

G. John Ikenberry and Takashi Inoguchi

The U.S.–Japan alliance is the most important pillar of security and political order in the Asia Pacific but it is increasingly subject to strains between the two countries and from a rapidly transforming region. Japan is in the process of redefining its political and security identity in the region and the United States is showing ambivalence about regional leadership. Added to this, a wide assortment of new challenges to regional security—such as arms proliferation, regional missile defense, unstable financial flows, rogue states, terrorism, and the growing prominence of China—are forcing the U.S.–Japan alliance to rethink its goals. The U.S.–Japan security partnership is 50 years old. If the alliance is to remain relevant to regional security for another 50 years, it will need to be renewed, redefined, and reconciled with the wider region.

This project brings together American and Japanese specialists to examine the relationship between the U.S.–Japan alliance and the wider regional environment. We pose a variety of questions. Can the alliance be preserved in a way that will allow it to continue to play a stabilizing role in East Asia but also accommodate—and even foster—wider multilateral security cooperation? What are the constraints and opportunities on the alliance as it attempts to operate more fully within the Asia Pacific region? These constraints and opportunities might include historical legacies, technological innovations, constitutional prohibitions, and shifting domestic political opinion. Can the domestic support for the alliance in both Japan and the United States be sustained in this period of regional transition? Security relations in the region will increasingly be multitrack and multilevel. The central question is whether and how the bilateral alliance can evolve and remain at the core of the region's security order.

This group study advances a series of conclusions and recommendations for U.S. and Japanese leaders.

1   First, the bilateral alliance is the most critical element ensuring regional security and order in East Asia. There are no obvious alternatives to the alliance system on the horizon that are sufficiently credible and operable. Alternative models of regional security do exist and they should continue to be explored and debated. But the preconditions for a stable regional multilateral security order are not yet in place nor will they be so for several decades.

2   Second, the U.S.–Japan alliance has been poorly defined and defended in recent years. The alliance is more than simply a military pact aimed at protecting the two countries from an external threat. The alliance is also a political partnership that provides institutional mechanisms that support a stable relationship between the countries inside the alliance. We argue that even if all the external threats in the region were to disappear, the alliance would still be important for regulating relations between the United States and Japan—the two largest economies in the world. Alliances are important mechanisms for establishing restraints and commitments on the use of power. The alliance projects American power into Asia but it also makes that power more predictable and reliable. The alliance allows Japan to solve its security problems without becoming a militarized Great Power and this stabilizes regional relations. The multifaceted roles of the alliance must be acknowledged and invoked in the explanation of the grand strategic role and value of the alliance.

3   Third, the alliance will not survive unless it evolves. Both U.S. and Japanese elites realize that Japan will need to rethink its regional security presence—to play a more active role in ensuring regional peace and security. How it does this is both tricky and critical. It will need to redefine its security identity in a way that allows it to be a more active state but not do it in a way that triggers regional instabilities and arms races. The most important next step in evolving Japan's regional security involvement is in UN-sponsored regional peacekeeping operations. The expansion of Japan's security role take place within agreed upon regional multilateral arrangements.

4   Fourth, it is useful to have a model of the future U.S.–Japan partnership. The Armitage Report of autumn 2000 argued that the

U.S.–British partnership was the best model for guiding the evolution of the U.S.–Japan relationship. We propose that the U.S.–German relationship is a better model. Germany is emerging from its World War II constraints to play a more active role in the region. The recent participation of Germany in the NATO bombing of Serbia, for example, allowed the world to glimpse the gradual expansion of Germany military responsibilities. But Germany has simultaneously signaled its willingness to work within regional multilateral frameworks, thereby providing stabilizing reassurances to neighboring countries. This is a model that the United States and Japan should look to in defining the direction of change.

5   Fifth, the rise of multilateral dialogues in the Asia Pacific are not a threat to but an opportunity for the alliance. These dialogues—such as the ASEAN Regional Forum—are an important supplement to the alliance. They provide institutional avenues for Japan to diversify its regional participation and strengthen its overall security identity. They provide opportunities for the United States to engage other regional players without throwing into question the core bilateral alliance partnerships.

6   Sixth, a variety of new issues are emerging—theater missile defense, peace keeping, revolutions in military technology—that will test old security patterns in the region. The United States and Japan should get "out ahead of the curve" on these issues and find ways to make them work for—rather than against—desired security partnerships.

In this introduction we expand on the problems and opportunities that confront the U.S.–Japan alliance in the decade ahead. We begin by looking at the current regional situation and the new challenges that are emerging. We turn next to the ideas and strategies that inform U.S. and Japanese foreign policy—toward each other and the region. After that, we turn to a discussion of the chapters in this volume and relate them to the broad themes and recommendations that we have just introduced.

One set of chapters looks at the problem from conceptual and historical angles. Chapters 2 and 3 look at the broad historical/conceptual possibilities for regional security (Mastanduno and Tsuchiyama). Chapter 4 looks at the historical legacies—regionally and within Japan itself—that shape and constrain Japan's role in the region (Berger). A second set of chapters looks more directly at the relations between security bilateralism and security multilateralism. Chapters 5 and 6 look at the U.S.–Japan alliance and explore how alliance reform can be made complimentary with regional multilateral security cooperation (Kamiya and Smith). Two additional chapters look at the same question from the perspective of the region—again asking the question about the constraints and opportunities for the bilateral alliance to mesh with regional security cooperation (see chapter 7 by Cha). A third set of chapters looks at regional function issues and they ask the question: how can Japan and the United States find ways to expand and deepen their cooperation in these new areas? Chapter 8 looks at the revolution in military affairs and the implications for alliance cooperation (O'Hanlon) and Chapter 9 looks at theater missile defense (Umemoto). Chapters 10 and 11 look at regional peacemaking and peacekeeping and how Japan and the United States might expand their cooperation with the framework of UN functional duties (Stedman and Fukushima).

Regional Security and Alliance Cooperation

The Asia-Pacific is one of the most dynamic and potentially unstable regions in the world today. The region encompasses a diverse mixture of rival Great Powers, thorny territorial disputes, unresolved historical memories, competing political ideologies, painful economic transitions, and shifting military balances. The unfolding relations between Japan, the United States, China, Russia, North and South Korea, Taiwan, and Southeast Asia would be a challenge to manage even if the region had well-established governance institutions. But these new and unsettling developments confront the U.S.–Japan alliance at a time when the alliance itself is under strain. To reinvigorate the alliance and at the same time respond to the rising demand for greater security governance in the region is a major challenge.[1]

The U.S.–Japan alliance grew out of postwar and Cold War circumstances, but even in the midst of dramatic global and regional change the alliance remains the most stable and coherent mechanism for the management of regional security order.[2] It is not surprising that in a recent discussion of the Asian financial crisis, Yoichi Funabashi argued that the most important source of stability in the region is the bilateral security pact.[3] But a stable status quo is not likely. The region is becoming increasingly unsettled by shifting economic, political, and technological developments. Arms proliferation, controversies over humanitarian intervention, the roller coaster ride of capital and trade flows, and the rising power of China are critical elements in the transformation of the region and make the tackling of regional security problems more difficult.

These new demands for regional security governance are emerging precisely at a time when the U.S.–Japan alliance is entering a new era of reconsideration. Japan is undergoing a national process of rethinking about its security, its reliance on the United States, and the specifics of the American military presence in Okinawa. Japan has slowly diversified its security contacts in the region and is involved in an array of annual and ad hoc ministerial talks.[4]

The United States is also starting to think more broadly about regional security. The United States and China have recently resumed high-level talks between their military establishments and various security experts, and political leaders have called for more formal trilateral talks between China, the United States, and Japan. The United States is currently exploring ways of establishing a G-8 dialogue—modeled on the Conference on Security and Cooperation in Europe—between the wider set of states in the region. Ideas about new multilateral institutions are in the air.[5] At the same time, the United States has shown less willingness to maintain its far-flung regional and global security and political commitments. It has not embarked on a dramatic return to isolationism but it is also less consistent and dependable in its exercise of leadership.

The American view toward multilateral military cooperation has fluctuated over the decade but it has generally been supportive of initiatives—as long as they do not undermine the core bilateral security order. The 1995 Pentagon report on East Asia spent more time discussing the positive contribution of these multilateral cooperative initiatives than the 1998 report. But overall, the United States has warmed up to soft security multilateralism. In 1991, when Japanese Foreign Minister Nakayama proposed at an ASEAN Post-Ministerial Conference that a forum be created to discuss regional security, American officials responded coolly. The American attitude warmed up in later years. The Clinton administration signaled its interest in multilateral security dialogues in April 1993 during the confirmation hearings for Assistant Secretary of State for East Asia and Pacific Affairs Winston Lord, who identified such initiatives as one of the major policy goals of the new administration for Asia. President Clinton himself gave voice to the multilateral vision in a speech before the Korean National Assembly in July 1993, when he called for the creation of a new Pacific community, built on "shared strength, shared prosperity, and a shared commitment to democratic values." He identified four aspects to this vision of community: continued U.S. military presence and commitment, stronger efforts to combat the proliferation of weapons of mass destruction (WMD), support for democracy and open societies, and the promotion of new multilateral regional dialogues on the full range of common security challenges.

In the following years, the United States has signaled its interest in organizing "coalitions of the willing" to address various regional security problems and to cautiously foster closer ties between its partners. It has given support to the ASEAN Regional Forum as a mechanism for dialogue. But the United States has also backed minilateral initiatives among its allies, including the U.S.–Japan–ROK Trilateral Coordination and Oversight Group (TCOG), the U.S.–Japan, ROK Trilateral Defense Talks, the Pacific Command's (PACOM) dialogue with Australia, Japan, Republic of Korea (ROK), and Singapore on establishing great interoperability for future collective humanitarian operations, and PACOM's Asia Pacific Security Center, where Asian militaries study the conceptual and operational aspects of confidence-building measures and cooperative security. These cooperative security undertakings reflect the general American government view that the bilateral alliances should be strengthened and coordinated as much as possible. "Foremost," argues the 1998 Pentagon strategic statement of East Asia, "the U.S. will continue to strengthen its strategic partnerships with allies, which serve as important pillars from which to address regional political and military challenges. All of our alliance relationships promise to expand both in scope and degree in coming years to encompass more comprehensive concepts of security cooperation."[6]

The security order in Asia is premised on unwavering American security participation and if this role becomes less certain the region begins to respond with unsettling arms races, security dilemmas, and renewed political tensions. In short, the U.S–Japan alliance is simultaneously caught between an increasing array of thorny regional security challenges and shifting domestic political environments in both Japan and the United States. It is useful to look more closely at the logic of American and Japanese thinking about the bilateral alliance and wider regional strategies.

American Policy Toward Asia

American policy toward East Asia is built around hard bilateral security ties and soft multilateral economic relations. Embedded in these policies are a set of political bargains between the United States and the countries within the region. The U.S.–Japan alliance is the cornerstone of the security order. The hub-and-spoke defense system has its roots in the early Cold War and the failure of more multilateral security arrangements that were intended to mirror the Atlantic security pact.[7] The U.S.–Japan alliance was established to deter the expansion of Soviet power and Communism more generally in the Asia-Pacific. This Cold War anti-Communist goal led the United States to use its occupation of Japan and military victory in the Pacific to actively shape the region—doing so more successfully in Northeast Asia than Southeast Asia. The United States offered Japan—and the region more generally—a postwar political bargain. The United States would provide Japan and other countries security protection and access to American markets, technology, and supplies within an open world economy. In return, Japan and other countries in the region would become stable partners who would provide diplomatic, economic, and logistical support for the United States as it led the wider American-center postwar order.

From the beginning, this bilateral security order has been intertwined with the evolution of regional economic relations. The United States facilitated Japanese economic reconstruction after the war and actively sought to create markets for Japanese exports, particularly after the closing of China in 1949.[8] The United States actively sought the import of Japanese goods into the United States during the 1950s so as to encourage Japanese postwar economic growth and political stability.[9] The American military guarantee to partners in East Asia (and Western Europe) provided a national security rationale for Japan and the Western democracies to open their markets. Free trade helped cement the alliance, and in turn the alliance helped settle economic disputes. In Asia, the export-oriented development strategies of Japan and the smaller Asian tigers depended on America's willingness to accept their imports and live with huge trade deficits; alliances with Japan, South Korea, and other Southeast Asian countries made this politically tolerable.[10]

The alliance system and the U.S.–Japan security pact in particular has also played a wider stabilizing role in the region. The American alliance with Japan has solved Japan's security problems, allowing it to forego building up its military capability, and thereby making itself less threatening to its neighbors. This has served to solve or reduce the security dilemmas that would otherwise surface within the region if Japan were to rearm and become a more autonomous and unrestrained Great Power. At the same time, the alliance makes American power more predictable and connected to the region. This too reduces the instabilities and "risk premiums" that countries in the region would need to incur if they were to operate in a more traditional balance-of-power order. Even China has seen the virtues of the U.S.–Japan alliance.

During the Cold War it was at least partially welcome as a tool to balance Soviet power—an objective that China shared with the United States. But even today, as long as the alliance does not impinge on China's other regional goals—most importantly the reunification with Taiwan—the alliance does reduce the threat of a resurgent Japan.

In the late 1940s, in an echo of today's situation, the United States was the world's dominant state with 45 percent of world GNP, leadership in military power, technology, finance, and industry, and brimming with natural resources. But the United States nonetheless found itself building world order around stable regional partnerships. Its calling card was its offer of Cold War security protection. But the intensity of political and economic cooperation between the United States and its partners went well beyond what was necessary to counter Soviet threats. As the historian Geir Lundstadt has observed, the expanding American political order in the half century after World War II was in important respects an "empire by invitation."[11] The remarkable global reach of American postwar hegemony has been at least in part driven by the efforts of European and Asian governments to harness American power, render that power more predictable, and use it to overcome their own regional insecurities. The result has been a vast system of America-centered economic and security partnerships.

The political bargain behind the East Asian regional hegemonic order was also aimed at making American power more predictable and user-friendly. If the United States worried about finding partners to help wage the Cold War and build an American-centered world order, these partners worried about American power—both domination and abandonment. Thus the East Asian regional bargain was also about the restraint and commitment of American power. The United States would agree to operate within bilateral and multilateral institutional frameworks and the junior partners would agree to operate within and support the American order. American hegemony would become more open, predictable, reciprocal, and institutionalized and therefore more benign and tolerable. But the United States would be able to lock other countries into operating within a legitimate and American-centered order.

The end of the Cold War and the shifting economic and political environment in East Asia has altered the region and presented challenges to this postwar regional hegemonic order. The geopolitical landscape has changed. The Soviet Union has collapsed and now Russia is a weakened Great Power—too weak to play a dominant role in the region. The peace negotiations between the Koreas also is likely to lead to the reassessment of relationships and bargains. The end of the Cold War makes it more difficult for some Americans to understand why the United States continues to provide security protection to Japan and the wider region. But in other ways, the relations and bargains remain critical to regional order—and they remain largely intact. The United States is even more powerful today than it was in the past, particularly with the ongoing economic malaise in Japan and the growth of America's new economy during the 1990s. The United States is still the world's leading military power. Fifty percent of world military spending takes place in the United States and it accounts for 80 percent of world military research and development. The United States also remains the leading destination for East Asian exports. There is a wide array of regional vested interests—on both sides of the Pacific—in favor of open trade and investment. This creates ongoing incentives for the countries of the region to engage the United States and attempt to establish credible restraints and commitments on American power.

The United States government clearly is convinced that its security and political presence in the region is as important as in the past, despite the end of the Cold War. The Nye Commission in the mid-1990s provides a critical intellectual and policy rationale for the continuation of the extended American leadership role in the region. As a result, the asymmetries of power and prevailing strategic interests make the basic bargain between the United States and its partners as relevant and valued as ever before. The alliance may have lost its Cold War function but it remains critical in forestalling security dilemma-driven conflict and arms races in the region and it makes the United States a more predictable and institutionalized superpower. The bargains behind the regional security order are evolving but they are also being recreated.

Japan's Ambivalent Multilateralism

Japan tends to prefer to operate bilaterally within the Asia Pacific region although it has begun to pursue a variety of multilateral diplomatic initiatives in recent years. The reasons why Japanese tend to see international relations in terms of bilateralism are several. First, there are historical and geopolitical reasons. The multilateral security system in Europe emerged out of centuries of balance-of-power politics that socialized the states of Europe into a common framework and created conditions for multilateral security cooperation. By contrast, there never has been a true balance-of-power system in Asia. China was too strong politically by the time of the Opium War. Likewise, Japan has been too strong economically after it became the first modernized power in Asia from the late nineteenth century onward and so there has never been a comfortable balance between the two. All other Asian powers have been too weak to balance against the big two. The absence of a working balance-of-power system has meant that one of the critical forces that fostered a tradition of regionalism and multilateral order in Europe did not take root in Asia. This situation has also contributed to the absence of a strong sense of shared identity and culture in Asia.

Second, Asia has existed as a so-called intrusive system—that is, the operation of security relations within Asia have been conducted as part of a wider Pacific and global system of Great Power relations.[12] Politically significant external states have helped shape relations within the Asian subsystem. Without the involvements of these states— European and American Great Powers—the Asian system would not have maintained regional order by itself. The leading states in this intrusive system—Japan and China—could gain greater leverage in seeking their interest in Asia by bringing Euro-American influence to bear on their regional policy objectives. The outside states that have been allied to either Japan or China have tended to play a relatively indirect and benign role in the region, allowing their regional partners to operate as they wished as long as larger global interests were not put at risk.

There are also cultural reasons for Japan's reluctant multilateralism. Japanese views of international relations has tended to be hierarchic, reflecting Japan's long experience with premodern Sino-Japanese relations. The Japanese also tend to see international relations as giving expression externally to the same cultural patterns that are manifested internally within Japanese society. As is often noted, Japanese society is characterized by the prevalence of vertically organized structures. Hierarchy is evident throughout its society. One of the most well-known relationships in Japanese business society is keiretsu (systematization). For example, besides the oligopolistic alignments controlled by financial groups, there are manufacturing keiretsu in such industries as chemicals and steel, and partial keiretsu in automobiles and electronics industries. In the keiretsu, a few hundred small plants and firms, called offspring companies, are aligned under a parent company in order to secure continuous order and technological and financial support.[13] If the images of international relations reflect the domestic power structure in a society, Japanese intellectual orientation in its foreign relations may be characterized as hierarchical. When the Japanese try to locate Japan in international society, their domestic model offers itself as an analogy. To the extent this is so, Japan's diplomatic behavior is biased toward vertically organized bilateral relations.

Japanese diplomatic experience also reinforces bilateralism at the expense of multilateral relations. When Japan has entered into a specific international order through geopolitical alignments, Japan's strategy is somewhat similar to the logic of keiretsu. Japanese thinkers situate Japan not only in the horizontally arranged international system (i.e., in terms of unipolar or multipolar order) but also in the stratified international system (i.e., patron–client relations). When Japan joins such an international system, alliance policy should come into play. At the turn of the century, Japan was considering two different states as a possible ally—England and Russia. In the end, Japan decided to go with Great Britain for a variety of reasons including its naval and economic power and the fact that Britain did not participate in the Triple Intervention by which Japan had to give up the Liaotung Peninsula.[14] In the case of the U.S.–Japan security treaty of 1951, the rationale was similar to the earlier Anglo-Japanese alliance. The United States could guarantee Japan's safety as well as economic growth. Hence, it was bandwagoning for profit once again. Even in the case of the Axis Pact of 1940, one may find the same logic in Japanese thinking. Though many of the mid-European powers turned to Nazi Germany out of fear, Japan did it to obtain expected military and economic gain. The Axis Pact had disastrous outcomes in Japan, while the alliances with England and the United States have been regarded as great successes.

This leads us to the current Japanese view of multilateral approaches to security. In spite of the fact that Japanese tend to deal with security issues by managing the bilateral relations of the U.S.–Japan alliance, the Japanese have come to have a more positive view of multilateral diplomacy in the years since the end of the Cold War. There are at least two reasons for this. First, the Japanese expected a decline of American hegemony in the early 1990s and this made foreign policy officials think more seriously of alternatives to the American-led security order. For example, the Report of the Advisory Group on Defense Issues (the Higuchi Report) made public in August 1994 stated, "the United States no longer holds an overwhelming advantage in terms of overall national strength." Then, it said, "[t]he question is whether the United States will be able to demonstrate leadership in multilateral cooperation." As the most distinguished institution of multilateral cooperation, the Report mentioned the United Nations, and indicated that "it is essential that multilateral cooperation be maintained under U.S. leadership." The report said Japan should "play an active role in shaping a new order" instead of playing a "passive role."[15] Partly because of this thinking, Japan has been very supportive to the ASEAN Regional Forum (ARF) security dialogue at the official level since its inception in 1994. Japan is also a member of the ASEAN-Post Ministerial Conference (PMC) since it started in 1978. The Asia-Pacific Economic Cooperation (APEC) that was organized in 1989 as a regional economic forum is expected to function as a confidence-building mechanism in this area.[16] At the private level, the Conference on Security Cooperation in Asia and the Pacific (CSCAP) was established in 1993, and is promoting dialogue with states that include Australia, Canada, Indonesia, Japan, South Korea, Malaysia, the Philippines, Singapore, Thailand, and the United States. Japan's Self Defense Agency has also launched security dialogues with China and Russia. All of those efforts will increase transparency in the security area. Japan's ODA and its policy in the UN's Peacekeeping Operations (PKO) activities are often regarded as part of Japan's multilateral commitments as well.

Taken together, one may be able to say that the Japanese are more positive toward multilateral diplomacy than they were in the past. Especially immediately after the Cold War ended, many pundits and political scientists in Japan predicted that multilateral security frameworks will take over the alliance networks in Asia. Today, however, no Japanese officials or researchers within the foreign policy establishment expect that multilateral arrangements can replace the bilateral security relations in the near future. It will continue to be a challenge to conduct both bilateral and multilateral relations at the same time without creating contradictions and thereby repeat the problems that Japan experienced in the first quarter of the twentieth century. To deal with North Korea and China, for example, the multilateral approach may function as a type of preventive diplomacy, at least to some extent. However, there is no great expectation that they will have a crisis management function. For example, there is some skepticism in Japan whether the Agreed Framework concluded among four governments including North Korea could produce the expected outcome.

Is the U.S.–Japan alliance and multilateral security dialogues compatible or contradictory? The multilateral security frameworks in Asia such as ARF is expected to work as a confidence-building measure and, as a result, they can decrease the chance of growing security dilemmas. However, they are not likely to have deterrence and defense functions in the near future. In other words, they do not have "teeth" yet. That is why those multilateral frameworks cannot do much once a crisis takes place—perhaps best seen in the case of East Timor in the summer of 1999. This is a more serious problem when long-range missiles and nuclear threats are involved. To deal with such problems, the U.S.–Japan alliance is expected to function. Therefore, there is a sort of division of labor between them. Conversely, if and when ARF has "teeth" in the future, it might create contradictions with the U.S.–Japan alliance. Even more importantly, when China gains influence within multilateral frameworks and begins to be more democratic, Japan may face a dilemma even though no party in Asia wants a China-centered multilateral arrangement at this point. Likewise, the deployment of Theater Missile Defense (TMD) in the area around Japan would make Sino-Japanese–U.S. relations more complicated.

On entering the new century three events took place, triggering some change in the nature and form of alliance with the United States. These three events took place a decade after the end of the Cold War. They are (1) the antiterrorist war, (2) China's accession to the World Trade Organization (WTO), and (3) Russia's quasi accession to the NATO. All these events have started to affect profoundly the form and substance of the alliance with the United States from the Japanese and German points of view.

1 The antiterrorist war is a new war. It de-territorializes alliance; it needs to treat all except rogue states as a cooperative partner. Special relationship as has been entertained of the alliance between the United States and some of its allies until the recent past seems to have lost its meaning. For instance, no one talks about the U.S.–Japan alliance in terms of Mike Mansfield, who called it the most important alliance bar none. The U.S. government has ceased to use the phrase special relationship. Instead, the word, partner, has been more or less uniformly used to characterize all the cooperative states in the antiterrorist war.

2 China's accession to the WTO has started to blur the erstwhile important distinction between security identity and commercial interests. The latter tends to acquire more importance. For instance, a spate of bilateral free trade agreement ideas has been flooding the Asia-Pacific, several involving China: China–ASEAN, China–Korea–Japan, Korea–Japan, Japan–ASEAN, ASEAN plus three, and the like. In some countries popular ranking of the United States have been recently reversed by those of China like in the ROK.

3 Russia's quasi accession to the NATO has started to blur the security identity of West Europeans. If Russia ceases to be a potential adversary, then why NATO? If NATO incorporates Russia, is Organization for Security and Cooperation in Europe (OSCE)

redundant? If NATO incorporates Russia, is Western European Union (WEU) becoming more important. If the United States acts in an unipolar and unilateralist fashion, what would be the best way for West Europeans to maintain their alliance with the United States?

Renewing The U.S.–Japan Alliance

The chapters that follow attempt to chart a course for the future of the security pact between Japan and the United States. Chapters 2 and 3 by Mastanduno and Tsuchiyama delineate the range of possibilities for future security organization in the region. Both provide arguments for why the bilateral alliance remains the most viable instrument of regional stability available in the decades ahead. But there are other conceptual possibilities. These include a more traditional balance-of-power system, a competitive Sino-American bipolar system, or a full-scale regional security committee. What Mastanduno and Tsuchiyama make clear is that security orders have specific political and power-related preconditions. It is not possible to simply agree to construct a security committee. Shared norms and convergent interests are also necessary. The critical issue in moving away from the bilateral alliance system toward something more multilateral is the role of China. Without movement toward compatible sociopolitical domestic systems and a resolution of lingering historical antagonisms, such a community-based security order will remain illusive. But chapters 2 and 3 also make it clear that without proper management of the bilateral arrangements it would be easy for the region to slip back into a more competitive and conflictual order. The alliance needs to be championed and renewed in order to sustain its position within the region.

Chapter 4 by Berger illuminates the diffuse antagonisms and lingering historical resentments that remain as obstacles to closer regional cooperation. Japan has not been able to put its history to rest. Symbolic gestures and concrete steps will need to be taken to overcome the resentments that remain in Japan's relations with China and Korea. Drawing stronger lessons from Germany's strategy of regional reconciliation would help. Berger makes clear that reconciliation in East Asia is possible. Some of the "history disputes" between Japan and China are created by elites for diplomatic advantage. But other aspects of these disagreements are rooted in issues such as textbooks and war memorials. In a very real sense, the level of conflict in the region hinges as much on these cultural and historical matters as the objective balance-of-power.

Deft diplomacy and enlightened leadership will be needed to heal wounds that linger and obstruct closer security cooperation in the region.

Chapters 5, 6, and 7 by Kamiya, Smith, and Cha probe the relationship between bilateral and regional multilateral security cooperation. One of the most important findings of these chapters is that the choice between bilateral and multilateral security arrangements is a false one. Both Japan and the United States have been traditionally suspicious of multilateral security activities. This is partly because they do not want to create slipshod mechanisms that erode the primacy of the alliance and because of the loss of control that a more diffuse security organization would entail. But the more firmly anchored the bilateral alliance is, the more that these two countries can participate in regional dialogues and use them to strengthen the alliance and the wider regional environment. A zero-sum relationship does not exist between the two types of security approaches if smart diplomacy is pursued.

If one of the important steps that Japan needs to take in the next decade is to expand its regional security responsibilities, regional multilateral arrangements will be important to ensure that all countries in the region are comfortable with the evolving Japanese security posture. The example of Germany is again relevant. Germany made a strategic decision to move toward early unification of West and East Germany in 1990. In doing so, however, Chancellor Kohl engaged the other countries in the region and sought their approval. Germany agreed to intensify its commitments to European monetary and political integration as a way to reassure France, Britain, and even Russia that a larger Germany would not be a larger threat to its neighbors. Likewise, Japan should use the multilateral fora in the region to consult with and reassure neighbors about its changing security orientation. Anchoring these changes within the U.S.–Japan alliance is critical. But fostering a dialogue with other countries about their interests and worries is also important to reconcile change and stability.

The final set of chapters 8, 9, 10 and 11 by O'Hanlon, Umemoto, Stedman, and Fukushima explore new issues that are creating challenges and opportunities for the alliance. O'Hanlon looks at the implications of the so-called revolution in military affairs (RMA) for alliance relations. It is possible that if the United States pushed the technological revolution sufficiently hard it could radically distance itself in terms of military capabilities and interoperable cooperation from its allies. O'Hanlon casts some doubt on whether a true revolution is in the offing. But he also argues that it is important to harness military innovation to alliance goals. Innovation is certainly a goal but it is not an end in itself.

Making sure that the United States and Japan are able to work together in training and operations is critical in the years ahead. The United States will continue to advance its high-technological capacities but it should make sure that its allies are not too far behind.

Tetsuya argues that missile defense is a delicate regional issue and that it should be dealt with in a way that strengthens rather than weakens the U.S.–Japan alliance. The United States should make sure that it pursues technologies that do not threaten China's deterrent capacities. Boost phase defense is the most reasonable approach that addresses potential missile threats from North Korea but does not—or at least should not—destabilize the wider region. At the same time, missile defense should be an alliance arrangement. The United States should consult with Tokyo and Seoul on the specifics of their plan and seek a joint approach to its development and deployment.

Stedman and Fukusima look at the opportunities that are opening up for Japan to play a more active role in regional peacekeeping. The idea here is to seek ways for Japan to be a more active security player in the region without triggering unnecessary new conflicts and antagonisms. Connecting Japan's peacekeeping duties to a region-wide UNs-sponsored mechanism is one sensible way to find a way forward. Japan's recessed security presence in the region—made possible by the alliance—has been a stabilizing feature of the region for 50 years. The goal is to not lose these advantages while also facilitating a more active and constructive Japan presence in managing regional conflict and cooperation.

Stepping back from the specific issues, this volume suggests that the United States and Japan need to discover a new model for the alliance partnership. One model has been advanced by the Armitage Commission: the U.S.–British relationship. Some of the features of this relationship do make sense in the context of the U.S.–Japan relationship. It is a special relationship built on deeply embedded trust and cooperation. But the U.S.–German relationship is probably a better model. Both Germany and Japan have labored under the weight of history. Germany is today modernizing its international position in ways that allow it to play a more active role in its region while also reassuring its neighbors. It is normalizing its role with the outside world but also building deeper connections with its region. The two processes go hand-in-hand. So too should Japan look to its institutionalized connections—first and foremost with the United States but also with the other countries in the region—as useful relations that should be strengthened, as its foreign and security presence in the region evolves.

Notes

1. For overviews of the changing security dynamics in the Asia Pacific region, see Paul Dibb, David D. Hale, and Peter Prince, "Asia's Insecurity," *Survival* (Autumn 1999); Matake Kamiya, "Hopeful Uncertainty: Asia-Pacific Security in Transition," *Asia-Pacific Review*, Vol. 3, No. 1 (Spring/Summer 1996); Aaron L. Friedberg, "Ripe for Rivalry: Prospects for Peace in a Multipolar Asia," *International Security*, Vol. 18, No. 3 (Winter 1993/94); Thomas J. Christensen, "China, the U.S.–Japan Alliance, and the Security Dilemma in East Asia," *International Security*, Vol. 23, No. 4 (Spring 1999); Barry Buzan and Gerald Segal, "Rethinking East Asia Security," *Survival* (Summer 1994); and Kent E. Calder, "The New Face of Northeast Asia," *Foreign Affairs* (January/February 2001), pp. 106–122; and Takashi Inoguchi, ed., *Japan's Asian Policy: Revival and Response* (New York: Palgrave, 2002).

2. For useful discussions of bilateralism and multilateralism in the Asia-Pacific region see William Tow, Russell Trood, and Toshiya Hoshino, eds., *Bilateralism in a Multilateral Era: The Future of the San Francisco Alliance System in the Asia-Pacific* (Tokyo: The Japan Institute of International Affairs, 1997).

3. Funabashi, "Tokyo's Depression Diplomacy," *Foreign Affairs*, Vol. 77, No. 6 (November/December 1998), pp. 26–36.

4. Multilateral security dialogues in which Japan is involved include the Forum for Defense Authorities in the Asia-Pacific Region, the International Seminar on Defense Science, the Asia-Pacific Seminar, and the Western Pacific Naval Symposium; for the latest developments in Japan's Asian policy, see Inoguchi, 2002.

5. For discussions of multilateral security arrangements in East Asia, see David Dewitt, "Common, Comprehensive and Cooperative Security," *Pacific Review*, Vol. 7, No. 1 (1994); Young Sun Song, "Prospects for a New Asia-Pacific Multilateral Security Arrangement," *Korean Journal of Defense Analysis*, Vol. 5, No. 1 (Summer 1993); Paul Evans, "Reinventing East Asia: Multilateral Security Cooperation and Regional Order," *Harvard International Review*, Vol. XVIII, No. 2 (Spring 1996); and Amitav Acharya, "A Concert for Asia?" *Survival* (Autumn 1999); Takashi Inoguchi, "Possibilities on Limits of Regional Cooperation in Northeast Asia: Security and Economic Access," in Tainjoon Kwon and Dong-Sung Kim, eds., *World Order and Peace in the New Millennium* (Seoul: Korean National Commission for UNESCO and Korean Association of International Studies, 2000), pp. 291–301.

6. *The United States Security Strategy for the East Asia-Pacific Region* (Washington, D.C.: Department of Defense, 1998), p. 61.

7. On the idea floated by the United States of a multilateral security institution in Asia in the early 1940s and during 1950–51 that was to be a counterpart to NATO, see Donald Crone, "Does Hegemony Matter? The Reorganization of the Pacific Political Economy," *World Politics*, Vol. 45 (July 1993).

8. See Micheal Schaller, *Altered States: The United States and Japan since the Occupation* (New York: Oxford, 1997); and Bruce Cumings, "Japan's Position in the World System," in Andrew Gordon, ed., *Postwar Japan as History* (Berkeley: University of California Press, 1993), pp. 34–63.
9. See Stuart Auerbach, "The Ironies that Built Japan Inc.," *Washington Post*, 18 (July 1993).
10. This argument is made in Robert Gilpin, *The Challenge of Global Capitalism: The World Economy in the 21st Century* (Princeton: Princeton University Press, 2000), chapter 2.
11. See Geir Lundestad, "Empire by Invitation? The Untied States and Western Europe, 1945–1952," *The Journal of Peace Research*, Vol. 23 (September 1986), pp. 263–277.
12. See Luise Cantori and Steven L. Smith, eds., *The International Politics of Regions: A Comparative Approach* (Englewood Cliffs, New Jersey: Prentice-Hall, 1970), p. 25.
13. Chie Nakane, *Japanese Society*, p. 96.
14. A comparison of Japanese security options in the early years of the twentieth and the twenty-first century can be seen in Takashi Inoguchi, "A Northeast Asian Perspective," *Australian Journal of International Affairs*, Vol. 55, No. 2 (July 2001), pp. 199–212.
15. Higuchi Report, Advisory Group on Defense Issues, *The Modality of the Security and Defense Capability of Japan: The Outlook for the 21st Century* (Tokyo: Defense Agency, August 1994).
16. The ASEAN plus 3 (Japan, China, and South Korea) meeting since 1997 is also expected in the near future to become a new mechanism for resolving not only economic issues but also security.

SECTION 1
HISTORICAL AND REGIONAL SETTING

CHAPTER 2

THE U.S.–JAPAN ALLIANCE AND MODELS OF REGIONAL SECURITY ORDER

Michael Mastanduno

Former U.S. ambassador to Japan, Mike Mansfield, frequently observed that the U.S.–Japan relationship was "the most important bilateral relationship in the world, bar none." Mansfield's statement rang true during the Cold War, and arguably through the first decade after the Cold War as well. Yet, as we move further from the structural setting of the Cold War, can we expect the U.S.–Japan relationship to remain as vital as it once was? Or will that alliance relationship, like so many others through history, become less relevant with the passage of time?[1]

The future stability of the Asia-Pacific region is highly uncertain and of great concern to scholars and policy makers. Major challenges are well known. They include the rise of China and the potential for a power transition between China and the United States. Other challenges relate to the uncertain status of the Japanese economy, unresolved disputes involving the Korean peninsula and Taiwan, and the historical suspicions and resentments that linger among states and peoples in the region some 50 years after the end of World War II. There is also some degree of uncertainty concerning the future regional role of the United States in light of the end of the Cold War, the absence of a central strategic threat, and, after September 11, 2001, the preoccupation of the United States with the struggle against terrorism. In light of these uncertainties, it is not surprising that some political scientists and policy analysts view the Asia-Pacific region as a potential zone for instability in the years ahead.[2]

An effective regional security order includes the absence of major war, the management and ideal resolution of conflicts short of war, and the peaceful accommodation of international change.[3] During the Cold

War, the U.S.–Japan security alliance was the foundation of each countries' strategy for regional order. The principal function of that alliance was to deter the expansion of Soviet and more generally communist power in the Asia-Pacific. The alliance was reasonably successful at this task, more so in Northeast than in Southeast Asia.

One could fairly characterize the bilateral relationship as a long-term political and strategic bargain. The United States provided for Japan's security, and assured that Japan would have access to markets, supplies, and technology in an open world economy. For its part, Japan proved to be a stable, non-Communist ally that provided diplomatic, economic, and logistical support to the United States as it carried out its bipolar struggle regionally and globally. The alliance was not balanced in that the United States pledged to defend Japan's territory, but Japan was not obligated to defend the United States. Nevertheless, the security strategies of the two sides complemented each other nicely. Any effort by the Soviet Union to break into the North Pacific from Vladovostok would necessitate a direct encounter with the forces and territory of Japan. Japan's commitment to self-defense and the U.S. commitment to global containment of the Soviet Union thus went hand-in-hand.

Even the Chinese, by the 1970s, came to see value in the U.S.–Japan alliance. That alliance helped to balance Soviet power—a critical strategic objective of China as well as of the United States. It also served to discourage Japan from adopting a more aggressive foreign policy posture. While the possibility of an aggressive Japan became increasingly remote to U.S. and Japanese officials as the Cold War progressed, Chinese officials, reflecting perhaps a sensitivity to China's historical experience, continued to exhibit concern over the potential for Japanese expansion and thus welcomed the alliance as a restraining influence.[4]

The end of the Cold War reconfigured the region's geopolitical landscape. The Russia that has emerged out of the collapse of the Soviet Union is currently too weak to play a major role in the Asian security order. The potential for Korean unification is a wild card that eventually could prompt a reappraisal of existing relationships. But for now, attention is appropriately focused on relations among three major players—China, Japan, and the United States. The U.S.–Japan security alliance has outlived the Cold War and remains a crucial factor in that triangular relationship.

This chapter makes three central arguments, developed in three subsequent sections. First, it places the U.S.–Japan alliance in a structural context by examining alternative future models of regional order. This is to emphasize that the status and role of the alliance will depend significantly on the characteristics of the wider regional order in which it is embedded. In some possible structures the U.S.–Japan alliance is crucial; in others, it is far less significant.

Second, I argue that the maintenance of regional order in the *current* structural context does depend on a strong bilateral alliance. The very nature of that structural context, however, makes it challenging for both countries to assure the continued health of their alliance. The significant asymmetry in the capabilities of the United States and Japan, coupled with the strategic uncertainty of the post–Cold War international environment, means that the two countries must devote considerable efforts to sustain their cooperation. In an uncertain setting, Japan and the United States need to work harder just to maintain the status quo of a stable relationship.

Third, because the durability of the current order is uncertain, I examine the prospects for a transition to an alternative order. I explore in particular the possibility and implications of transforming U.S.–Japan relations from their current hierarchical state to that of a more meaningful and equitable partnership. A genuine partnership would be more stable and desirable, but will be difficult to attain.

Alternative Models of Regional Order

The U.S.–Japan alliance relationship must be placed in a broader strategic context, because in different contexts, the character of that relationship will differ significantly. In some future models of regional order, the U.S.–Japan alliance is a crucial element. In others it is less important, and in still others we might expect the alliance to disappear altogether. This section briefly illustrates that point by sketching five models of future regional order in the Asia-Pacific and noting the likely role that the U.S.–Japan alliance would play within each. The sequence in which I present the models represents a progression from those in which the U.S.–Japan alliance is least critical to those in which it is most critical.

Model I: Regional Order Through Multipolar Balance-of-Power

Some analysts anticipate the emergence of a multipolar balance-of-power system in the Asia-Pacific. In this view, the current international system, dominated by a single power, is an unnatural one. Power tends to balance power in international relations, and challengers to American dominance are destined to emerge. The major players in a multipolar Asia would likely include an engaged but less preponderant United States, a China that maintains its economic development and territorial integrity, a Russia that recovers its role as a regional and global power, a Japan more willing to project its power and influence, and perhaps an India or Indonesia that realizes its economic and geopolitical potential.[5]

Order in this system would be maintained through diplomatic maneuvering and shifting alliance commitments among the constellation of these major powers. The historical referent is nineteenth-century Europe. Europe's past, in effect, becomes Asia's future. Multipolar optimists point to flexible diplomacy among roughly equivalent powers as the basis for European peace (defined as the absence of major war among Great Powers) and prosperity between 1814 and 1914. Multipolar pessimists point to the collapse of the balance in the late nineteenth century and, despite growing levels of economic interdependence, the coming of total war.[6]

In this structural context, the U.S.–Japan alliance would recede in significance and in all likelihood wither away. In multipolar balances, states have permanent interests, but not permanent friends. Japan and the United States might find themselves cooperating on some security and diplomatic issues, but lining up against each other on others. Bilateral cooperation would be time- and issue-specific, rather than institutionalized and enduring.

Model II: Regional Order Through Pluralistic Security Community

A security community transcends the balance-of-power as a mechanism for assuring regional order. A group of states that are part of a security community, share interests and values with sufficient commonality that cooperation becomes a matter of routine, and the use of force to settle conflicts among them becomes unthinkable.[7] In this model, Europe's present becomes Asia's future. The Asia-Pacific would take on some of the attributes of the contemporary European Union (EU)—a self-conscious political community organized around shared values, interconnected societies, and more robust regional institutions.

Order would be maintained in an Asian security community through the transmission of norms and the effective functioning of legitimate regional institutions.[8] One might imagine the further development of APEC and ARF such that these institutions come to play a central rather than peripheral role in Asian economic and security affairs. They would become mechanisms to foster integration and resolve political conflict. We might also anticipate the development of standards of acceptable state behavior, with regard both to foreign policy and to the treatment of individuals and groups within domestic societies.

The U.S.–Japan alliance would necessarily become less significant in this strategic context. Multilateral institutions and initiatives would take on greater political salience than bilateral ones. The U.S.–Japan alliance might serve as an impetus to regional community, perhaps in the way that the Franco-German partnership did for postwar Europe. Over time, however, that alliance would be subsumed and overtaken by the larger regional political entity as that entity came to take on a life and identity of its own. France's emerging anxiety over whether the very success of European integration has rendered the Franco-German special relationship unnecessary is a symptom of the likely pattern as it plays out in Europe.[9]

Model III: Regional Order Through Hegemony[10]
Order in this model would be based primarily on the capabilities and behavior of a dominant state. The United States emerged from the Cold War as the dominant state in the international system, in possession of material resources and power projection capabilities considerably more advanced than those of any other major power. U.S. officials made clear throughout the 1990s that they intended to remain fully engaged in Asian affairs militarily, economically, and diplomatically. They view the United States as the primary source of regional order, and worry that in the absence of a U.S. forward presence, the stability of the Asia-Pacific will be jeopardized.[11]

Hegemonic order is maintained through the active engagement of the dominant state. That state takes responsibility to discourage major power competition, to defuse regional conflicts, and to reassure smaller states. Leaders must have followers for hegemony to function effectively. The more other states are willing to recognize the hegemonic project as legitimate and share its purposes, the more durable it will be. In this sense, U.S. hegemony in Asia must be characterized as incomplete.[12] Some states (e.g., Japan) recognize in fairly explicit terms the legitimacy of a U.S. leadership role in the region. But others—China and India come to mind—suggest by their rhetoric and behavior that they are unwilling to accept a U.S.-centered global and regional order.

The United States has centered its hegemonic strategy in Asia around a series of special bilateral relationships. Bilateral ties are primary, and the cultivation of multilateral institutions is secondary. The U.S.–Japan relationship, in this context, is undoubtedly of major importance. This Cold War alliance has carried over to the post–Cold War era. In the new era, however, there is necessarily a significant degree of uncertainty in the relationship. The U.S.–Japan alliance must coexist with other "special" relationships that the United States might wish to cultivate in the interest of its broader hegemonic strategy. During the 1990s, U.S. officials promoted a special partnership with China. In the wake of the terrorist attacks of September 2001, the United States moved very close to a new partnership with Russia. These initiatives reflect the simple fact that after the Cold War, the preponderantly powerful United States has considerable discretion in its foreign policy strategy. As discussed in the following, this reality cannot help but affect the status of the U.S.–Japan relationship.

Model IV: Regional Order Through a Bipolar Balance

The United States and Soviet Union maintained a de facto international order through their rivalry for over four decades. Some foresee the return of this model of order with China replacing the Soviet Union.[13] An obvious precondition would be continued political stability in China and the sustained development of Chinese economic, technological, and military capabilities. China, in effect, would need to develop the capacity, not just the rhetoric, to challenge the United States. A more powerful China would not necessarily be hostile to the United States. But one could easily imagine an action–reaction process, triggered by a conflict over Taiwan or some other type of crisis, which would lead each to view the other as a formidable adversary.

In this model the Asia-Pacific region would likely become polarized, with most states forced to line up on one side or the other. Order would be maintained primarily through the balance-of-power between the two blocs. As was the case during the Cold War, the two dominant powers might develop a set of tacit rules of engagement to regulate their own behavior and that of their allies. For example, the United States and the Soviet Union tended to engage in military conflict by proxy rather than directly, in order to minimize the risks of escalation to an all-out war.

It is plausible to imagine the U.S.–Japan alliance playing a central role in a future bipolar order. Japan's economic, technological, and even military capabilities would make it the most prized alliance asset in any bipolar struggle. For the United States, the alliance with Japan would become as crucial as that with NATO in the European context during the Cold War. Japan, for its part, would likely be forced to choose sides. Its long and enduring postwar alliance with the United States, and its deeper history of tension in relations with China, suggest the greater likelihood of a U.S.–Japan alliance to contain China rather than a China–Japan alliance to contain the United States.

Model V: Regional Order Through U.S.–Japan Partnership
In this scenario, the dominant role of the United States would be transformed into a "co-leadership" arrangement between the United States and Japan.[14] A necessary precondition is that Japan be prepared, within the alliance context, to take on the capacity and willingness to play a more active role in the resolution of regional security and economic problems. The United States would need to accept a meaningful sharing of decision-making authority, rather than simply expect Japan to practice "checkbook diplomacy" in support of U.S. foreign policy initiatives.

Regional order would be maintained through an effective burden-sharing arrangement between Japan and the United States. These two states, in combination, control an overwhelming preponderance of economic, financial, and military resources. Order would depend on their ability to reach sufficient agreement on both the purposes of foreign policy and the means by which to pursue it. One might imagine coordinated U.S.–Japan responses to financial instability, military standoffs, humanitarian crises, and other sources of regional instability.

In this model the U.S.–Japan alliance is at the very core of the regional security order. It would function not only to defend the two states, but also to solve regional problems "out of area," in much the way NATO evolved during the 1990s as an instrument devoted to broader European security.

Alliance Management in a Hegemonic Order

Today, the character of regional order in the Asia-Pacific fits most closely the features of the third model, that of U.S. hegemony. The United States possesses a clear preponderance of material capabilities, both militarily and economically. It has sought to maintain a regional and global order that is consistent with its core values and interests.[15] U.S. hegemony is incomplete in that not all the major players in the region are prepared to accept a role as subordinate partners in a U.S.-centered order. U.S. officials, nevertheless, perceive the United States as the principal source of regional order and developed a strategy during the 1990s to assure that this all-important region would remain sufficiently stable to serve the geopolitical and economic interests of the United States.

The U.S. intention to serve as the principal source of regional order is symbolized and reinforced by the American forward military presence. Early in the 1990s, the United States scaled back its troop commitments in East Asia and about the same time relinquished its naval facilities in the Philippines at the request of that government. These moves were read in the region and elsewhere as the beginnings of U.S. withdrawal. By 1995, U.S. officials made clear that this was not the case, and in fact that their intention was the opposite. The United States planned, in the words of the Pentagon's East Asia strategy document, to maintain a forward political and military commitment to East Asia of "indefinite duration."[16] This included the stabilization of the U.S. troop presence in the region at about 100,000. The United States also intended to maintain its dominant position in maritime East Asia. U.S. alliances with Japan and South Korea provided secure access in Northeast Asia. In Southeast Asia, the U.S. Navy would rely on "places, not bases." By the end of the 1990s, U.S. officials had concluded access agreements for naval facilities in Indonesia, Malaysia, Singapore, and Brunei, along with a status-of-forces agreement with the Philippines.[17]

A second component of the U.S. strategy for regional order might be called a commitment to a forward *economic* presence in Asia. U.S. officials have consistently and aggressively promoted the spread of liberal international economic policies in Asian states inclined to be more comfortable with the practices of developmental capitalism. Economic openness plays into U.S. economic interests, particularly given U.S. competitiveness in the export of services, agriculture, and advanced technology. It plays into U.S. security interests since U.S. officials have consistently held that liberalism and economic interdependence promote more peaceful and cooperative political relations. It is not surprising that U.S. officials have reacted negatively and decisively to initiatives that seemed to suggest closed regionalism. In the early 1990s the United States opposed, and worked hard to assure that Japan would oppose, Malaysia's proposal for an East Asian Economic Group that would exclude the United States. The role of the United States in APEC has been to push member states more decisively and quickly in the direction of "open regionalism."

A third component of U.S. strategy has been the cultivation of a set of special relationships with key states in the region. The overall U.S. approach might be thought of in terms of a "hub and spokes" arrangement.[18] U.S. officials have sought to establish a series of relationships designed to assure key regional players that their connection to the United States is both crucial and indispensable. The most important of these bilateral relationships is with Japan, reflecting the continuity between America's Cold War and post–Cold War regional strategy. U.S. officials similarly have maintained their bilateral alliance structure and commitment to South Korea. They have reaffirmed their so-called unique partnership with Australia. And, instead of using these alliances to balance China, the U.S. strategy, at least through the 1990s, was to develop a special relationship with China as well.

Fourth, it is important to note that U.S. officials view regional security institutions as supplements to, not substitutes for, their core bilateral security relationships. They have supported the ARF as a vehicle for ASEAN members to voice their security concerns and explore the potential for preventive diplomacy and maritime cooperation. Similarly, they have supported the Northeast Asia Cooperation Dialogue (NEACD) among China, Japan, Russia, the United States, and the two Koreas. But, in times of crisis they turn not to these regional institutions but prefer instead to rely on U.S.-led diplomatic efforts and institutional structures that the United States can more comfortably control. In the North Korean nuclear crisis of 1994, the United States relied on ad hoc diplomacy and established a new entity, KEDO (Korean Peninsula Energy Development Organization) to implement its agreement.[19] During the Asian financial crisis, U.S. officials rebuffed Japan's proposal for a regional financing facility and instead concentrated on the management of the crisis on the more familiar terrain of the International Monetary Fund (IMF).

A healthy and stable U.S.–Japan alliance is clearly a central component of the U.S. strategy to develop and strengthen a U.S.-centered order in the Asia-Pacific. The very nature of that order, however, makes it difficult to sustain the health and stability of the alliance. Four key challenges for the management of the alliance arise out of the current asymmetry in the U.S.–Japan relationship.

The first challenge is that of triangular diplomacy among the United States, Japan, and China. Japan can make a legitimate claim to being the most important Asian alliance partner of the United States. But American attention is necessarily divided, and Japan must share the stage with China. This follows logically from the fact that U.S. strategy in Asia has been to develop special relationships with each of the key regional actors. The United States wants some kind of special partnership, if not a full-blown alliance, with China as well as with Japan. The U.S.–China relationship, of course, is a potential source of uncertainty and anxiety for Japan. As the preponderant global as well as regional actor, the United States has considerable discretion in its foreign policy. The obvious concern for Japan is that the United States might ignore or downplay Japanese interests. At the extreme, the fear is that of outright abandonment.

Japan's experience during the Clinton administration demonstrates the plausibility of these concerns. During its first term, the administration paid considerable attention to Japan, primarily through its efforts to force economic change on Japan. By the time of the 1996 Clinton–Hashimoto summit, U.S. officials reconsidered their aggressive economic strategy and pledged to place greater positive emphasis on the security aspects of the U.S.–Japan relationship. Japanese officials, it is fair to say, were encouraged by the summit initiative but were subsequently disappointed by the inability of the United States to follow through and maintain a focus on U.S.–Japan relations. The attention of the Clinton administration shifted decisively to China, as U.S. officials, starting with the president, sought to develop a comprehensive partnership with China. Clinton's ten-day visit to China in 1999, without even a stop in Japan, was troubling to Japanese officials. The fear that the United States might "bypass" Japan was expressed routinely by the Japanese.[20] By the end of the Clinton administration, influential Asian specialists within the U.S. foreign policy community became more sensitive to this problem, as evidenced by the so-called Armitage Report of 2000 and the attention it received from the incoming Bush administration.[21]

Japanese fears will necessarily persist as long as the United States cultivates China as a strategic partner. But what if, instead, the United States follows the instincts of some members of the Bush administration and adopts a more confrontational stance toward China? From the perspective of Japan, this might solve the abandonment problem, but it creates another—that of entrapment. Neither the Japanese government nor Japanese society is currently prepared to participate in a new Cold War with China as the target. Japan has cultivated growing economic ties with China, and its diplomatic instinct is that engagement is preferable to containment as a means to manage relations with a large, rapidly growing, and potentially unstable neighbor. Japan needs the United States to be not too confrontational—yet not too cooperative—in its approach to China.

It is worth noting that the same concerns apply, from the perspective of China, in U.S. relations with Japan. The Chinese fear containment if the U.S.–Japan alliance develops and expands forcefully. But they also fear the consequences of a more unilateral Japanese foreign policy, in the event the U.S.–Japan alliance weakens or dissolves altogether.[22]

These triangular dynamics pose a delicate diplomatic problem for the United States. It must steer as carefully and consistently as possible between the two extremes. The general tendency of U.S. diplomacy, however, is to be anything but subtle. U.S. policy is typically characterized by wide swings in the direction of either extreme. U.S. officials tend to oversell engagement strategies and raise expectations at home that economic engagement will transform potential adversaries into close friends. All the talk of U.S.–China "partnership" inevitably leads to disappointment when China acts contrary to U.S. interests. At the other extreme, U.S. officials tend to overinflate threats and raise concerns that potential challengers pose an imminent and profound threat to U.S. security. When the pendulum swings in this direction, the U.S. public becomes mobilized for a confrontation in a way that becomes a self-fulfilling prophecy.[23]

The diplomatic problem suggests a second challenge—the maintenance of domestic support for U.S. foreign policy in the aftermath of the Cold War. In most opinion polls, the U.S. public expresses strong support for U.S. alliances and the continuation of an internationalist foreign policy. There is no strong public sentiment calling for the end of the U.S. forward strategy in Europe, Asia, or the Middle East. This bodes well for the management of the U.S.–Japan alliance. At the same time, there are two important trends in U.S. public sentiment with the potential to complicate alliance management.

One trend is that the U.S. public is generally disinterested in foreign affairs. In a 1999 poll conducted by the Chicago Council on Foreign Relations, the most common response by Americans to the question "what are the most important foreign policy issues facing the United States today?" was "I don't know."[24] The relative apathy of the U.S. public is in part a function of the end of the Cold War. The American people—until the terrorist attacks of September 2001—viewed themselves as secure and reasonably prosperous. Their attention was focused more on domestic than foreign policy issues. After September 11, it is likely that the foreign policy issues that will generate public attention will be all the more closely related to domestic concerns—the problems of terrorism, nuclear proliferation, and, depending on developments in the domestic economy, the loss of jobs through international trade. Almost overnight, "homeland defense" and "homeland security" moved to the forefront of the national policy agenda. In short, the post–Cold War American public has proven in overall terms to be sympathetic to internationalism, but generally not engaged. This leads to the possibility that domestic support for international engagement of the type represented by the U.S.–Japan alliance is fairly broad, but also rather shallow.

A second trend is the general public reluctance to bear the costs of foreign policy. There is consistent public and congressional pressure on the ability of the United States to fund international aid initiatives or to make payments to international institutions such as the UN or the IMF. Popular sentiment, accuracy notwithstanding, seems to be that the

United States overpays while other countries "free ride." The reluctance to bear costs is all the more evident over questions of military intervention. The notion that foreign interventions should be quick and almost casualty-free became conventional wisdom in the United States after the Cold War. Whether the intervention in Afghanistan that began late in 2001 will reinforce or undermine that conventional wisdom remains to be seen.

The implication of these trends is that U.S. foreign policy officials must play a two-level game. As they maintain a forward foreign policy strategy and manage alliance relations, they must also be sensitive to general public sentiment at home and placate the more specific demands expressed by interest groups through the Congress. There is an obvious potential for conflict and that, in turn, complicates the management of the U.S.–Japan alliance.

With American public opinion in mind, a serious military conflict in Northeast Asia—say, over Korea or Taiwan—remains the nightmare scenario for U.S. foreign policy strategists. For the United States to take significant casualties in such a conflict would arouse a public that until now has proved willing to tolerate a forward engagement strategy in Asia that has seemed to carry modest costs. U.S. casualties would necessarily raise the political salience of that strategy and lead Americans to ask why the United States, in the absence of the Soviet threat, continued to defend states perfectly capable of their own defense. This political problem, of course, would become all the more difficult in the event that the U.S. forces took casualties while Japan, for constitutional or other reasons, felt compelled to stand aside or offer only minimal logistical assistance to the United States. Officials on both sides of the alliance recognize the danger of this scenario and the need to revise alliance commitments in order to meet it.

This scenario points to a more general sensitivity in U.S. public opinion—alliance burden sharing. The U.S. public and particularly its representatives in Congress perceive rightly or wrongly that the United States bears more than its "fair" share of the costs of global and regional stability. This sentiment reflects America's alliance relations in Europe as well as in Asia. In relations with Japan, it leads to continual pressure on Japan to contribute more, and at the same time to expressions of resentment that Japan is not doing enough. The result, not surprisingly, is resentment in Japan and conflict within the alliance. The Persian Gulf War offers an apt illustration. The Japanese perception is that Japan's financial contribution to the coalition effort was generous yet underappreciated; the American public perception was that Japan did too little, too late. Similarly, a prevailing U.S. attitude is that Japan did not do enough to restore stability during the Asian financial crisis. The Japanese can justifiably claim that their efforts to do more—in their own way—were discouraged by the United States, which insisted on controlling the political response to the crisis.

The governments of the United States and Japan, faced with a new crisis some ten years after the Persian Gulf conflict, seemed determined to avoid falling into a similar diplomatic trap. After September 11, U.S. officials made clear the urgency of a Japanese response that went beyond the financial realm. The Japanese government, for its part, took a very helpful first step by passing antiterrorist legislation that enabled the Japanese navy to provide direct military support to U.S. forces engaged in the waters proximate to Afghanistan.

However the Afghanistan intervention turns out, it is worth noting that underlying sentiments of economic nationalism within the U.S. public and Congress have the potential to complicate further the task of alliance management. These concerns came to the political forefront during the 1980s and early 1990s in the forms of complaints about Japanese unfair competition and demands that Japan change not only its behavior but also its domestic economic and social institutions. From the perspective of the alliance, the low point was probably the 1989 FSX dispute, which simultaneously threatened bilateral economic and security cooperation.[25] The economic pressure continued and escalated during the early years of the Clinton administration. The 1996 Clinton–Hashimoto summit was a turning point, however, as concerns over the stability of the Asian security environment led U.S. officials to downplay economic conflicts and focus squarely on strengthening the security side of the U.S.–Japan relationship.

The potential for economic conflict to return to centerstage is real. During the 1990s, the United States enjoyed a powerful and prolonged economic expansion. In that context trade deficits and economic conflicts with Japan lost their political salience. But economic expansions do not last forever, and any protracted slowdown in the U.S. economy will bring the old concerns to the forefront.[26] Japan's own economic predicament gives it strong incentives to emphasize exports, and this will exacerbate any potential economic conflict.

The challenge of U.S. domestic politics is compounded by a third problem—that of unilateralism in U.S. diplomacy. Unilateralism is a continual temptation for states that enjoy preponderant power. Hegemonic states are less constrained than "normal" states in the international system. They can act unilaterally and defy international norms without facing the kind of sanctions or other forms of international disapproval to which weaker states would be subject. The United States might sometimes act like a rogue state, but in the current international system it is too powerful to be treated by others as a rogue state.

U.S. unilateralism takes various forms—the rejection of widely supported international initiatives such as the Comprehensive Test Ban Treaty or the Kyoto Treaty, the application of extraterritorial trade sanctions in defiance of international trade law, or the contemplation of a national missile defense system that would undermine existing arms control agreements. Although the United States can "get away" with this kind of behavior, the behavior nevertheless inspires resentment and frustration internationally and complicates U.S. relations with other major powers, in particular its allies.

U.S. unilateralism is a familiar problem in U.S.–Japan relations. The so-called Nixon shocks of the early 1970s (the closing of the gold window, pressure on Japan to revalue the yen, and the abrupt diplomatic opening to China) created anxiety and insecurity in a highly dependent Japan. As Japan has become stronger, U.S. unilateral action has tended to inspire frustration and resentment in Japan and consequently friction in the alliance. Alliance conflict over Super 301, the Structural Impediments Initiative, and the Persian Gulf War are apt examples.

The alliance problem that results from U.S. unilateralism is more profound in the current unipolar context than it was in the prior bipolar context. In the bipolar context, both U.S. behavior and the Japanese response to it were constrained by the overriding need to coalesce in the face of the Soviet threat. In the absence of that threat, the United States, feeling less constrained, is even more tempted to act unilaterally. Japan, facing greater security uncertainty and possessing greater power than it did 20 or 30 years earlier, may become tempted to explore diplomatic or other initiatives outside the U.S.–Japan alliance context.

A fourth and final challenge to alliance management concerns the economic predicament of Japan. Ten years ago, Japanese economic strength was a great source of tension in the bilateral relationship. Americans feared that Japan would overtake the United States economically and thereby pose a threat to U.S. economic security and foreign policy autonomy. Those concerns dissipated during the 1990s, as U.S. economic growth and especially technological dominance seems to have been restored, while Japan seemed incapable of generating a meaningful recovery from the economic recession of the early part of the decade.

In light of the alarm over the "Japanese economic challenge" that pervaded U.S. political discourse a decade ago, it is somewhat ironic that today Japanese economic weakness poses as much, and arguably more, of a challenge to the stability of the alliance than did Japanese economic strength. A Japan beset by an intractable economic crisis at home is a less effective alliance partner than an economically powerful and more self-confident Japan. An economically weakened Japan has less options in response to regional economic problems. During the Asian financial crisis, for example, a more vibrant Japanese domestic economy could have served as an engine of growth to help pull the struggling, smaller economies of Asia out of recession. U.S. officials were both quick to take credit for stimulating the recovery and to criticize Japan for not doing enough it carry its share of the load. A Japan incapable of significantly growing its home market will itself be tempted to emphasize an export-led response to economic stagnation. That strategy will be a source of alliance friction to the extent it leads to penetration of U.S. markets during a possible U.S. growth slowdown.

Japanese economic weakness spills over to the security aspects of the U.S.–Japan relationship as well. It is unlikely that Japan's already weakened political system can handle two major sets of policy initiative at the same time. That is, it is unlikely that Japanese officials can pay significant attention to the need to reform and expand the U.S.–Japan alliance while they are transfixed by the thus far unsolvable problem of restoring Japanese economic vitality. Alternatively, Japanese officials might choose to focus public attention on security issues, precisely as a way to deflect attention from intractable economic problems. The longer-term stability of the U.S.–Japan relationship depends, of course, on the extent to which Japanese government and society can effectively address both economic and security problems.

Japanese economic weakness, if it persists, might also become something of a "wild card" in terms of Japanese political identity and foreign policy ambition. For decades, Japan's political identity has been based on its successful economic performance and the desirability of its economic model. What are the foreign policy implications if Japan can no longer rest comfortably on that foundation? We can imagine, at one extreme, a Japan that becomes withdrawn and passive in foreign policy, lacking the political will and confidence to join with the United States in strengthening the bilateral alliance to address regional crisis or meet new threats. At the other extreme, we might anticipate a frustrated Japan searching for a new international identity, and that search leading it to a foreign policy orientation considerably more independent than that preferred by the United States.

These challenges, taken together, suggest that the long-term stability of the U.S.–Japan alliance should not be taken for granted, and that the alliance relationship must be actively and carefully managed. There is an inclination on the U.S. side to presume that Japan will always be there as a faithful partner, regardless of U.S. behavior. Domestic and international politics are simply too unpredictable to rest great weight on that reassuring assumption.

From Hegemony to Partnership?

U.S. hegemony is by no means an ideal solution to the problems of regional order in the contemporary Asia-Pacific. It is incomplete, and there are limits to what it can achieve. It makes other states uncomfortable, and in some ways it makes the United States uncomfortable as well. The future of the U.S. hegemonic order is uncertain. It is not clear that other major states will embrace the legitimacy of an American-centered system. Dominant powers are naturally resented in the international system, even if they believe their intentions are benign.

The hegemonic order poses challenges for the U.S.–Japan relationship as well. Hegemony tempts the United States to act unilaterally. It leads the American public to take national security and international stability for granted, and to resent having to make any but the most perfunctory sacrifices to promote international order. It tempts the United States to take the relationship with Japan for granted as one simple part of a more ambitious and comprehensive design. The current international structure confronts Japan, for its part, with contradictory temptations. There is the tendency, on the one hand, to remain passive on the assumption that the United States will take care of any security challenges. On the other hand, Japanese officials must face the inevitable uncertainty over how durable the American commitment is, and the nagging question of whether and how to provide for Japanese security more independently. Japan's security predicament is compounded by a profound uncertainty over the prospects for the Japanese economy and for the evolution of Japanese national identity.

The first section of this chapter presented, in addition to hegemony, four possible models of regional order. Are any preferable to the hegemonic model? Two of these models—the security community and the U.S.–Japan partnership models—are arguably more attractive than hegemony. But one can question the extent to which they are feasible in the short- to medium-term regional context. Two other models—the bipolar and multipolar balance models—may be somewhat more feasible. But here we can question the extent to which they are desirable as approaches to regional order.

The potential for a new bipolarity in Asia, while still somewhat remote, seems to increase as China becomes more powerful and as U.S.–China interests conflict, whether over Taiwan, nuclear proliferation, or, as the crisis of April 2001 suggested, control of the airspace and sea lanes in proximity to China. The United States and China could stumble into a bipolar conflict. Would the resulting order be a desirable one?

The maintenance of order through bipolarity would be difficult. The two major powers would need to manage the kind of risks that made the Cold War so dangerous. Bipolarity encourages nationalism, intense ideological competition, and tests of resolve. The United States and Soviet Union managed these tensions without a major war, but they just may have been lucky. The United States and China would face additional challenges as long as their nuclear capabilities remained highly asymmetrical and the United States claimed as an ally a political entity that China considers part of its own territory. Bipolarity would also carry high economic costs, since it would likely lead to the disruption of the economic interdependence that has come to characterize the region as a whole.

The feasibility of a future multipolar order in Asia rests on the popular assumption in international relations theory that hegemonic and even bipolar orders are historical anomalies. Eventually, international relations revert to the familiar pattern of a balance-of-power among multiple major states. Even if we grant, for the sake of argument, that the regional balance will move toward multipolarity, it would still be a mistake to assume that this new multipolar order in the Asia-Pacific would operate similarly and provide the kind of stability associated with the classic European balance-of-power of the nineteenth century.

As a mechanism for order, a multipolar balance would face significant challenges in the contemporary Asia-Pacific. Sources of instability include the uneven spread of military and especially nuclear capabilities among the major contenders. There are also numerous regional flashpoints that increase the potential for conflicts to begin and escalate. The potential inflexibility of alliance commitments due to long-standing friendships (e.g., the United States and Japan) and long-standing rivalries (e.g., Japan and China) is another likely constraint.

Unlike bipolarity and multipolarity, the vision of an Asian security community is extremely attractive. It would in fact be difficult to find a basis for regional order that was more preferable than the prospect of a "European Union like" resolution of long-standing security resentments among the major states of the Asia-Pacific. The obvious problem is that the EU is an extraordinary exception. In general, the circumstances required for the emergence of pluralistic security communities are difficult to attain. The existence of a political community across the borders of sovereign states is an elusive condition that cannot easily be engineered by state leaders.

History and geography make this a special challenge in the Asia-Pacific. Would shared political identity be trans-Pacific or East Asian? What are its core values, and on what common cultural, religious, or other type of foundation would it rest? Pluralistic security communities also rely on the robust presence of democratic government. The Asia-Pacific is marked instead by a significant diversity of regime types. An Asian security community is an attractive ideal that would require considerable time and political transformation to be realized.

What, then, of a transformation from hegemony to a more balanced U.S.–Japan partnership? A more symmetrical U.S.–Japan partnership would in many ways be more attractive, for both parties, than the current unequal one. Mutual dependence would create incentives for more equitable burden-sharing. It would help to constrain unilateral behavior and the resentments that naturally arise on both sides of an unequal partnership. And, the effective combination of U.S. and Japanese resources and instruments would increase the options for addressing regional economic, security, and diplomatic problems.

The authors of the recent Armitage Report find such a partnership extremely attractive. They view it as a way to "redefine and reinvigorate" the bilateral alliance for a new era. They call upon the United States to exercise genuine leadership, defined as "excellence without arrogance." It must "welcome a Japan that is willing to be a more equal alliance partner." Japan, for its part, needs to develop a stronger and more responsive political system, economy, and commitment to collective self-defense. The two sides must eliminate surprises in their diplomacy, and turn burden shifting into power sharing. The bilateral model envisioned by the authors of the Report is the special relationship between the United States and Great Britain.[27]

The vision is indeed an attractive one, but there are many challenges to the realization of this model of security order. Would the United States accept the meaningful sharing of decision-making authority necessarily involved in an equal partnership? To do so would require U.S. officials to overlook the considerable asymmetry in the bilateral *power* relationship—an asymmetry that has left U.S. officials, as well as their Japanese counterparts, conditioned to accept as natural an approach to alliance management in which the United States always leads and Japan always (albeit reluctantly) follows. Under what conditions would Japan step into a more prominent role, notwithstanding the political immobility and economic stagnation that have characterized its predicament since the beginning of the 1990s? To do so requires a fairly significant change, not only in policy but in the political identity and culture that has come to characterize postwar Japan.[28]

It also must be recognized that the U.S. special relationship with Great Britain is based not only on the complementarity of strategic and economic interests, but also on a shared culture, and, more importantly, on the shared historical experience of fighting side by side in major armed conflicts. It is sensible to put forth the U.S.–British relationship as a model, to which the United States and Japan can aspire, in the long term. To attain it will require dedicated and persistent efforts from the governments and societies on both sides of the Pacific. Crises sometimes become opportunities; the U.S. response to the 2001 terrorist attacks presents the United States and Japan with the opportunity not only to foster diplomatic cooperation, but also to begin to gain the experience of fighting side by side.

The development of a deeper U.S.–Japan partnership must also account for the reaction of other states in the region. In light of historical legacies, would the weaker states of the Asia-Pacific embrace a more forward Japanese foreign policy role, even one coordinated with that of the United States? China would likely consider a stronger and more active U.S.–Japan partnership a source of profound anxiety rather than a welcome source of regional stability.

Conclusion

The U.S.–Japan alliance must resist the obvious, post–Cold War temptation to drift without purpose, driven forward only by the force of inertia. The development of a more equal partnership is an ambitious, worthy goal. To achieve it will require both the United States and Japan to manage their alliance relationship more aggressively and effectively. The United States could help by devoting to the alliance the priority diplomatic attention that it deserves. U.S. officials might also work to counter Japan-passing and -bashing at home, and to lower any expectations the U.S. public might have that the U.S. relationship with China will transform itself rapidly either into a meaningful partnership or an all-out confrontation. Japan, for its part, confronts the obvious but intractable problems of political stalemate and economic stagnation— domestic problems with profound foreign policy implications. A weak

Japan poses greater challenges for alliance management than does a strong one. It is essential for each country to recognize that the road to genuine partnership begins at home.

Notes

1. I wish to thank the project organizers, Takashi Inoguchi and John Ikenberry, along with Michael O'Hanlon, Thomas Berger, Jitsuo Tsuchiyama, Victor Cha, and Umemoto Tetsuya for comments and suggestions.
2. As an authoritative survey recently put it, "the most serious threats to U.S. security are likely to come from Asia, where an increasing proportion of the world's economic and military power has come to reside, and where domestic instability and international conflict are virtually certain." Richard J. Ellings and Aaron L. Friedberg, *Strategic Asia: Power and Purpose, 2001–02* (Seattle: National Bureau of Asian Research, 2001), p. i.
3. John A. Hall and T.V. Paul, "Introduction," in Paul and Hall, eds., *International Order and the Future of World Politics* (Cambridge: Cambridge University Press, 1999).
4. For discussion see Neil E. Silver, *The United States, Japan, and China: Setting the Course*, Occasional Paper (New York: Council on Foreign Relations, 2000).
5. See Aaron Friedberg, "Ripe for Rivalry: Prospects for Peace in a Multipolar Asia," *International Security*, Vol. 18, No. 3 (Winter 1993–94), pp. 5–33; Richard K. Betts, "Wealth, Power, and Instability: East Asia and the United States After the Cold War," *International Security*, Vol. 18, No. 3 (Winter 1993–94), pp. 34–77; and more generally, Kenneth N. Waltz, "Structural Realism after the Cold War," *International Security*, Vol. 25, No. 1 (Summer 2000), pp. 5–41.
6. The main arguments are summarized in Charles W. Kegley, Jr. and Gregory Raymond, *A Multipolar Peace? Great Power Politics in the Twenty-First Century* (New York: St. Martin's, 1994), chapter 3.
7. Emmanuel Adler and Michael Barnett, eds., *Security Communities* (Cambridge: Cambridge University Press, 1998).
8. As Blair and Hanley argue, "The process will be one of building upon bilateral security relationships to form a web of regional relationships and capabilities that reinforce security for individual states, discouraging armed aggression as a way of settling disputes, and developing habits of regional military cooperation and professional military behavior." Dennis C. Blair and John T. Hanley, Jr., "From Wheels to Webs: Reconstructing Asia-Pacific Security Arrangements," *The Washington Quarterly*, Vol. 24, No. 1 (Winter 2001), pp. 7–17, quote at p. 16.
9. See, e.g., "France and Germany: Scenes from a Marriage," *The Economist*, March 14, 2001, pp. 27–30.
10. I use the term "hegemony" in this chapter as a social scientific term to describe a certain type of international order. I also recognize that some

scholars and political actors use the same term pejoratively, to condemn behavior of which they disapprove.

11. A good example of official U.S. thinking on regional order in Asia is the so-called Nye Report. See U.S. Department of Defense, *United States Security Strategy for the East Asia-Pacific Region*, Report, Office of International Security Affairs (Washington, D.C.: Government Printing Office, 1995). See also Joseph S. Nye, "The 'Nye Report': Six Years Later," *International Relations of the Asia-Pacific*, Vol. 1, No. 1 (2001), pp. 95–103.

12. I develop this argument at length in Michael Mastanduno, "Incomplete Hegemony: The United States and Security Order in Asia," in Muthiah Alagappa, ed., *Asian Security Order: Instrumental and Normative Features*. (Stanford: Stanford University Press, 2003).

13. See, e.g., Robert S. Ross, "The Geography of the Peace: East Asia in the Twenty-First Century," *International Security*, Vol. 23, No. 4 (Spring 1999), pp. 81–117. An alternative view is Thomas J. Christensen, "Posing Problems Without Catching Up: China's Rise and Challenges for U.S. Security Policy," *International Security*, Vol. 25, No. 4 (Spring 2001), pp. 5–40.

14. Takashi Inoguchi uses the term "bigemony" to describe a version of this model of regional order. See Inoguchi, "Four Japanese Scenarios For the Future," *International Affairs*, Vol. 65, No. 1 (Winter 1988–89), pp. 15–28.

15. See, e.g., Bruce Cumings, "The United States: Hegemonic Still?" in Michael Cox, Ken Booth, and Tim Dunne, eds., *The Interregnum: Controversies in World Politics, 1989–1999* (Cambridge: Cambridge University Press, 1999).

16. See U.S. Department of Defense, *United States Security Strategy*, and Joseph S. Nye, Jr., "The Case for Deep Engagement," *Foreign Affairs*, Vol. 74, No. 4 (July/August 1995), pp. 90–102.

17. Ross, "Geography of the Peace," pp. 85–86.

18. The logic of "hub and spoke" foreign policy strategies is described in Josef Joffe, "Bismarck or Britain? Toward an American Grand Strategy After Bipolarity," *International Security*, Vol. 19, No. 4 (Spring 1995), pp. 94–117.

19. A good discussion of the Korean case is in Robert Litwak, *Rogue States and U.S. Foreign Policy: Containment after the Cold War* (Washington, D.C.: Woodrow Wilson Center Press, 2000), chapter 6.

20. See Silver, *The United States, Japan, and China*, and Yoichi Funabashi, "Tokyo's Depression Diplomacy," *Foreign Affairs*, Vol. 77, No. 6 (November–December 1998), pp. 26–36.

21. *The United States and Japan: Advancing Toward a Mature Partnership*, INSS Special Report (Washington, D.C.: Institute for National Strategic Studies, National Defense University, October 11, 2000).

22. See Thomas J. Christensen, "China, the U.S.-Japan Alliance, and the Security Dilemma in East Asia," *International Security*, Vol. 23, No. 4 (Spring 1999), pp. 49–80.

23. U.S. foreign policy toward the Soviet Union during the détente of the 1970s and the "new Cold War" of the 1980s illustrates this dynamic. See

Michael Mastanduno, *Economic Containment: CoCom and the Politics of East–West Trade* (Ithaca: Cornell University Press, 1992).

24. See John E. Rielly, ed., *American Public Opinion and U.S. Foreign Policy 1999* (Chicago: Chicago Council on Foreign Relations, 1999), p. 11.

25. A detailed discussion of the FSX dispute, from an economic nationalist perspective, is found in Clyde V. Prestowitz, Jr., *Trading Places: How we are Giving our Future to Japan and How to Reclaim it* (New York: Basic Books, Second Edition, 1990).

26. An argument anticipating this outcome is C. Fred Bergsten's, "America's Two-Front Economic Conflict," *Foreign Affairs*, Vol. 80, No. 2 (March–April 2001), pp. 16–27.

27. *The United States and Japan: Advancing Toward a More Mature Partnership*, INSS Special Report.

28. Arguments suggesting the difficulty of this transition include Masaru Tamamoto, "Ambiguous Japan: Japanese National Identity At Century's End," in John Ikenberry and Michael Mastanduno, eds., *International Relations Theory and the Asia-Pacific* (New York: Columbia University Press, 2003).

CHAPTER 3

FROM BALANCING TO NETWORKING: MODELS OF REGIONAL SECURITY IN ASIA

Jitsuo Tsuchiyama

Post–Cold War East Asia has attracted the attention of security specialists, because the political landscape in East Asia has kept changing, especially in the Korean peninsula and China.[1] Realists in International Relations expect an increasing number of future conflicts and crises in this area, so that for example Richard K. Betts predicts "it [East Asia] is becoming less stable as an area of great power interaction."[2] On the other hand, liberal theorists tend to see a more stable Asia that is based on fast economic growth, democratization, and the American commitment. For example, G. John Ikenberry elegantly analyses that the constitutional features of American postwar order provided mechanisms and venues to build political as well as economic relations. Hence, he said they produced massive "increasing returns."[3] Depending upon approaches and perspectives one may adopt, different future security frameworks in Asia will be expected to emerge, ranging from a balance-of-power system to a security community.[4]

Though we have not reached a consensus as to what kind of security frameworks are emerging in Asia at the opening of the twenty-first century, there appears to be an agreement that Asian security frameworks have been constructed by Asians themselves for the first time in their history despite the fact that in the past Asian security frameworks used to be formulated largely by non-Asian forces.

In this chapter, first, I shall examine the various models of Asian security frameworks in the past. Then I shall draw the prevailing models for the present time and for the near future. In doing so, I shall try to shed light on the new roles of the U.S.–Japan alliance in the emerging security frameworks, focusing particularly on the multilateral character of the alliance. To identify the more persuasive rationale of the U.S.–Japan relations for the twenty-first century, I shall use two concepts at the end of this chapter, namely the "bandwagon effect" and "network externalities," both of which are borrowed from microeconomics.

The Asian Regional System in the Past

Prior to the nineteenth century, Asia had not been considered as a solid region. The concept of Asia itself was rather ambiguous for many centuries. It was only after Asian forces encountered European powers that the concept of Asia took shape in the West. Considering this fact, one might say that Asia is a counter-concept of Europe. The interactions among Asian countries in the mid-nineteenth century had been comparatively lower than the European interactions during the same period. Even today, what Asia means is not always the same even among Asian specialists. In other words, the meaning of Asia differs according to the perspectives or fields that we deal with such as politics, economy, and culture. Australia, for example, is usually excluded from Asian culture, but it is included in Asian economy and security. Despite the distant geographic location of the United States from Asia, it has been deeply rooted in Asian politics as well as economy, especially after World War II.

As I pointed out earlier, the interactions among Asia-Pacific powers have shaped a new security framework in Asia for the first time in the modern era.[5] Before getting into detailed discussions of the current security system, let me briefly review the international order that existed or that was believed to have existed in Asia in the past.

Tribute System

As one of the models of the political system in the premodern period, one might quickly recall the Sino-centric order that existed in Asia before the Opium War. John K. Fairbank and his associates, for example, regarded China's tribute system as an international order in East Asia, locating China at the center and other units at the periphery.[6] It is arguable whether this is the concept of the international order in the correct sense of contemporary International Relations, due for example to the fact that England was one of the tribute countries but Japan was not. Nonetheless, even during the Tokugawa period, Japan in practice identified itself with the hierarchical order advanced by physically large and culturally progressed China. In this regard, most Asian countries in the premodern era were on the Chinese "bandwagon" at least in terms of culture, and, to some extent, economy. That system however collapsed as a result of the Opium War and the events that followed, which created an "identity crisis" for countries such as Japan.

Absence of the Balance-of-Power

Relating to the arguments stated earlier on the tribute system, many political scientists pointed out that there had never been a comfortable balance-of-power in Asia. For example, William Chapin wrote in *Adelphi Paper* in 1967 that "[i]t is also unlikely that Asia will develop any really independent balance system."[7] According to Coral Bell who wrote in *Adelphi Paper* in 1968, "the centrality of the Chinese position [was] the prime obstacle to the belief in a workable Asian balance of power."[8] It also pointed out that Japanese economic strength after it became modernized has been too "heavy" to make a balance. As I will discuss later, mere existence of powers does not constitute a balance-of-power. As the European balance-of-power system during the eighteenth-nineteenth centuries has eloquently demonstrated, a balance-of-power system is not just a power configuration among the member states. Rather, the balance-of-power system in Europe is an international institution within which member states regulate disputes among themselves.[9] Without such a mechanism, a balance-of-power system does not function effectively, and conflict resolution is not easy. Compared with the case in Europe, the fact that there was no workable balance-of-power system in Asia prevented the formation of a sensible security framework in the past.

The Intrusive System

Instead of a balance-of-power, Asian political system could be better characterized by what Louis Cantori and Steven Spiegel call the "intrusive system."[10] This is the system in which security relations are managed as a part of the global system. According to their arguments, non-Asian (Euro-American) Great Powers shaped the Asian subsystem. Without external powers' involvements, the Asian powers alone could not construct their own regional order.

There are two distinct characteristics in this system. First, Asian "core" powers such as Japan and China could use the external power's influence on behalf of Japanese/Chinese interests inside the system. Nonetheless, non-Asian Great Powers maintained a benign attitude toward their Asian allies as long as their strategic interests, such as their local interests or global strategic balance, were not put at risk. Japan's alliance policy with England in 1902–22 and Japan's entente diplomacy with Russia and France were such examples.[11]

Second, this system was entirely lacking in local international relations. As Oran R. Young pointed out in his analysis of political discontinuities in post–World War II Asia, the most important interstate relations in Asia—the Sino-Japanese relations—had been shattered by the War and the events that followed. Young wrote that the War destroyed the preconditions of the previous pattern of European dominance in Asia, but it did not produce the new autonomous Asian subsystem.[12] Therefore, Asian interstate relations had been unable to function effectively as a political system. Furthermore, most Asian politics bore the imprint of the dominance of European states in earlier years. Accordingly, many governments, namely China, Indonesia, Malaya, Philippines, and Vietnam have been preoccupied with internal conflicts and civil strife. In addition, the strategic rivalry between the United States and the Soviet Union divided Asian countries into two camps during the Cold War period, and they even fought the most severe wars—Korea and Vietnam—in Asia during the period 1950–70. Asian interstate politics after World War II started from these rather chaotic bases.[13] Young's political discontinuities model was relevant to analyze the Asian situation roughly by the end of 1960s.

Because of these historical as well as strategic reasons, the American commitment to Asian politics, which is basically the outgrowth of the Pacific War, loom larger. It is true that American military presence in Asia had provided a source of stability. And yet, as Chapin pointed out, it has been a source of tension in Asian politics, too.[14]

The Asian Power Balance Today

To a certain extent, the characteristics of Asian security models explained earlier are still relevant to comprehend certain aspects of the current Asian security relations. However, none of those arguments reflect the dynamics of Asia's reality correctly today, because Asia has emerged as a distinct region in the recent past. The reasons are obvious. Japan reemerged as an economic power in the 1960s and 1970s, and the Japanese GNP had grown to about half of the U.S. GNP in the 1980s. Japan also expanded its security role in the U.S.-led alliance in the mid-1990s. Chinese economic as well as military capabilities are still steadily growing. ASEAN countries have developed not only a strong economy but also a security framework known as the ARF. India's economy is growing fast, and its military is becoming strong enough to make a balance vis-à-vis its rival states, China in particular. As a result, the volume of trans-Pacific trade became larger than that of trans-Atlantic trade. Defense expenditures in Asia have grown by more than 40 percent in real terms in 1985–95, while defense spending in the United States and Europe had fallen during the same period. Hence, to use Aaron Friedberg's words, "Asia is ripe for rivalry."[15]

Most security specialists now recognize that the balance-of-power in Asia has emerged. For example, Paul Dibb wrote in his *Adelphi Paper* published in 1995: "the complex five [China, Japan, India, Russia, and the United States]-sided balance-of-power that will now extend right across Asia is a new phenomenon in the region's international order."[16] He also pointed out, "in Asia, it is power balancing and economic growth that are the main security variables."[17] Kenneth Waltz also recently wrote, "the actions and reactions of China, Japan, and South Korea, with or without American participation, are creating a new balance-of-power in East Asia, which is becoming part of the new balance-of-power in the world."[18]

Here, the question is what they meant by the balance-of-power. In order to make clear the meaning of a balance-of-power, it appears to be useful to examine the Asian balance-of-power applying three models of the balance-of-power system that Michael W. Doyle conceptualized.

Doyle's first model is the structural balance that is rooted in the neorealist (Hobbesian) conception of international politics. This model suggests that an anarchic international system can be stable when agonistic powers oppose each other, resulting in a balance. Here the balance is mechanical artifact. The second is the sociological balance that can be rooted in the sociological realist's thinking à la Rousseau. This model requires preconditions in addition to the assumptions of the structural model, which include a shared sense of common interest and identity, a sense of shared legitimacy, and a cultural commitment among member states. "Blood, commerce, arts, and colonies" writes Doyle, "make the balance sufficiently important that states naturally want to reproduce it."[19] Here the balance-of-power is a sociological circumstance. The third is the strategic balance that can be found in Henry Kissinger's writings and in the fox-like diplomacy of Metternich or Castlereagh. Here the balance is a work of diplomacy—"a product of finesse."

Which model describes the case of Asian power balance well? When Waltz wrote that a balance-of-power is emerging in Asia, he obviously meant a structural balance, that is Asian countries have accumulated substantial military and economic capabilities in addition to critical mass (territory and populations) to form a balance among themselves. In this sense, most observers would come to admit that there is a balance-of-power in Asia today. However, one should accept this view with some reservations, because for example one may wonder if Japan is actually "balancing" vis-à-vis China. Christopher P. Twomey, for instance, writes, "Japan has neither significantly strengthened the alliance to allow it to face potential Chinese expansion through the region nor has it allowed it to wither completely."[20] Since Japan avoids strong countervailing alliances and offensive strategy and ignores an opponent's growth, Twomey calls Japan's behavior as "circumscribed balancing."[21] In short, as long as Japan is appeared to be "hiding," one may have difficulty admitting that there is a structural balance in Asia. Because of this reservation, Kenneth Waltz wrote in 1993 that for a country like Japan, to choose not to become a Great Power is a "structural anomaly."[22]

When Dibb writes that the Asian system is "not yet capable of promoting common policies because there is no agreement on what might constitute interests,"[23] he is perhaps considering the system from a sociological viewpoint. Indeed, Asian balance-of-power lacks not only a shared concept of interest, but also a mechanism or an institutional setting for crisis management and conflict resolution in the region. Nor could most Asian countries share the experience of a rule-based balance-of-power game in the region. Since sociological "bonding" is weak, the balance-of-power system in Asia will remain ineffective. As we will see later, the concept of security community is applicable to Asia only in a limited sense. Increased economic interdependence alone does not guarantee security cooperation either. Therefore, Henry A. Kissinger may be right in writing: "the stability of the Asia-Pacific region . . . is not a law of nature but the consequence of an equilibrium."[24] And yet, considering all of the factors mentioned here, Asian security is likely to depend more on the structural balance, especially U.S. military presence in Asia-Pacific and its willingness to use military forces in Asia. Last but not least, no diplomat or statesman has succeeded in creating a legitimized and stable balance-of-power in Asia, since there has been no Metternich or Bismarck in Asia yet.

To sum up, the balance-of-power in Asia has been emerging only in terms of the structural balance in a limited sense, that is with which the level of violence in Asia could be mitigated, but also heightened.

Security Dilemma for Tomorrow?

One of the familiar critiques of the balance-of-power is that it defines power too narrowly: that is, power is mostly considered as military capability. As a result, managing a power balance often produced military competition between rival countries, because as Hans J. Morgenthau pointed out more than four decades ago, every party must try to have "a margin of safety" in making a power balance. Therefore, if one increased its level of security, the rival state may decrease its security. So Morgenthau writes, "all nations must actually aim not at a balance, . . . but at superiority of power in their own behalf."[25] Similarly, Kissinger points out that in the balance-of-power system, "[a]ny significant increase in strength by one of them is almost certain to evoke an offsetting maneuver by the others."[26] Hence, balance-of-power politics breeds power competition that could invite instability. In fact, this was the case that took place between Japan and the United States after they failed to keep the arms control regime known as the Washington Treaty system. By the late 1930s, the security framework in the Asia-Pacific collapsed and that brought two countries to the War in 1941. From 1951 onward, however, the U.S.–Japan security arrangement has prevented both nations from repeating the mistakes they made before the War. In this sense, the U.S.–Japan alliance has succeeded in coordinating interest and action of two states during the past five decades.

In the Asia-Pacific region, most noncommunist countries have security relations with the United States but not with each other; the exception is security cooperation in ASEAN countries. Two bilateral relations are especially important for power balance in this area—the Sino-U.S. relations and the Sino-Japanese relations.

To maintain a balance-of-power, the leadership of these three countries need to carefully assess their partners' power and intentions. When China became second not only in military but also in economic capabilities, "management of the conflicting strategies of economic hardball and security softball will become all the more delicate,"[27] especially for the U.S. leadership, as Michael Mastanduno points out. Or, should the U.S. relative strength be reduced in the future, China and Japan may have to confront each other more directly. Since America's preponderance will not last indefinitely, it may be unavoidable to achieve balance between China and Japan in the years to come. When U.S. primacy became unsustainable, the credibility of U.S. extended deterrence may also be reduced.

To cope with the relative decline of U.S. power, Christopher Layne is advocating an "offshore balancing" strategy for the United States, which is, according to Layne, less expensive than the strategy of preponderance.[28] As an "offshore balancer," Layne advocates that the United States should disengage from its military commitment in Europe, Japan, and Korea. The United States should, especially, reduce the size of U.S. ground forces in those areas. If such a policy option became reality, the Japanese may have to face a more difficult situation than the present one both politically and psychologically. This is one of the worries shared by some American strategists. For example, Samuel P. Huntington wonders if Asian countries, Japan in particular, are going to bandwagon with "hegemonic" China, should the U.S. predominance be lost in Asia. Though we cannot be sure if China will become a "hegemon" in Asia again, Friedberg and Huntington suggest that Asia's future resembles Asia's past when most Asian powers were subordinated to China.[29]

As long as balancing characterizes the relationship between East Asia's two most powerful states, "a cooperative regional order will remain out of reach" as Charles A. Kupchan writes.[30] Whether they can construct cooperative security relations will depend on the following three factors: (1) the manner in which China exercises its surplus power in the future, (2) Japan's tolerance of its relative decline, and (3) U.S. capabilities to formulate appropriate security concepts with China and Japan. If the leadership of the three countries fails to produce satisfying security relations, there could be a security dilemma especially in American/Japanese relations with China.

Since mid-1990s, there have been a number of studies that pointed out a potential development of the security dilemma in Asia, especially between Japan and China. They stress the Chinese "fear" of the U.S.–Japan alliance on the one hand, and the rise of the China "threat" on the other. For example, Thomas J. Christensen writes that Chinese worry increased when the United States and Japan revised the guidelines for the U.S.–Japan defense cooperation. Christensen says that Chinese analysts view the revised guidelines as troublesome, "because they can facilitate U.S. intervention in a Taiwan contingency."[31] In a similar vein, the Chinese leadership fears the future deployment of the TMD in East Asia, Japan in particular, again in conjunction with their Taiwan problem.[32]

There are many reasons for the troubles that the Sino-Japanese relations are going to encounter in the years to come. First, there is a power shifting: China's power is continuously rising in both economic as well as military terms, while Japan's economy has stopped growing for more than ten years and its military strength lacks credibility. Second, they are still suffering from the legacy of the War, since they have unresolved issues. In other words, China and Japan have not overcome their political and historical difficulties yet. As Kupchan wrote, it is true that "[s]uspicion and political cleavage still characterize relationships among the area's major powers."[33] Third, in addition to old problems, they faced new ones: the revised guidelines for the U.S.–Japan defense cooperation, the missile defense controversy, and the Taiwan issue. All of them could fuel the security dilemma between the two. Both sides believe that the other party is "offensive," whereas our side is "defensive." Even worse, both sides worry that the strategic environment of each is not improving as time goes by.[34]

Misperception and misunderstanding on both sides have also negatively impacted their relations. Especially Chinese misperception and the ambiguity on the U.S.–Japan side are worth mentioning here. When the review of the guidelines began in 1994–95, Tokyo, and probably Washington too, had no particular concern with the Taiwan contingency problem, but were involved with the Korean contingency plan. However, when the Hashimoto–Clinton meeting was held, the focus of the new guidelines appeared to have, perhaps unintentionally, shifted from North Korea to China. This was primarily because of the "Taiwan missile crisis" just a month before the meeting, which was originally planned to be held in November 1995. Since Chinese foreign policy makers repeatedly claimed that the revised guidelines attempted to expand Japan's military roles both operationally and geographically making it possible for Japan to "intervene" in a Taiwan contingency, the revised guidelines of September 1997 came to be considered as such even among non-Chinese elites.

TMD may have a similar problem of misperception on the Chinese side. Shortly after North Korea fired a missile known as Taepodong 1 over Japan in August 1998, the Japanese government decided to collaborate with the United States for research on TMD. Again, there was no serious argument in Japan as to how to "use" TMD in a Taiwan contingency at that particular time. Only after the Japanese were told did they come to realize that the actual (or potential) deployment of ship-based TMD in the Japan area would have serious strategic implications in a cross-strait crisis, even if the Japanese government had no such political will. As Thomas Christensen predicts, with TMD deployed, Japan may face a severe strategic dilemma between the U.S.–Japan alliance commitment and risk avoidance in the Sino-Japanese relations, when a cross-strait crisis occurred.[35] The United States has a legal commitment to defend Taiwan, whereas Japan does not have a legal commitment to Taiwan. Nevertheless, if a future Japanese government decided that a Taiwan contingency would not be included in "situations in areas surrounding Japan" which was imposed in the new guidelines, it would have a devastating impact on the U.S.–Japan alliance.

The Bi-Multilateral Security System

To prevent a security dilemma in the U.S. as well as Japanese relations with China, it is desirable to have a security arrangement besides the U.S. bilateral alliances. Though the current security in Asia is guaranteed in large part by the bilateral security arrangements with the United States, there is hope for making workable multilateral security arrangements in the future. As a candidate model for such a security institution, Japan's entente diplomacy in 1907–17, which took place prior to the Washington Treaty system of the 1920s, may be worth mentioning here.

Two years after the conclusion of the Anglo-Japanese alliance, the Russo-Japanese War erupted in February 1904. Two months after the war started, England concluded an entente with France (Russia's ally) partly to avoid being entrapped in the Russo-Japanese War. Based on the Anglo-French entente of 1904 and the Anglo-Japanese alliance of 1902, Japan concluded an entente treaty with France in June 1907, which made it possible for Japan to conclude a Russo-Japanese entente a month later. Finally, based on these entente treaties, England came to conclude an entente treaty with Russia in August, which completed the entente system among France, Russia, England, and Japan. Yet, neither Japan nor England wanted to leave the alliance, in spite of the fact that they realized the theoretical contradictions between the Anglo-Japanese alliance and their entente relations with Russia. This whole round of entente diplomacy was one of the landmarks of Japan's multilateral diplomacy in Japanese eyes. As a diplomatic historian Morinosuke Kajima wrote in 1969, it was the most peaceful time for Japanese diplomacy since the Meiji Restoration.[36]

By concluding the Four Powers Treaty of 1923, Japan joined a multilateral naval arms control regime known as the Washington Treaty system. But, the important difference between the entente system mentioned here and the Washington Treaty system was the fact that the Anglo-Japanese alliance had to be terminated in the latter. To read the future course of the U.S.–Japan alliance, the entente diplomacy in 1907–17 could offer an analogy for future models of Asian security frameworks in which the U.S.–Japan alliance could continue to play a central role.[37]

If the Asian security arrangement follows European experience, a multilateral security arrangement may be in order. Institutionalization of regional security will be strengthened through multilateral frameworks rather than bilateral frameworks. A high level of institutionalization of security arrangements would reduce uncertainty, ambiguity, and the fear of being cheated, and increase credibility and confidence among the parties.[38] But, the current multilateral security frameworks in Asia such as the ARF do not have basic security functions, namely deterrence, crisis management, and defense functions. As long as they remain to be this way, a shift from bilateralism to multilateralism is unlikely in the near future.

Networking

Despite the end of the Cold War and the collapse of the Soviet Empire, the Cold War alliances, NATO, and the U.S.–Japan alliance in particular, have remained alive. Why? To solve this puzzle, there appear to be three arguments: (1) a hegemonic order based on the U.S. preponderance of power continues to sustain the alliance commitments, (2) behavior of small/mid powers are still on the American bandwagon, and (3) the network that the United States developed during the past half century is expanding even after a dramatic power shift took place recently. Each perspective is explained in the following.

Hegemonic Order

With the end of the Cold War, the United States remains as the only superpower, enjoying a substantial surplus of power vis-à-vis all other would-be Great Powers. The size of the Russian economy has shrunk to be about 1 or 2 percent of the U.S. economy. Japan that was once regarded as a number one future economic rival of the United States in the early 1990s has suffered from economic stagnation over the past ten years. There is still a wide gap between U.S. and Chinese nuclear capabilities. Extending Kenneth Waltz' argument, it is now widely believed that the international system has been transformed from bipolarity to unipolarity.[39]

Based on a hegemonic order model, U.S. allies in Asia continue to play a subordinate role. In other words, the United States is the "hub," while its allies are the "spokes" as a recent U.S. secretary of state characterized it. In this context, according to this argument, the U.S.–Japan alliance was redefined in 1996–2000 to suit the new security environment. For example, Japanese Self Defense Forces (SDFs) were sent to Cambodia and Mozambique to participate in the UN peacekeeping activities, despite the fact that the Japanese government had formerly held that Japan cannot send the SDFs abroad due to constitutional constraints. The 1997 new Guidelines for the U.S.–Japanese defense cooperation made it possible for the SDF to extend its "rear-area" supports and search-and-rescue operations to U.S. forces in "situations in areas surrounding Japan." Not only Japan, but also other U.S. allies in the Asia-Pacific such as Korea, Taiwan, and Australia will be expected to play a similar role individually or collectively in the near future. As has been seen at the 1999 Kosovo operation, NATO is also expanding its area of responsibilities beyond NATO members' territories.

Nonetheless, there are difficulties in adopting a hegemonic model in Asia as it is today, because, for example, this model cannot find an appropriate role for China, or to a lesser extent one for North Korea. For the countries that do not accept U.S. hegemony in Asia, notably China, there cannot be a hegemonic order, but there is a balance-of-power in their relations with the United States.

Bandwagoning

In International Relations theory, bandwagoning is a counter-concept of the balance-of-power. For balancing, a country should align with a weaker side against a stronger side: for bandwagoning, a country should align with a stronger power (or threat). In other words, balancing limits the power or influence of states and prevents one from overcoming the others, while bandwagoning increases a stronger side's power by creating a stronger coalition. In short, as Daniel M. Jones writes, "balancing denies others the ability to gain power or influence: bandwagoning offers the opportunity to gain power or influence."[40]

For example, England is known as a "balancer" in European diplomacy. Whenever any powers on the European continent appeared to have a dominant influence, England came to form a counter-coalition with the powers that were against such domination. In a similar vein, the United States after World War II has also played the role of a balancer in the international system.

By contrast, one may discern the logic of bandwagoning in Japanese alliance behavior without any difficulty, whenever Japan joined international coalitions. For the Japanese, international coalitions are regarded either as ways to increase its power and influence, or as opportunities to gain spoils from the conflicts, although it is not difficult to find balancing behavior vis-à-vis Japanese ally's potential enemy. Overall, Japan's alliance rationale has been bandwagoning; Japan has always bet on the "winning horse" when it entered an alliance. Through alignment with a dominant power in the international system, Japan attempted to obtain not only security guarantee from the allied partner, but also used an alliance to enter nonmilitary international regimes in such areas as international finance, trade, and technology. This is why Japan's alliance policy in the first quarter and the last half of the twentieth century placed heavy emphasis on its relations with Anglo-American powers. From such a viewpoint, the Axis alliance was an exceptional case in Japan's alliance policy, because Germany had never been a hegemonic power that controlled the international system. Japan got on Britain's bandwagon in 1901, and on the American bandwagon with the conclusion of the U.S.–Japan security treaty of 1951.[41]

Network Externality
The bandwagoning concept employed by political scientists is borrowed from the economists' concept of the "bandwagon effect." For economists, however, the bandwagon effect has slightly different meanings from the bandwagoning understood by political scientists. According to economist Harvey Leibenstein, the bandwagon effect refers to the situation whereby the utility of some goods increased when more people purchased the same goods.[42] In other words, one's demand depends upon the demands of other people. One's demand is especially affected by the number of other people who purchased the good. For example, the more people who have FAX machines, the more FAX machines will be manufactured, and the greater will be the value of the FAX to their users. The same thing can be said for computer software; the more people who bought Windows for example, the more Windows will be made, and more will be the utility for those users. The bandwagon effect also arises with children's toys (e.g., Pokemon). If almost everyone has it, the desire to have Pokemon will increase. For the same reason, American computer software had a larger market, while Japanese software did not because the latter had a smaller bandwagon effect.[43]

Applying this rationale to alliance behavior in International Relations, we may be able to say that countries enter into or remain in a particular alliance system because many other countries are members of that alliance. Likewise, the more the number of countries coming to depend on the security obtained from, for example, the U.S.-led security institutions, then those security institutions will get larger "market value," and therefore the more useful the security institutions will be for those members.

Today, economists call the bandwagon effect a "network externality." A positive network externality exists if the quantity of a good demanded by a typical consumer increases in response to the growth in purchase of other consumers.[44] Michael Katz and Cal Shapiro write, "the utility that a given user derives from a good depends upon the number of other users who are in the same network."[45] To describe the positive feedback process, economists also use the term "increasing returns." When institutions have increasing returns, it is difficult for other institutions to replace it. Some theorists point out that increasing returns are a source of path dependence, while some others pay attention to the fact that costs of switching from one institution to another increase over time.[46] In other words, once one computer software gained a larger market, or one institution came to be accepted widely (e.g., the Qwerty System), it is hard to switch to another.

The network externality as well as increasing returns arguments provide powerful reasons why VHS, not Beta, Microsoft, Macintosh, and Ethenet, nor TokenRing got a larger market. As Ikenberry points out, American postwar order exhibited this phenomenon of increasing returns to its institutions.[47] If the opposite is the case, there is a negative network externality (e.g., environmental problems).

Without regard to the end of the Cold War and the collapse of the Soviet Union, the network externality of the U.S. security institutions, especially alliances, significantly increased in the recent past. This rationale of network externality does not necessitate a stronger (or weaker) power (or threat) of a rival coalition. Therefore, alliance rationale depends on this logic and does not require the power (in terms of material) assessment of a counter-coalition. Because of this, network externality can better explain the puzzle as to how the Cold War alliances outlived the Cold War.

As various goods and products from electric appliances to weapon systems are competing over "de facto standards," the ways in which governments manage the international security compete over their "standards" in world politics. Hans J. Morgenthau might call this a struggle for power. Today, international actors who can set the standards in each issue area and can form crosscutting coalitions will become winners of the game. Sometime it is up to the "market" that determines the de facto standards, while in other cases de facto standards could be obtained through negotiations and agreements.

Such complex institutions as alliances are made up of many de facto standards over not only weapon systems, but also the rules, procedures, and obligations in the case of crisis and war. Most of the standards in alliance management are either negotiated with, or sponsored by the U.S. government. Acquisition and Cross-servicing Agreement (ACSA), Pre-positioning of Oversea Material Configured to Unit

Sets (POMCUS), and Host Nations Support (HNS) are such examples that the United States has successfully set certain models of alliance cooperation, which are functioning as de facto standards of U.S. alliance management.

Furthermore, as the United States spreads its alliance networks, "the virtual alliances" are now emerging among some countries that are not legally allied to each other. For example, though Australia, South Korea, and Japan are not official allies, their alliance relations with the United States could make them de facto allied partners to one another in such circumstances as an "out of area" situation. Like the Combined Joint Task Force (CJTF) plan in NATO, a similar arrangement in U.S. alliances in the Asia-Pacific is likely to create a "virtual alliance" among them.

For instance, the operations in East Timor demonstrated that many countries in the Asia-Pacific, namely Australia, New Zealand, the Philippines, Singapore, South Korea, Thailand, and the United States contributed to the international forces there. For the East Timor operation, Japan provided C-130 aircraft for transporting humanitarian supplies, South Korea provided a battalion of troops, and China provided police forces.

This regional security cooperation can be strengthened by the U.S. military exercises with the powers in the region. In 2001, the exercise called "Team Challenge" was held between Thailand, the Philippines, Singapore, and the United States, while Japan and South Korea sent observers. Likewise, key U.S. bilateral security arrangements in the Asia-Pacific are moving beyond bilateralism. This is the situation that Dennis C. Blair, the commander-in-chief of the U.S. Pacific Command, calls "security community" and is aiming at creating in the Asia-Pacific region. Blair and his colleague wrote that the security challenge in the Asia-Pacific region is to transform the balance-of-power approach to produce security community.[48] Nonetheless, it is needless to say that security-community building increases the United States' capabilities to manage international security as well as safety problems ranging from military disputes to international terrorism.

This rationale neither contradicts the realists' argument of bandwagoning nor the liberals' concept of institutional "stickiness."[49] This is in line with Joseph S. Nye's "soft power" argument, too. Nye wrote "co-optive power is the ability of a country to structure a situation so that other countries develop preferences or define their interests in ways consistent with its own." Hence, "when one country gets other countries to want what it wants," it has soft power.[50] Network externality basically explains the same phenomenon in a different fashion. Figuratively speaking, Japan continues to "purchase" security from the security mechanism that the United States built and maintains. If this is the case, whatever happened for example to the Soviet Union, does not make much difference in the U.S. allies' calculation of whether they are to stay in alliances after the Cold War. Thus, the United States is able to increase its power by maintaining and expanding its security networks in the post–Cold War world. One may call the United States a "hegemon" after the Cold War, while another may call it an "invisible empire."

Conclusion

In this chapter, I have presented four models of regional security frameworks in post–Cold War Asia, namely the balance-of-power system, the security dilemma, the bi-multilateral security system, and the network externality model. Each perspective shed light on one aspect of the Asian security framework in general and the U.S.–Japan alliance in particular. The chance to go back to the balance-of-power struggle is always there, either when the United States lost its primacy or when China gained significant influence in Asia. If a negative spiral began to grow between China, the United States, and Japan, it would increase instability not only in Asia but also in the international system.

A bi-multilateral security framework appears to be a realistic policy option for Japan in the near future. Japan's experience of its entente diplomacy in 1907–17 may offer a useful analogy in order to make use of both bilateral arrangement (U.S.–Japan alliance) and multilateral arrangements at the same time. Yet, one may wonder if the current Japanese government has the diplomatic skill to conduct such a nuanced diplomacy today. The Multilateral security framework in Asia will remain to be seen as weak, because the multilateral arrangements in Asia have severe limitations to become effective security institutions. In the meantime, bilateral U.S. alliances in Asia, the U.S.–Japan alliance in particular, are expected to play a central role. As has been pointed out, when the Guidelines for the U.S.–Japan defense cooperation are revised, this alliance would add more multilateral character for Asian regional security. In such a way, the security network based on U.S. ideas, information, and economic as well as military power will be expected to expand, in Asia. As I have suggested earlier, this security network is not necessarily going to take the form of a unified alliance as has been the case in Europe. Rather, this is a more flexible mechanism that can cope with the various types of disputes at ad hoc bases. This network should be able to control not only regional security issues, but also to deal with "the operations other than war" type of safety problems, such as international terrorism, international crimes, international transportation safety, and disease (e.g., AIDS) control. Peace enforcement, noncombatant evacuation operation, humanitarian assistance, and disaster relief are other areas of responsibilities that the security network should pay more careful attention to in Asia. Thus, we have entered into an era where we are experimenting if a new security network that has never existed in our history works in Asia. Whether we can make use of the existing institutions to create the security network mentioned here depends mostly upon our capabilities to foresee the security/safety problems of Asia in the years to come.

Notes

1. See e.g., Aaron L. Friedberg, "Ripe for Rivalry: Prospects for Peace in a Multipolar Asia," *International Security* (Vol. 18, No. 3, 1993/94), pp. 5–33; Richard K. Betts, "Wealth, Power, and Instability: East Asia and the United States after the Cold War," *International Security* (Vol. 18, No. 3, 1993/94), pp. 34–77; Thomas J. Christensen, "China, the U.S.–Japan Alliance, and the Security Dilemma in East Asia," *International Security* (Vol. 23, No. 4, 1999), pp. 49–80, 63; and Thomas Berger, "Set for Stability: Prospects for Conflict and Cooperation in East Asia," *Review of International Studies* (Vol. 26, 2000), pp. 405–428.

2. Betts, "Wealth, Power, and Instability," p. 34.

3. Kenneth W. Waltz, "The Emerging Structure of International Politics," *International Security* (Vol. 18, No. 2, Fall 1993), pp. 44–79, 67.

4. See, e.g., G. John Ikenberry and Jitsuo Tsuchiyama, "Between Balance of Power and Community: The Future of Multilateral Security Co-operation in the Asia-Pacific," *International Relations of the Asia-Pacific* (Vol. 2, No. 1, 2002), pp. 69–94.

5. Aaron L. Friedberg, "Will Europe's Past be Asia's Future?" *Survival* (Vol. 42, No. 3, 2000), pp. 147–159, 147.

6. John K. Fairbank, ed., *The Chinese World Order: Traditional China's Foreign Relations* (Cambridge: Harvard University Press, 1968).

7. William Chapin, "The Asian Balance of Power: An American View," in Louis J. Cantori and Steven L. Spiegel, eds., *The International Politics of Regimes: A Comparative Approach* (Englewood Cliffs, New Jersey: Prentice-Hall, 1971), pp. 335–350, 335, 348.

8. See, e.g., Corall Bell, "Asian Balance of Power: A Comparison with European Precedents," *Adelphi Paper* (No. 44, 1968).

9. Hedley Bull, *The Anarchical Society* (New York: Columbia University Press, 1977), chapter 10.

10. Cantori and Spiegel, *The International Politics of Regimes*, pp. 1–41.

11. For detailed discussions on Japan's diplomacy, see G. John Ikenberry and Jitsuo Tsuchiyama, op.cit.
12. Oran R. Young, "Political Discontinuities in the International System," in Richard A. Falk and Saul H. Mendlovitz, eds., *Regional Politics and World Order* (San Francisco: W.H. Freeman, 1973), pp. 34–49, 40.
13. Ibid., p. 40.
14. Chapin, op. cit., p. 48.
15. Friedberg, "Ripe for Rivalry," p. 7.
16. Paul Dibb, "Toward a New Balance of Power in Asia," *Adelphi Paper* (No. 295, 1995), p. 10.
17. Dibb, "Toward a New Balance of Power in Asia," p. 11.
18. Kenneth N. Waltz, "Structural Realism after the Cold War," *International Security* (Vol. 25, No. 1, 2000), pp. 5–41, 36.
19. Michael W. Doyle, "Balancing Power Classically: An Alternative to Collective Security?" in George Downs, ed., *Collective Security Beyond the Cold War* (Ann Arbor: University of Michigan Press, 1997), pp. 133–165, 143.
20. Christopher P. Twomey, "Japan, a Circumscribed Balancer: Building on Defensive Realism to Make Predictions About East Asian Security," *Security Studies* (Vol. 9, No. 4, Summer 2000), pp. 167–205, 200–201.
21. Ibid., "Japan, a Circumscribed Balancer," pp. 167–168.
22. Kenneth N. Waltz, "The Emerging Structure of International Politics," *International Security* (Vol. 18, No. 2, Fall 1993), pp. 44–79, 66.
23. Dibb, op. cit., p. 8.
24. Henry A. Kissinger, *Diplomacy* (New York: Simon Schuster, 1994), p. 826.
25. Hans J. Morgenthau, *Politics Among Nations* (New York: Knopf, 1948), p. 227.
26. Kissinger, op. cit., p. 826.
27. Michael Mastanduno, "Preserving the Unipolar Moment, Realist Theories and U.S. Strategy after the Cold War," *International Security* (Vol. 21, No. 4, 1997), pp. 49–88, 87.
28. Christopher Layne, "From Preponderance to Offshore Balancing," *International Security* (Vol. 22, No. 1, 1997), pp. 86–124, 112–113.
29. See e.g., Aaron L. Friedberg, "Will Europe's Past be Asia's Future?" p. 151.
30. Charles Kupchan, "After Pax Americana, Benign Power, Regional Integration, and the Sources of a Stable Multipolarity," *International Security* (Vol. 23, No. 2, 1998), pp. 40–79, 64.
31. Thomas J. Christensen, "China, the U.S.–Japan Alliance, and the Security Dilemma in East Asia," *International Security* (Vol. 23, No. 4, 1999), pp. 49–80, 63.
32. Ibid., esp., pp. 64–69, 74–80.
33. Kupchan, op. cit., p. 62.
34. On power shift, see, e.g., Stephen Van Evera, *Causes of War* (Ithaca: Cornell University Press, 1999), chapter 4.
35. Thomas Christensen, op. cit., pp. 64–69.
36. Morinosuke Kajima, *Nihon no Heiwa to Anzen* (Peace and Safety of Japan) (Kajima Peace Research Institute, 1969).

37. Jitsuo Tsuchiyama, "Ironies in Japan's Defense and Disarmament Policy," in T. Inoguchi and P. Jain, eds., *Japanese Foreign Policy Today* (New York, Palgrave: St. Martin's Press, 2000), pp. 136–151, esp. 140–141.

38. G. John Ikenberry, "Institutions, Strategic Restraints, and the Persistence of American Postwar Order," *International Security* (Vol. 23, No. 3, 1998), pp. 43–78.

39. Michael Mastanduno, op. cit., pp. 49–88.

40. Daniel M. Jones "Balancing and Bandwagoning in Militarized Interstate Disputes" in Frank W. Wayman and Paul F. Diehl, eds., *Reconstruction Realpolitik* (University of Michigan Press, 1994), pp. 227–244, 229.

41. Tsuchiyama, op. cit., pp. 140–142.

42. Harvey Leibenstein, "Bandwagon, Snob, and Veblen with Network Externality," *Journal of Industrial Economics*, XL, pp. 55–83.

43. Carl Shapiro and Hal R. Varian, *Information Rules* (Cambridge: Harvard Business School Press, 1998), chapter 7.

44. Robert S. Pindyck and Daniel L. Rubinfeld, *Microeconomics*, 3rd ed. (New Jersey: Prentice-Hall International, 1995), p. 118.

45. Michael L. Katz and Carl Shapiro "Network Externalities, Competition, and Compatibility," *American Economic Review* (Vol. 75, No. 3, June 1985), pp. 424–440. Quoted in S.J. Liebowitz and Stephen E. Margoils "Network Externality: An Uncommon Tragedy," *Journal of Economic Perspective* (Vol. 8, No. 2, Spring 1994), pp. 133–50, 133.

46. Paul Pierson, "Increasing Return, Path Dependence, and the Study of Politics," *American Political Science Review* (Vol. 94, No. 2, June 2000), pp. 251–267.

47. Ikenberry, op. cit., pp. 43–78, 73. See also Pierson, op. cit., pp. 251–267.

48. Dennis C. Blair and John T. Hanley, Jr., "From Wheels to Webs: Reconstructing Asia-Pacific Security Arrangement," *The Washington Quarterly* (Vol. 24, No.1, Winter 2001), pp. 7–17, esp. 15–16.

49. Ikenberry, op. cit. See also his *After Victory: Institutions, Strategic Restraint, and the Rebuilding of Order after Major Wars* (New Jersey: Princeton University Press, 2001), chapter 3, pp. 50–79.

50. Joseph S. Nye, Jr., "Soft Power," *Foreign Policy* (No. 80, Fall 1990), p. 168.

CHAPTER 4

THE CONSTRUCTION OF ANTAGONISM: THE HISTORY PROBLEM IN JAPAN'S FOREIGN RELATIONS

Thomas Berger

Over the past decade, Japan has moved toward greatly enhancing its regional security role within the framework of the U.S.–Japan security treaty.[1] Japan's provision of logistical support to U.S. forces fighting in Afghanistan is one important, concrete reflection of this trend, and provides a welcome contrast to Japanese inaction during the Gulf campaign a decade earlier.[2] Japan's willingness to assume such a role greatly strengthens the U.S. ability to maintain a stabilizing presence in Asia at a price that is acceptable to the American public. More importantly, it removes one of the main sources of tension in the U.S.–Japan alliance, namely the charge that Japan is a free rider on an international security order paid for largely with American money and defended with the lives of American men and women.

This transition, however, from passive participant to active contributor to the international order is not devoid of risk. The memory of Japanese aggression before 1945 continues to weigh heavily on its relations with the rest of Asia, in particular on its relations with China and the two Koreas. The widespread perception that Japan has no sense of remorse for its past actions, feeds suspicions that it easily could revert to its earlier, more belligerent patterns of behavior. As a result of this gap in historical perceptions, many Asian leaders have been deeply suspicious of any efforts to enhance Japan's military role. As Singaporean Prime Minister Lee Kuan Yew famously put it, encouraging Japan to do more militarily is like offering chocolate liqueurs to a reformed alcoholic. Japan's emergence as a military power, even if it is in partnership with the United States, therefore runs the risk of triggering a regional arms race. To put it another way, the "history problem," as it is sometimes referred to, exacerbates regional tensions and acts as a major potential obstacle to strengthening and expanding the U.S.–Japan alliance.[3]

Fortunately, such antagonisms are not carved in stone. As the European experience demonstrates, even deeply rooted, protracted conflicts eventually can be overcome, if not totally eradicated. Franco-German relations prior to 1950 were burdened by a history of conflict and mutual grievances that rivals the Sino-Japanese relationship in length, acrimony, and complexity. Likewise, German–Polish relations and German–Czech relations have been marked by the memory of atrocities and mass expulsions that match or exceed anything experienced in Asia in the past century. Nonetheless, today the nations of Western and Central Europe have achieved a far-reaching conciliation and are engaged in a historic enterprise of transnational institution building that is transforming interstate relations in that region.[4]

Political developments in Asia since the end of the Cold War have created the possibility for a similar process to occur. Whether this potential will be realized, however, depends on a variety of factors. Above all, regional leaders must recognize that security has not only military and economic dimensions, but a critical societal and ideational one as well. In order to enhance regional stability they will have to confront the history problem and explore ways by which its disruptive impact can be minimized. Confronting the burdens of the past, however, is likely to require a long and protracted effort. Moreover, the prospects for success are uneven. Because of their strong common interests and common democratic institutions, the chances for conciliation between Japan and South Korea are relatively good. Sino-Japanese relations, on the other hand, are more problematic, and dispelling historically grounded feelings of animosity are likely to prove far more difficult.

The Construction of Conflict

Scholars and policy makers alike have been slow to recognize the importance of historically based animosities and rivalries in international affairs. Academic analyses of the causes of conflict have been long dominated by structural theories of international relations that largely discount ideas and culture as causal variables or sees them as being reflective of other, underlying forces (the balance-of-power, opportunities for trade, etc.). This gap in academic analyses has practical consequences. In the absence of theoretically grounded models that can explain which particular factors are important and why, it is impossible to articulate a foreign policy that addresses them as issues.

The first step is to recognize that ideas have consequences. Socially held beliefs and values, including feelings of hatred and victimization, have implications for international relations and state policy.[5] Such socially held beliefs, however, do not float freely in a society. They emerge out of the interaction between various groups within a given society or political system and are shaped and sustained by a host of often conflicting goals, beliefs, and concrete material interests. To put it another way, antagonisms between groups and nations are not naturally occurring phenomenon, they are socially and politically constructed.

While the nature of that interaction needs to be investigated on a case by case basis, it is nonetheless possible to identify some common patterns and causal mechanisms by which antagonistic relations between groups are typically created. Although such patterns are not the same as the universal laws of physics, they can be identified for heuristic purposes to analyze the structure of antagonism in different societies separated in time and space.

These patterns can be seen as falling into two broad categories. In the first pattern, intergroup animosity develops at the mass societal level and bubbles up to create conflict. Often these feelings of antagonism well up in what appear to be sudden eruptions of hatred. In the second category, animosities are deliberately created by elites, often for instrumental purposes. For the purposes of the present discussion, we can call such top-down causes of hostility "the mobilization of antagonism."[6]

Perhaps the simplest and most direct way in which antagonisms develop from the bottom up occurs when there are collective memories of past injustices, whether real or imagined, that have been visited by one group on another. Such memories may be based on actual direct experiences of the victims of such injustices. Alternatively, they may be transmitted to others by means of stories told in families, through movies, novels, and other works of art, as well as through school texts and history books. They act as a potential well of hatred that can poison relations between groups, often over the space of generations.[7]

Another bottom-up mechanism that generates eruptions of intergroup hatred results from competition between members of different groups for scarce resources, such as housing, jobs, or public services.[8] While typically they are of greater concern for domestic politics than for international relations, such domestic-level tensions can spill over into interstate conflict in a variety of ways. For instance, if ethnic conflict in one country involves members of an ethnic group who also reside in another country, then sympathy for their fellows can lead the members of the same ethnic group residing in the second country to place pressure on their government to intervene in the affairs of the first country.[9]

In addition to such bottom-up eruptions of hatred, there are numerous reasons why elites may choose to mobilize antagonisms from the top down. Often this type of antagonism may be of use in harnessing societal energies for a collective purpose, such as fighting a war or embarking on some other difficult enterprise.[10] In other instances, elites may chose to mobilize antagonisms for narrow parochial interests, such as strengthening their hold on power and diverting attention away from domestic social, economic, and political problems.[11] Elites may then tap existing memories of injustices that already exist, amplifying and redirecting them through use of the media, the educational system, and so forth.

Once a sense of antagonism is generated, however, elites often find it difficult to reign in the passions they have unleashed.[12] This is particularly so when the elites are disunited and in competition with one another. Under such conditions there exists the temptation of one elite to use such sentiments in order to strengthen their own position vis-à-vis other elites who adopt a more moderate position. In some (but not all) cases a kind of symbolic bidding war may ensue, as each side tries to demonstrate that it has stronger nationalist credentials than its rivals. Eventually, elites themselves may come to believe in the images and ideas that they created originally for cynical, instrumental purposes. This is especially so if there has been a generational shift where the new rising cohort of elites have been socialized to view such ideas as being true.[13] In this way, antagonisms that originally were generated at the elite level filter down to the mass level only to circulate back up to the elite level, thereby reinforcing them and creating a particularly potent culture of animosity.

Obviously, these patterns often overlap. Generally speaking, the more mechanisms are at play in a given case, the more complex the structure of antagonism between two or more groups is likely to be, and the more difficult it is to defuse the resulting tensions. Depending on the causal mechanisms by which these tensions were generated, very different types of policies may be needed to defuse them. In cases of elite mobilization of antagonisms it will be necessary to first win the cooperation of the elite, typically through a process of political bargaining. While one side may bear the brunt of the burden for achieving reconciliation, the other side needs to be ready to reciprocate in kind. At a minimum, there can be no genuine reconciliation if both sides are not committed to the process.[14] On the other hand, when the roots of animosity exist at the grassroot level, it will be necessary to implement a variety of public policies designed to reduce the level of tension in addition to gaining the support of elites. Beyond symbolic demonstrations of reconciliation by leaders, it may be necessary to offer compensation to the victims of past injustices and to punish their perpetrators. The improvement of treatment of other countries' nationals may be needed. Similarly, grassroot contacts through student and scholarly exchanges, as well as the extensive efforts at reeducation through the school system and the media can play a critical role in tackling negative images at the mass societal level.[15]

Where a deep-rooted culture of antagonism has been created, it will be necessary to engage on both levels at once. Even then, progress is likely to be slow and difficult. In such cases, if the commitment to reconciliation exists only at the elite level, while the societal roots of antagonism are not addressed, the reconciliation process is likely to be undermined at some point by bottom-up pressures.

Having briefly outlined some of the general pathways by which deep-rooted intergroup antagonisms become established, the next task is to explore how they developed in East Asia. For analytical purposes it may be useful to examine first the broad international framework in which the structure of antagonisms developed over the course of the Cold War before looking at the specific mechanisms that have helped generate antagonisms in the Japanese–Korean and Sino-Japanese contexts.

The Structure of Conflict in Asia During the Cold War

The end of World War II and the onset of the U.S.–Soviet superpower rivalry brought about far-reaching changes in the global strategic environment. Yet, these changes were far from uniform in nature. In different parts of the world the Cold War took on a drastically different character, with far-reaching ideational as well as geostrategic implications. Three factors in particular made the structure of the Cold War in Asia very different from that of Europe: the relative looseness of the U.S.-led coalition, the paucity of democracies in the region, and the deep divisions among the Communist nations in Asia. Together these factors served to discourage regional leaders from confronting historically rooted feelings of animosity.

The relative looseness of the U.S.-led alliance system in Asia resulted above all from the nature of the principal security threat faced by countries in the region. In Europe, the massed forces of the Soviet Red Army posed a clear and present danger in the eyes of America's European allies. In the Asian context, however, for much of the Cold War the main threat was posed by divisions within Asian countries, either in the form of guerilla movements or of conventional armies seeking to reunify the divided nations of China, Korea, or Vietnam. As demonstrated first in Korea and then again in Vietnam, this threat was fueled by deep nationalist passions and could not be easily deterred. Although the U.S. military enjoyed overwhelming conventional military superiority over the armies of North Korea and Vietnam and was able to inflict vastly greater casualties on the enemy than it itself suffered, it was unable to beat them into submission. On the other hand, conventional Soviet forces in the Far East posed a less significant direct threat to U.S. allies in the region. This was especially true for America's principal Asian partner, Japan, which as an island nation was relatively insulated from the threat of invasion. As a result, the fear of becoming entangled in fierce, protracted conflicts in which they had only a relatively marginal interest made U.S. allies leery of committing themselves to a tightly integrated military structure like NATO, even as they sought to bind themselves tightly to the United States for their own defense.[16]

The United States as well was fearful of becoming overly entangled in Asian conflicts. From an American perspective the loss of one of the less developed Asian nations would have less of an impact on the global balance-of-power than the loss of one of its European allies. Whereas the United States might have been willing to contemplate risking nuclear war to prevent West Germany from falling into the hands of the Soviet Union, it was unwilling to take such chances for the sake of Vietnam.

As a result, the United States created a system of bilateral security relations with various Asian countries, instead of a single, multilateral framework as in Europe. This so-called hubs and spokes arrangement placed the United States at the center of regional politics. The bilateral diplomatic dialog with the United States was the single most important point of contact with the larger international system for virtually every one of its regional allies, including South Korea, Japan, and the Philippines. One consequence of the hubs and spokes arrangement was that the pressure for political dialogue between America's Asian allies was much weaker than was the case in Western Europe.

Under these circumstances, as long as the United States was willing to subordinate justice and international reconciliation to the larger goal of defending against Communism there was little structural reason for Asian nations, including Japan, to pursue issues of historical injustice. In contrast, already in the 1940s and 1950s the Federal Republic of Germany was compelled to seek reconciliation with its western neighbors (most importantly France).

Even if the Japanese and the United States had been eager to pursue a dialog on historical issues the authoritarian, antidemocratic character of many of America's Asian allies during the Cold War did little to encourage them. It might have seemed highly incongruous for Japan to pursue a dialog on past injustices with regimes like those of South Korea's Park Chung Hee or China under Mao Zedong at a time when those governments were engaged in the brutal repression of their political opponents. In addition, it was possible for authoritarian regimes to repress any grassroot anti-Japanese sentiments that may have been present in their societies if they felt that this was in the larger national interest. In 1965, when South Korea and Japan finally normalized relations, the Park Chung Hee government was able to ignore vehement public criticism and large-scale demonstrations. In the case of China, Mao and Zhou En Lai were able to waive the issue of reparations without provoking the slightest visible public reaction.

The looseness of the U.S.-led alliance structure in Asia was paralleled by even greater divisions on the Communist side. In Eastern Europe most Communist governments—with the important exceptions of Albania and Yugoslavia—were created and sustained by Soviet power. In contrast, in Asia most Communist governments were established by indigenous revolutionary movements, typically emerging out of anticolonial movements. They enjoyed a considerable degree of independence from the Soviet Union. Over the course of the Cold War, differences within the Communist camp increased, culminating in the Sino-Soviet split followed by bloody conflicts between the People's Republic of China (PRC) and Vietnam as well as Vietnam and Cambodia.

The divisions on the Communist side reduced the incentive for regional leaders to address questions of guilt, justice, and compensation. During the 1950s and 1960s, the high point of détente in Europe, the Federal Republic of Germany felt compelled to address its responsibility for the horrific crimes perpetrated by Germany in Eastern Europe during World War II. Chancellor Willi Brandt's much celebrated self-prostration before the monument to Jewish victims of the Warsaw uprising was not simply an act of contrition by an individual statesman, but rather a crucial part of the Federal Republic's campaign to improve ties with the Soviet Union in the late 1960s and early 1970s. In contrast, during the same period in Asia the pressure on Japan to acknowledge its crimes during World War II in certain respects actually weakened. The Sino-Soviet split encouraged Chinese Communist leaders to bury the issue of a Japanese apology and compensation for the suffering caused by Imperial Japanese forces during the war in the Pacific in return for economic aid and investment. North Korea appeared as hostile as ever toward the United States and its allies. Finally, tensions throughout the region rose following the fall of Saigon in 1975. Justice and reconciliation were generally crowded off the political agenda by more pressing geostrategic considerations, allowing mutual animosities and feelings of resentment to smolder long after 1945.

There were some countervailing trends. The PRC's opening of relations to the outside world allowed individual Japanese, such as the Asahi newspaper reporter Tachibana, to meet directly with the victims of the worst atrocities committed by Japanese forces in Asia prior to 1945.[17] During the 1980s, increased intra-regional economic interdependence and intensified regional political dialog put the history issue on the international political agenda, as reflected by the controversy that erupted between Japan and the PRC over Japanese textbooks in the early 1980s. On balance, however, the relative weakness of political ties between U.S. allies in the region, as well as the divisions in the Communist world simply did not create the same sort of incentives for seeking reconciliation that existed in Europe during the Cold War era.

These structural factors alone, however, do not explain the origins of the animosities that exist between Japan and its neighbors. They provide only a partial explanation of why they have been able to smolder on for more than half a century after the end of the War. To better understand these factors it is necessary to look at how these sentiments are rooted at the national-political and bilateral levels.

Japan and South Korea—Unwilling Partners

Japan and Korea have had a particularly troubled relationship in modern times. As Japan developed into a Great Power in the late nineteenth and early twentieth century it sought to catch up with the Great Western Powers by carving out an imperial sphere of its own.[18] Korea became the first target of Japanese expansionism, and eventually was annexed by Japan in 1910. Opposition to Japanese rule was squelched with brutal efficiency, and the economic and strategic needs of the Japanese home islands, rather than the interests of the Korean population, dictated the course of Korean economic and social development.[19]

The exploitation of Korea on the political and economic level was exacerbated by popular Japanese feelings of superiority vis-à-vis Koreans and other Asians on the societal level. It was widely felt in Japan that the superior qualities of the Japanese nation had been demonstrated by the fact that among the peoples of Asia, Japan alone had successfully industrialized and learned to compete with the Western powers on an equal, or near-equal footing. Koreans, Chinese, and other Asian peoples were viewed as superstitious and backward in comparison. These feelings of superiority were translated into everyday discrimination against Koreans and others in the education and labor markets. Asian citizens of the Japanese empire living on the main islands were granted more extensive rights. Yet, with some important exceptions, Korean immigrants to Japan were typically relegated to menial tasks and hard manual labor and generally occupied the lowest rungs of the social hierarchy.[20]

As the colonial subjects began to resist Japanese rule, Japan's sense of superiority came to be mixed with feelings of fear and mistrust. Korean (and Chinese) anticolonial protests were seen as evidence of the irrationality of the subject peoples. Moreover, the political radicalization of at least part of the Korean community in Japan fed fears that the Koreans could become a subversive Fifth Column in Japanese society and posed a threat to the social and political order. These apprehensions led to increasingly strict police supervision of Koreans both in Korea and on the home islands. They also fueled anti-Korean violence, most notoriously in the wake of the great Kanto earthquake of 1923, when thousands of resident Koreans were hunted down and killed by Japanese militias.

The oppression of the Korean population worsened during the militarist era of the 1930s and 1940s. Forced assimilation policies were adopted and efforts were made to eradicate Korean culture. Hundreds of thousands of Koreans were forcibly conscripted into the Japanese armed forces and used as slave laborers in Japan and other parts of the Japanese empire. Most notoriously, as many as 200,000 women were lured or kidnapped to serve as sexual slaves for the Japanese army (the so-called Comfort women).[21]

At the end of the war Japanese rule over Korea collapsed and many Koreans were repatriated. However, a considerable number—as many as 800,000—remained in Japan. The pattern of discrimination against Koreans that was established before 1945 lingered on in the postwar period. Fears of a Korean Fifth Column reemerged when Korean workers joined in the Communist workers movement or formed criminal gangs.[22] Prime Minister Yoshida Shigeru famously compared the resident Korean population to ants residing in the belly of a lion, ants who potentially could kill the lion from inside. Yoshida and other Japanese leaders actively lobbied General MacArthur to increase the powers of the police so that they could clamp down on the so-called Three People's Problem,—the resident Korean, Chinese, and Taiwanese populations. The emergence of a Communist North Korea, which could command the loyalty of a substantial portion of the resident Korean population, and the outbreak of the Korean War, eventually persuaded the American occupation authorities to accede to these requests. Resident Koreans, including those who had served in the Japanese military or had been victims of the atomic bombings of Hiroshima and Nagasaki, were stripped of their Japanese citizenship and associated rights and benefits.[23]

Although ostensibly aligned with Japan through its security relationship with the United States, South Korean elite and popular sentiment was overwhelmingly colored by a powerful anti-Japanese feeling. In a very real way modern Korean nationalism had been forged in the crucible of Japanese colonial domination of Korea, and many of the new ROK's most revered figures were former leaders of the anticolonial movement. Japan's continued mistreatment of the resident Korean population, as well as remarks by senior Japanese government officials that reflected a continuation of condescending attitudes toward Korea, did little to change both grassroots and elite level anti-Japanese animosity in South Korea.[24]

In Korea, the symbols of the new republic drew actively on anti-Japanese symbols. For instance, a national monument was erected in honor of An Jungkun, the Korean assassin of the first Japanese consul general of Korea, Ito Hirobumi, and his image was widely used in Korean currency. The import of Japanese cultural products, including music and theater, was outlawed, despite a large potential audience for such goods. Japanese–Korean diplomatic relations were hampered by deeply rooted feelings of mutual antipathy and bitter recriminations. One episode that poignantly reflects these tensions occurred in 1953, when the United States was able to lure Japanese Prime Minister Yoshida Shigeru into a conversation with his South Korean counterpart, President Synghman Rhee at U.S. military headquarters in Tokyo. Reportedly, the two men sat silently without exchanging a word. Finally, Yoshida, in order to make some conversation, asked, "Are there any tigers in Korea?" "No," Rhee replied, "the Japanese took them all." With that brief exchange all conversation between the two leaders ended.[25]

The strategic realities of the 1950s and 1960s supported such a distant relationship. For the Japanese government, a closer strategic relationship with South Korea carried with it the very real risk of becoming entangled in a land war in Asia. Indeed, it was precisely in order to reduce that risk that Yoshida Shigeru slowed down the pace of Japanese rearmament so that the Japanese SDFs did not formally come into existence until 1955, well after the armistice of 1953 had ended military operations on the Korean peninsula.[26] In the 1960s, however, pressures for closer relations between the two countries mounted. Confronted with a worsening situation in South Vietnam, the U.S. State Department stepped up its efforts to foster a regional dialog between its two chief partners in East Asia. At the same time, the new military government of President Park Chung Hee was willing to make greater concessions in order to secure Japanese aid and increase Japanese investment.

In both countries, domestic opposition to closer ties was strong. In South Korea, demonstrators accused the Korean government of selling out the Korean nation to its archenemies. In Japan, leftist students and protestors warned that the treaty would further lock Japan into America's strategy of regional domination. Japanese and Korean leaders persevered, however, and in 1965, after 14 years of bitter and often tumultuous negotiations, the two countries finally signed a treaty normalizing their diplomatic relations.

The treaty brought many benefits. Beyond establishing the framework for increased economic trade and investment, it dealt with a wide variety of issues, including fishing rights and the return of stolen art treasures and other valuable cultural objects to South Korea. The treaty also led to a significant improvement in the legal status of ethnic Koreans residing in Japan and claiming South Korean citizenship. At the same time, however, the treaty laid the foundations for avoidance of the issue of historical injustices and future acrimony.

Under the terms of the Agreement on Economic Cooperation and Property Rights, Japan extended $500 million in aid to the Korean government and arranged for the resolution of outstanding property claims. The Japanese government insisted that these payments were not to be understood as reparations or compensation for past injustices, flatly contradicting public statements being made by the Korean negotiators. In particular, the Japanese government insisted that demands for compensation by Korean comfort women and other Korean individuals had been resolved under the terms of the agreement and that the Japanese government was under no legal obligation to recognize such claims. The Korean government, on the other hand, argued that although the Korean government had relinquished the right to compensation, the treaty did not apply to individual Korean citizens, including the Comfort Women, Korean A-bomb survivors, and others.

The two sides also had sharply divergent views of the meaning of Article 2 of the 1965 Basic Relations Treaty, which stated that "all applicable treaties and agreements, including the Treaty of Annexation of August 22, 1910, and all previously signed treaties between the Korean Empire and the Empire of Japan, are considered to be already null and void." The Korean side interpreted the phrase "null and void" to mean that Japan now recognized that the Treaty of Annexation and previous treaties had been illegal and invalid. The Japanese government, however, in Diet interpellation insisted that "null and void" meant that the treaties had been legally valid and signed on the basis of mutual agreement, but had ceased to be in effect with the establishment of the ROK in 1948. According to this interpretation of history, since the Japanese takeover of Korea had been mutually agreed upon, there should be no need for Japan to apologize for its past actions nor to pay compensation for the alleged injustices perpetrated by its colonial administration.[27]

These differences in interpretation helped ensure that the history issue would remain a chronic source of bilateral tension. In a pattern that would repeat itself throughout the Cold War and beyond, Japanese policy makers—including even quite liberal members of the Japanese political elite such as Socialist Prime Minister Murayama Tomoichi—would claim that the compensation and colonial guilt issue had been resolved by the 1965 treaty and espouse a sanitized version of modern Japanese history that ignored or downplayed the suffering inflicted on the Korean people.

Such claims would enrage ordinary Koreans and prompt the Korean government to lodge emotional protests. In response, conservative Japanese politicians and interest groups, such as Veterans groups and the Japan Bereaved Family Association, would put pressure on the Japanese government to resist such demands.[28] In the end the Japanese government would find some face-saving mechanism—typically officials responsible for making provocative statements would be forced to resign and new monetary assistance would be offered to placate the most vocal groups of protestors—to appease Korean protestors. At the same time, Japanese officials would retreat behind opaque legalistic arguments based on the 1965 treaty in order to avoid admitting that Japan bore any legal or moral obligation for its past actions, thus laying the groundwork for the next cycle of bilateral acrimony and recrimination.

Over the course of the Cold War, Japan and the ROK were inevitably led to increase their ties with one another. Common geopolitical and economic interests, buttressed by active U.S. encouragement of dialog between the two, made the case for greater cooperation strong and compelling.[29] The depth of the historically rooted animosity between the two sides, and the strength of the perverse political mechanisms that sustained such hostile sentiments, helped ensure that the two sides never managed to get beyond a thin, U.S.-mediated alignment against the backdrop of bitter antagonism.

Japan and the PRC

Sino-Japanese relations have been at least as contentious and acrimonious as Korean–Japanese relations. After Korea, China became the principal target of Japanese imperial aggression. Huge swathes of Chinese territory, beginning with Taiwan after the Sino-Japanese War, came under Japanese imperial control before virtually the entire Chinese coastal area was seized by Japanese forces after the Marco Polo bridge incident in 1936.

As in Korea, Japan justified its imperial expansion on the grounds that it was the only Asian nation that had managed to transform itself into a major military and industrial power able to compete with the Western imperial powers. As in Korea this imperial myth transformed itself into a general sense of superiority vis-à-vis the Chinese that permeated relations between ordinary Japanese and Chinese on a day-to-day level.[30]

Not surprisingly Japanese encroachment on Chinese territory as well as the wounds inflicted on Chinese national pride by Japanese attitudes of superiority provoked a powerful nationalist backlash among the Chinese population. One of the cathartic moments in the formation of the modern Chinese sense of national identity, the May Fourth Movement of 1919, was triggered by popular outrage over the Chinese government's acceptance of Japanese territorial demands after World War I.[31] Chinese national identity defined itself in opposition to Japan.

Because Japanese control over its Mainland Chinese possessions were never as complete as its hold on Korea, Chinese resistance to Japanese rule provoked even bloodier reprisals designed to beat the Chinese population into submission. According to conservative estimates offered by Japanese as well as Chinese historians, approximately 200,000 Chinese, the majority of them civilians, were killed after the fall of the Nationalist Chinese capital of Nanjing in 1936. Thousands more were raped, tortured, and brutalized during a ten-day campaign of terror that de facto was sanctioned by the Japanese field commanders. And Nanjing was merely the most notorious incident during the brutal nine-year struggle between Japanese and Chinese forces. In all, an estimated total of ten million Chinese soldiers and civilians died during the Japanese invasion of China, leaving behind a residue of bitter memories that would continue to feed anti-Japanese resentment more than 50 years after the end of the War.

In the post-1945 period, Japan and the PRC found themselves on opposite sides of the Cold War. Yet, for many of the same reasons that Japanese ties to South Korea were so weak, its rivalry with China was restrained. At the elite level, some Japanese politicians developed close ties with the Republic of Taiwan and espoused a strongly anti-Communist ideology. Yet others, including such influential figures inside the ruling Japanese Liberal Democratic Party as Prime Ministers Yoshida Shigeru and Ishibashi Tanzan, were reluctant to adopt an overly antagonistic stance toward China for fear that Japan could become entangled in a land war in Asia.[32] Influential Japanese business leaders who either had commercial relations with China or were interested in it as a potential market and source of raw materials similarly pushed for a measured approach to relations with the PRC.

At the same time, the same leftist groups who opposed closer military links to South Korea and the United States supported improved dialog with the PRC. Beyond any ideological affinity that some leftists may have felt for the Communist regime, many also felt genuine remorse over the atrocities committed by Japanese forces in Mainland China.

Japanese public opinion data from the 1950s and 1960s showed that the PRC was one of the least liked and least trusted nations. Yet, anti-Chinese sentiments in many respects were less salient than anti-Korean sentiments, in part because the resident Chinese population at under a 100,000 was so much smaller than the resident Korean population. In addition, there existed a considerable reservoir of sympathy in some quarters in Japan, especially among left-wing intellectuals and the media.

During the first half of the Cold War, this penchant for moderation on the Japanese side was not reciprocated by the PRC. Japan's alignment with the PRC's archenemies, Taiwan and the United States, placed it fully on the side of capitalist imperialism from a Chinese ideological standpoint. China's political leaders were happy to draw on the rich wellsprings of popular anti-Japanese sentiments to help mobilize the country for its own ideological purposes.[33]

In the aftermath of the Sino-Soviet split and the reopening of ties with the United States, however, these attitudes were quick to change. Senior Chinese officials such as Zhou En Lai quietly informed their erstwhile allies in the Japanese Socialist Party that they no longer opposed the U.S.–Japanese Security Treaty because they saw it as a useful check on Soviet "hegemonism."[34] The Chinese regime sharply moderated its previously anti-Japanese position and over the next few years worked out a series of agreements leading up to the full normalization of Sino-Japanese diplomatic relations in 1978.

Following on the precedent already set by Taiwan, South Korea, the Philippines, and other U.S. Asian allies in the 1950s and 1960s,[35] the PRC dropped its demands for compensation in return for economic aid and assistance. Once again, however, the two sides differed on what they had agreed to. Whereas the Japanese side insisted that with the 1978 normalization treaty the issue of Japanese formally taking responsibility for the actions of the Japanese imperial army had been settled, the Chinese leadership felt free to continue to criticize what it saw as evidence of Japan's evident unwillingness to face up to its past. Consequently, the 1980s witnessed a string of incidents that brought into the open these differences between Chinese and Japanese views of the past. Chief among these were the controversies over Prime Minister Nakasone's 1985 visit to the Yasukuni Shrine; the Japanese Ministry of Educations approval of an allegedly revisionist history textbook for adoption in Japanese schools; and various comments made by Senior Japanese politicians that downplayed or denied Japanese moral culpability for the events of the Pacific War.

A variety of factors lay behind the PRC's decision to pursue the history issue. Chief among them was the fear that a number of senior Chinese leaders, including Deng Xiaoping, felt that the propagation of historically revisionist view were the first steps toward a possible remilitarization of Japanese society. In addition, the Sino-Japanese relations became intertwined with internal Chinese political battles, as rival leaders within the Chinese Communist Party accused their opponents of lacking in patriotic spirit for an overly moderate stance toward Japan.[36] At the same time, outside the ranks of the Communist Party, student demonstrators, in an echo of the May Fourth Movement nearly 70 years earlier, used Sino-Japanese relations to criticize their own government.[37]

At the end of the Cold War in 1989, despite the normalization of relations, increased economic ties, and a wave of popular Japanese interest in China, Sino-Japanese relations remained filled with potential tensions. Disagreements loomed on a broad range of issues, from trade to military spending. Increased Sino-U.S. tensions inevitably spilled over into the Sino-Japanese relationship. And while a modus vivendi had been worked out on the issue of reparations, the two sides remained far apart in their understanding of history and their images of each other.

The Possibility of Conciliation after the Cold War

During the 1990s, the end of the Cold War together with a number of other domestic and international political developments seemed to set the stage for a genuine transformation of Japan's relations with its neighbors. At the domestic level, a number of mass societal trends in both Japan and Asia promised to reduce the level of antagonism between Japan and its neighbors. Chief among these was the passing away of the generation that had been directly involved in the War and Japan's colonial domination of Asia. This generational shift had a number of consequences. First, it led to an increased readiness in Japan, to openly discuss the more gruesome aspects of Japan's domination of East Asia. Those who could be charged with criminal responsibility for atrocities that occurred prior to 1945—including most importantly Emperor Hirohito—had passed from the scene. Meanwhile a new generation of younger Japanese grew up who were largely ignorant of the War, but in many cases were interested in learning about it. Second, the passage of time meant that outside of Japan, those who had personally suffered at the hands of the Japanese had passed from the scene, creating at least the possibility of a de-escalation of emotional anti-Japanese sentiment.

Another important development was gradual liberalization of Japanese attitudes toward foreigners as reflected in both changes in official government policy and in societal behavior. Foreign residents regained access to most of the social and welfare services provided by the Japanese state. Naturalization procedures were clarified and simplified. The legal status and rights of resident Koreans and Chinese were strengthened (including those resident Koreans pledging loyalty to North Korea). Finally, police controls on foreigners residing in Japan were systematically loosened if not entirely abolished.[38] On the level of everyday life, discriminatory attitudes and behavior continued to be strongly in evidence, but they had changed greatly compared to the Japan of the 1950s, 1960s and even 1970s.[39] As a result a major, if subtle, source of tension between Japan and its neighbors, in particular South Korea, was removed.

Reinforcing these domestic political developments were a number of changes in Japan's international environment, both on the geoeconomic and geostrategic levels. Whereas until the 1980s most of the economies of the East Asian economies were oriented toward boosting exports to the West, after 1980 intra-regional trade and investment began to skyrocket. With increased economic interdependence came the growth and development of regional economic and political institutions, and increased dialog between Asian elites on a broad range of issues, including trade, the environment, and security. In the past Korean and Chinese complaints about Japanese attitudes toward the past were voiced primarily on a bilateral level. Beginning in the 1990s the two countries could make use of multilateral venues, such as the ARF to place concerted pressure on Japan. Likewise, as their investments in Asia grew, Japanese business elites became increasingly sensitive to the issue.

Just as important as these geoeconomic considerations was the change in the geostrategic logic of Japan's position in East Asia. During the

Cold War Japan's fear of entanglement through its alliance commitments outweighed its fear of abandonment by its allies. The disappearance of the Soviet military threat, however, threatened to gravely weaken the U.S. resolve to maintain its overseas military presence. At the same time a host of old and new security problems troubled the region, as reflected first by the Gulf War in 1991, followed by the escalation of tensions on the Korean peninsula in 1994 and in the Taiwan straits in 1996, and finally and most dramatically by the War against Terrorism that began in 2001. Japanese policy makers came under increased pressure to bolster their regional security role beyond merely assisting in the defense of Japanese home islands.

For Japan to take on such an enhanced military security role is immensely difficult. Despite the collapse of the old Japanese Left centered on the Japanese Socialist Party, domestically Japanese popular resistance to assuming a greater security role remains strong. While few Japanese leaders today continue to espouse the old pacifist ideal of unarmed neutrality, the majority of Japanese remain unconvinced of the need to assume a greater military burden or doubt that Japan would be able to effectively cope with its security problems were it to do so. Moreover, many Japanese fear that if Japan increases its military role solely within the context of its bilateral security relationship with the United States, it runs the risk of being dominated by its far larger and more powerful alliance partner. Externally a more active Japanese military role could provoke fears of renewed Japanese adventurism in other parts of Asia, especially in Korea and the PRC. Such a reaction could lead to an increase in regional tensions and possibly spark a military arms race.

As a result, since the end of the Cold War there has been renewed interest in Japan and other parts of Asia in finding a new multilateral security framework that would allow Japan to assume a greater military role without alarming its neighbors or its own citizens. One important prerequisite for the creation of such a multilateral framework, as a number of prominent Japanese politicians including Ozawa Ichiro and Kakizawa Koji have come to realize, is a new willingness to resolve the differences between Japan and its Asian neighbors regarding the history issue. Beginning with the inauguration of the Hosokawa Morihiro government in 1993 Japan has embarked on an extended diplomatic campaign designed to demonstrate its increased willingness to acknowledge at least some measure of responsibility for the War while underlining Japan's commitment to the ideal of peaceful coexistence with its neighbors.

These efforts are plagued by the vast gulf between the ways in which Japan and its neighbors saw history. Despite the new openness to debating the historical issue, after decades of neglect many ordinary Japanese continued to feel a lack of direct responsibility for the past and were only vaguely aware of the extent and scale of the suffering that Japan had inflicted on the rest of Asia.[40] Moreover, conservative elements in Japanese politics and Japanese society frequently undermined efforts by the Japanese government to symbolically come to grips with the history issue. One dramatic example was provided by the passage in 1995 of a Diet resolution condemning World War II–related aggression and pledging that never again would such acts be repeated. While there was broad political support for the resolution, the measure was met with fierce conservative criticism. A signature campaign condemning the resolution reportedly was signed by five million Japanese citizens, while threats from more conservative members of the ruling coalition threatened to topple the government of Socialist Prime Minister Murayama Tomiichi. In the end Murayama persevered, but he was forced to water down the wording of the resolution considerably, and the intense and highly public political controversy sparked by the initiative arguably negated any symbolic value that it might have had.[41]

Despite the problems encountered in Japan's diplomatic campaign these efforts eventually bore fruit. During a historic visit to Tokyo in October 1998 by the newly inaugurated South Korean President Kim Dae Jung Japanese–Korean ties appeared to take a big step toward reconciliation on the history issue. During his trip Kim and Japanese Prime Minister Obuchi Keizo⁻ issued a joint statement in which the Japanese government offered a clear and forthright apology for the pain and suffering that its colonial rule had inflicted upon the Korean people. More importantly, more than any Korean leader before him, Kim Dae Jung suggested that Korea was willing to accept such an apology and use it as the basis for an improved bilateral relationship.[42] Subsequently both sides undertook a number of steps designed to further reconciliation between the two peoples. Later that summer, amidst much fanfare, South Korea lifted its ban on the import of Japanese cultural items. Around the same time Japan in turn offered aid and compensation to Korean A-bomb victims and Korean Veterans of the imperial army, two groups that previously had been barred from receiving such aid on the basis of their nationality. Likewise, a new debate was initiated on giving resident Koreans increased civil rights, including possibly the right to vote in Japanese local elections. Movement on the history issue paved the way for increased cooperation on strategic and diplomatic issues as the two sides intensified the joint planning and training between their armed forces.

The visit to Tokyo by PRC leader Zhang Zemin a few weeks later provided a sharp contrast to the apparent progress made by the Kim Dae Jung visit. Like Kim, Zhang sought to make the history issue the center-piece of his visit, hoping to use it to extract concessions on the issue of Taiwan. Unlike Kim, however, Zhang was unwilling to commit himself to a "final resolution" of the history issue, and there was a general impression in Japan that China was not ready to embark on a genuine process of conciliation. In addition, as the leader of a democratic nation, Kim Dae Jung appeared to have greater legitimacy in the eyes of many Japanese. Even in the eyes of relatively liberal Japanese, the PRC's demands for an apology for the historical misdeeds of Japanese mili-tarism seemed a bit rich in light of China's continued military build-up and increased military assertiveness in Asia today. As a result relatively little progress was made on the history issue during Zhang's visit. Although Japan did offer signs of remorse, it stopped short of making the kind of full-fledged apology that it had offered to South Korea a few weeks earlier. More importantly, while the Kim Dae Jung visit was widely hailed in the media as a major step forward in the two countries' bilateral relations, the Zhang visit was seen as disappointing at best.[43]

The comparison between the Kim and Zhang visits suggests that while Japan today may be more ready to move closer to its neighbors on historical questions, such efforts are as likely to be motivated by calcu-lations of political interest as they have been in the past. Without a firm fundament of common interest and credible promise of reciprocity, efforts to achieve reconciliation on this issue is likely to flounder. In the case of South Korea, the two countries saw strong common interests in not only their economic relationship, but in preserving the U.S.-led security order on which both countries had come to depend. In the case of China, tensions remained over Taiwan and potentially Japan's security relationship with the United States. Zhang's unwillingness to commit himself to a lasting resolution of the history issue seemed to signal that cooperation on economic and other issues was tactical in nature and did not reflect a readiness to realign long-term strategic interests. Under such conditions, capitulating to Chinese pressures on the history issue would be counterproductive.

Subsequent developments in spring and summer 2001 suggest that even under favorable conditions, however, attempts at reconciliation can be undermined by a lack of sustained leadership. Conservative scholars in Japan under the directorship of Nishio Kanji produced a draft textbook offering a decidedly revisionist view of modern Japanese history that downplays or ignores the negative aspects of Japan's period of imperial expansion and the atrocities committed by its forces during World War II. After requiring only relatively minor revisions, the Japanese Ministry of Education then approved the use of this text in Japanese schools, sparking a new round of sharp criticism from South Korea and the PRC. Soon thereafter Prime Minister Koizumi Junichiro undertook a controversial visit to the Yasukuni shrine dedicated to the Japanese war dead. In doing so he made good on his promise to conservatives in his party, whose support he needed in order to rally support in his campaign for the party presidency but at the price of further antagonizing Japan's neighbors. Japan was made to pay a significant and heavy diplomatic price for its actions. The criticism from Beijing was scathing, but the tone in Seoul was hardly any less harsh. Military to military talks between Japan and Korea were suspended. The ban on Japanese cultural items was reimposed. And the South Korean ambassador was temporarily recalled to Seoul for "consultations."[44]

Signs soon appeared that the immediate diplomatic storm would eventually subside.[45] Efforts to patch up Japanese–Korean and Sino-Japanese relations accelerated in the wake of the September 11 attacks on the United States. Both Japan and South Korea, as close U.S. allies, came under pressure to cooperate more closely on how to provide a regional response to the terrorist threat. Of particular concern was defusing possible regional tensions arising from Japan's unprecedented dispatch of warships to the Indian Ocean in support of the U.S. military campaign in Afghanistan. In addition, the two countries were intensely aware of the need to orchestrate policy on the thorny issue of North Korea, which was defined as part of the new "axis of evil" and made the primary targets of the second round of the American war on terror. For its part, the PRC was eager to capitalize on America's need for allies and to use the opportunity to crack down on Islamic separatists in Xinjiang.

As a result, in October Koizumi visited both South Korea and China to arrange for a resumption of normal relations. In Korea, Koizumi reiterated previous apologies for Japanese past misdeeds and paid his respects to Korean freedom fighters celebrated at a museum in Seoul. Thereafter the two sides agreed to renew cooperation on a wide range of issues, including joint historical research, counter terrorism, and fishing rights.[46] In Beijing once again the tone was markedly cooler. The two sides agreed to concentrate on future cooperation without proposing any concrete suggestions on seeking reconciliation on the history issue.[47] Once again, as in 1998, the Japanese perception was that the prospects for achieving genuine reconciliation were greater with South Korea than with China. But even with Korea there was a marked coolness in the atmosphere after the events of the previous year, and the goal of achieving a genuine reconciliation between the two nations seemed further off than it had in over a decade.[48]

Conclusions

The history of Japan's relations with its Asian neighbors strongly suggests that security has not only military and economic dimensions, but a critically important social cultural component as well. This finding has practical as well as analytical consequences. From the point of view of scholars and analysts of international affairs it suggests that greater systematic attention needs to be given to the ways in which particular constructions of identity and interests interact to produce structures of either cooperation or conflict. In terms of its implications on the practical level, the forgoing analysis suggests that political leaders and foreign policy practitioners need to treat the politics of reconciliation as more than just an afterthought. To be sure, in some instances it is neither desirable nor necessary to expend political capital for this purpose. In particular, when it appears that there is a lack of willingness or capacity on the other side to pursue reconciliation, then it should be postponed, at least for the time being. Apologies must be accepted, as well as given, if a genuine reconciliation is to be achieved.

Policy makers also need to be aware that in instances where a culture of antagonism has taken root there will be no easy, one-step solutions that will sweep away decades of distrust and antipathy. One of the underlying causes of the setback of relations between South Korea and Japan in 2001 was the widespread assumption on the part of many Japanese that the issue had been essentially resolved in 1998. Instead, to use the phrase that was employed at the end of the first compensation talks between Germany and Israel, policy makers must realize that any given agreement is likely to be only the first step on the long path toward reconciliation.[49] The time has come for Japan and its neighbors to begin to walk that path together, beginning with the ROK. Asian political leaders, beginning with the Japanese prime minister, must be willing to support such efforts and prevent them from being sabotaged by conservative political forces that oppose such a dialog or deny the need for reconciliation. We can only hope that in time such leadership will emerge in Japan and that the other nations of East Asia can join them in this effort.

It remains an open question, however, whether Japan on its own will be able to muster sufficient leadership to undertake such a sustained and arduous effort. After nearly a decade of wrestling with only limited success with the history issue, a sort of "apology fatigue" has taken hold in Tokyo. Japanese elites have come to appreciate the intractability of the history issue, while many ordinary Japanese, especially among the younger generation, have become increasingly frustrated by what they see as a lack of appreciation by the outside world of Japan's efforts to forge a more healthy relationship with its neighbors. It is in this atmosphere that revisionist views may find root in Japan. While the revisionist textbook issued by Nishio Kanji has won only limited acceptance (less than 0.1 percent of Japanese schools have actually adopted the textbook), the popularity of right wing manga-comic books, and in particular the works of Kobaysahi Yoshinori, reflects a disturbing trend toward revisionism among young Japanese.[50]

The United States, together with Japan's other security partners in the region, have a strong interest in preventing this trend from going too far. While by itself the historical issue is unlikely to lead to military conflict, it can have a serious corrosive impact on the region and is likely to hinder efforts to forge a stronger regional alliance system. Instead, the United States, together with South Korea, the Philippines, Australia, New Zealand, and possibly Thailand should seek to encourage a regional dialog on the history issue in tandem with existing discussions on cooperation in the trade and economic areas. Only in this way will it be possible to place the existing set of relationships on a firmer ideological footing and create the political climate that will allow the adaption of the present security system to the challenges of the twenty-first century.

Notes

1. For an excellent overview of this shift in Japanese strategy, see Michael Green, *Japan's Reluctant Realism: Foreign Policy Changes in a Era of Uncertain Power* (New York: St. Martin's Press, 2001).
2. The Bush administration has taken special care to thank Japan for its efforts in this regard.
3. See Thomas Christensen, "China, the U.S.–Japan Alliance and the Security Dilemma in East Asia," *International Security* 23:4 (Spring 1999). See also Gerrit W. Gong, ed., *Remembering and Forgetting: The Legacy of War and Peace in East Asia* (Washington, DC: CSIS, 1996).
4. For German nationalists France long figured as the arch villain responsible for national division after the horrible destruction inflicted by the Thirty Years War. For its part, France in the contemporary era felt it had been victimized by German aggression three times in the space of less than a century. See Lillian Gardner Feldman, "The Principle and Practice of 'Reconciliation' in German Foreign Policy," *International Affairs* 75:2 (April 1999).

5. While this might appear to many a self-evident observation, in fact it represents a radical departure from the way in which most political scientists have viewed the role of ideas since the late 1960s. Belief systems have been portrayed as largely epiphenomenal—the reflections of the concrete, objective interests of groups and interests understood primarily in terms of material benefits or power relationships. Over the past decade, however, there has been a revival of interest in the impact of ideas. For an overview see Jeff Chekel, "The Constructivist Turn in International Relations Theory," *World Politics* 50:2 (January 1998).

6. These two types of patterns are reflective of two different views of how political cultures function. For a discussion of the theoretical lineage of these different schools, see David Laitin, *Hegemony and Culture: Politics and Religious Change Among the Yoruba* (Chicago: University of Chicago Press, 1986). Scholars studying the process of reconciliation in post–civil war societies similarly stress the importance of both top-down and bottom-up approaches. See John Paul Lederach, *Building Peace: Sustainable Reconciliation in Divided Societies* (Washington, DC: The United States Institute of Peace Press, 1997).

7. For instance, when Yugoslavia disintegrated in the late 1980s, long-suppressed memories of the brutal conflict between Albanians, Croats, Serbs, and Slovenes during World War II helped fuel a new round of violence that cost over 200,000 lives in the 1990s. Laura Silber and Allan Little, *Yugoslavia: Death of a Nation*, revised edition (New York: Penguin Books, 1997).

8. For a classic analysis of this type of conflict mechanism, see Myron Weiner, *Sons of the Soil*. For a detailed and nuanced discussion of the origins of ethnic conflict, see Donald L. Horowitz, *Ethnic Groups in Conflict* (Berkeley: University of California Press, 1985), chapters 3–5.

9. Myron Weiner has labeled this pattern "the Macedonian Syndrome." See Myron, Weiner, "The Macedonian Syndrome: An Historical Model of International Relations and Political Development," *World Politics* 23:1 (1970). For a brilliant discussion of this process, see Rogers Brubaker, *Nationalism Reframed* (New York and Cambridge: Cambridge University Press, 1996).

10. For instance, Thomas Christiansen has argued that Mao Zedong used the sense of threat from the United States and Taiwan to mobilize the Chinese populace for his program of rapid industrialization, The Great Leap Forward. See Thomas Christiansen, *Useful Adversaries* (Princeton, NJ: Princeton University Press, 1996).

11. For a particularly clear example of this line of argumentation applied to the case of German Imperialism, see Hans-Ulrich Wehler and Kim Traynor, trans., *The German Empire, 1871–1918* (Anna Arbor, MI: Berg Books, 1985). See also Jack Snyder, *Myths of Empire: Domestic Politics and International Ambition* (Ithaca, NY: Cornell University Press, 1993).

12. One should not underestimate, however, how quickly such sentiments can be suppressed. See e.g. John Dower's fascinating study of U.S.–Japan wartime propaganda, *War Without Mercy* (New York: Pantheon Books, 1986).

13. For an extensive articulation of this point of view, see Snyder, *Myths of Empire*, pp. 41–42, 107–108.

14. For a similar argument regarding the importance of elite reciprocity in achieving reconciliation, see Herbert Kelman, "Transforming the Relationship Between Former Enemies: A Social-Psychological Analysis," in Robert I. Rotberg, ed., *After the Peace: Resistance and Reconciliation* (Boulder, Co: Lynne Rienner, 1999).

15. For discussions of the varieties of reconciliation policies see Lederach, *Building Peace in Divided Societies*; Joseph Montville, "Reconciliation as Realpolitik: Facing the Burdens of History in Political Conflict Resolution" and Louis Kriesburg, "Paths to Varieties of Intercommunal Reconciliation," both in Ho-won Jeong, ed., *Conflict Resolution Dynamics* (Aldershot: Ashgate 1999); and Martha Minow, *Between Vengeance and Forgiveness* (Boston: Beacon Press, 1998).

16. The failure of the Manila Pact and the SEATO alliance provides an excellent illustration of these problems. See Leszek Buszynski, *SEATO: Failure of an Alliance Strategy* (Singapore: Singapore University Press, 1983).

17. For an excellent overview, see Takashi Yoshida, "A Battle over History: The Nanjing Massacre in Japan," in Joshua A. Fogel, ed., *The Nanjing Massacre in History and Historiography* (Berkeley: University of California Press, 2000).

18. The debates over why Japan chose to carve out an empire are many and complex. For an overview, see W.G. Beasley, *Japanese Imperialism, 1919–1945* (Oxford: Clarendon Press, 1987). For an account focusing on economic-strategic factors, see Michael Barnhart, *Japan Prepares for Total War: The Search for Economic Security* (Ithaca, NY: Cornell University Press, 1987). For a fascinating cultural–ideological account of the dynamics of Japanese imperialism, see Louise Young, *Japan's Total Empire: Manchuria and the Culture of Wartime Imperialism* (Berkeley: University of California Press, 1998).

19. There is considerable debate over the extent of the benefits brought on by Japanese rule. For a balanced overview, see Ramon Myers and Mark Peattie, eds., *The Japanese Colonial Empire, 1895–1945* (Princeton, NJ: Princeton University Press, 1984).

20. See Michael Weiner, *Race and Migration in Imperial Japan* (New York and London: Routledge, 1994).

21. See George L. Hick, *The Comfort Women: Japan's Brutal Regime of Enforced Prostitution in the Second World War* (New York: Norton, 1995).

22. On the Korean link to organized crime see David Kaplan and Alec Dubro, *Yakuza* (New York: Macmillan, 1987).

23. See Tanaka Hiroshi, *Zainichigaikokujin: Ho⁻ no Kabe, Kokoro no Mizo*, 2nd edition (Tokyo: Iwanamishoten, 1995).

24. For a more detailed analysis of the development of anti-Japanese sentiments in Korea in the early Cold War period, see Cheong Sung-Hwa, *The Politics of Anti-Japanese Sentiment in Korea: Japanese-South Korean Relations under American Occupation, 1945–1952* (Westport: Greenwood, 1991).

25. As related by John Welfield, *An Empire in Eclipse: Japan in the Postwar American Alliance System* (Atlantic Highlands, NJ: Athlone Press, 1988), pp. 91–93.

26. See Frank Kowalski, *Nihon no Saigumbi* (Tokyo: Simul Press, 1969), especially pp. 72–73. Likewise, Michael Green, *Japan's Reluctant Realism*, pp. 113–114.

27. For a recent articulation of this point of view, see Fujioka Katsuo and Izawa Motohiko, *"No" to ieru Kyo‾kasho e: Shinjitsu no Nikkan Keankeishi* (Tokyo: Sho‾dansha, 1998).

28. For an important new study exploring the role of domestic political-interest groups in shaping Japanese views on these issues, see James J. Orr, *The Victim as Hero: Ideologies of Peace and National Identity in Postwar Japan* (Honolulu: University of Hawaii Press, 2001). For an analysis focusing on the role of Japanese intellectuals and cultural figures in shaping Japanese views, see Yoshikuni Igarashi, *Bodies of Memory: Narratives of War and Postwar Japanese Culture, 1945–1970* (Princeton, NJ: Princeton University Press, 2000). For a lively comparison of German and Japanese attitudes, see Ian Buruma, *The Wages of Guilt* (New York: Farrar, Giroux and Strauss, 1992).

29. Paradoxically, while the United States worked hard to encourage cooperation between its two chief regional allies, the existence of each country's bilateral security relationship may have allowed the two sides to keep their distance. Arguably without the United States to fall back on, Japan and South Korea would have had a stronger incentive to cooperate with one another. For an example of a similar mechanism at work in a very different institutional and geostrategic context, see Ronald R. Krebs, "Perverse Institutionalism: NATO and the Greco-Turkish Conflict," *International Organization* 53:2 (Spring 1999).

30. For a fascinating study of the influence of stereotypes on popular culture in imperial Japan, see Jennifer Ellen Robertson, *Takarazuka: Sexual Politics and Popular Culture in Modern Japan* (Berkeley, CA: University of California Press, 1998).

31. See Vera Schwarz, *The Chinese Enlightenment: Chinese Intellectuals and the Legacy of the May Fourth Movement of 1919* (Berkeley, CA: University of California Press, 1990). A similar moment in the development of Korean national consciousness can be seen in the anticolonial March First Movement of the same year.

32. See John Welfield, *An Empire in Eclipse: Japan in the Postwar American Alliance System* (London and Atlantic Heights, NJ: Athlone Press, 1988), especially chapter 5. On Yoshida Shigeru's attitudes toward the PRC, see John Dower, *Empire and Aftermath: Yoshida Shigeru and the Japanese Experience 1878–1954* (Cambridge, MA: Council on East Asian Studies, Harvard University Press, 1979).

33. On the periodic use of anti-Japanese sentiments by the Chinese state, see Nathan and Ross, *The Great Wall and the Empty Fortress*, pp. 87–89, 91.

34. See Kamanishi Akio, *GNP 1% Waku: Bo‾eiseisaku no Kensho* (Tokyo: Kakugawa, 1986), part II.

35. See Yin Yan-Jun, *Chu‾nichi Senso‾ Baisho‾ Mondai* (Tokyo: Ochanomizu Shobo‾, 1996), pp. 255–312.

36. For a brief overview of the controversies that emerged during this period, see Kojima Tomoyuki, *Ajia Jidai no Nichu‾ Kankei* (Tokyo: Saimaru Shupankai, 1995), pp. 90–118.

37. See Willem van Kamenede, *China, Hong Kong, Taiwan, Inc.* (New York: Alfred A. Knopf, 1997), p. 381.

38. For a more thorough discussion of these issues, and a comparison of the Japanese experience with that of the Federal Republic of Germany, see Thomas Berger, "Parallel Pathways to Pluralism?: The Politics of Immigration in Germany and Japan," in The Japan Association of International Relations, *Japan, Asia and the World in the 21st Century* (Tokyo: Kokusai Shoin, 1998), pp. 585–607.

39. One reflection of this trend was the sharp increase in intermarriage between the Japanese and resident Korean populations. Miya Hiroto, *65manjin Zainichicho˜senjin* (Tokyo: Ko˜do, 1977), pp. 65–71.

40. On the relatively slow evolution of Japanese views regarding its history, see Yoshida Yutaka, *Nihonjin no Senso˜kan* (Tokyo: Iwanami Shoten, 1995).

41. For brief overviews of the politics of Japan's apology campaign of the 1990s, see William Lee Howell, "The Inheritance of War : Japan's Domestic Political Politics and the Domestic Political Ambitions," in Gerrit W. Gong, ed., *Remembering and Forgetting: The Legacy of War and Peace in East Asia* (Washington, DC: Center for Strategic and International Studies, 1996), and Michael Mochizuki, "Dealing with a Militarist Past" (forthcoming), Brookings Institution, (2002). On the political importance of the campaign to the Japanese Socialist Party, see Asano Atsushi, *Renritsu Seiken: Nihon no Seiji 1993* (Tokyo: Bungeishunju, 1999), part II, chapter 3.

42. For the text of the statement and initial press reactions see *Asahi Shimbun and Yomiuri Shimbun*, October 8, 1998, p. 1. A cynic might observe that Kim did not go unrewarded for his tact. In return for softening his demands for an apology Korea received an additional three billion dollars in aid from Japan, thus continuing a pattern of Japanese money in return for Korean circumspection that dates back to 1965.

43. For a comparison of the Japanese reaction to the two visits, see Wakaiyama Yoshibumi, *The Postwar Conservative View of Asia* (Tokyo: LTCB Library Foundation, 1998), pp. 256–261; and Michael Green, *Japan's Reluctant Realism*, pp. 96–98.

44. See *The Korean Herald*, August 15, 2001.

45. See *Asahi*, September 4, 2001, p. 1

46. See *Asahi*, October 22, 2001, p. 3.

47. *Asahi*, October 22, 2001, p. 3.

48. See *The Korean Herald*, October 16, 2001 and *Asahi*, October 20, 2001.

49. Ronald W. Zweig, *German Reparations and the Jewish World: A History of the Claims Conference* (Boulder, CO: Westview Press, 1987).

50. See e.g. Kobayashi Yoshinori, *Sensoron* (Tokyo: Gentosha, 1998).

SECTION 2
SECURITY BILATERALISM AND MULTILATERALISM

CHAPTER 5

REFORMING THE U.S.–JAPAN ALLIANCE: WHAT SHOULD BE DONE?

Matake Kamiya

The U.S.–Japan Alliance During the Clinton Years

The end of the Cold War and the collapse of the Soviet Union that followed generated a pressing need for policy leaders in Tokyo and Washington to reevaluate and restructure the U.S.–Japan alliance so that it would fit the post–Cold War security environment in the Asia-Pacific and globally. First, the two governments had to find a new rationale for the alliance in the world where the Soviet threat no longer existed. Second, with the rapid development of regional security cooperation in the Asia-Pacific since the end of the Cold War, they had to define the relationship between such multilateral security efforts and the bilateral security arrangement between them. Third, Tokyo and Washington had to deal with the issue of alliance reform and restructuring, including the long-standing question of burden-sharing between the two allies. They had to determine how the alliance had to be changed in order to maintain its vitality and its effectiveness for a long time in the future.

For more than a year since its inauguration, however, the Clinton administration's Japan policy mainly focused on economics rather than security. Clinton, who won the presidential race against Bush with his pledge to reconstruct the American economy, advocated the concept of "economic security" and gave the highest priority in his dealing with Japan to the issue of economic friction. Showing little interest in the security relations with Japan, the Clinton administration adopted a "result oriented trade strategy" and stubbornly sought Japanese acquiescence to the U.S.-led trade agreements. The aggressive and high-handed attitude of Clinton's trade negotiators put off the Japanese, who viewed the "result oriented trade strategy" as propelled by U.S. arrogance. When the summit meeting between Prime Minister Hosokawa and President Clinton in February 1994 failed to produce any agreement on the new "trade framework talks," the U.S.–Japan relations were nearly at a deadlock. It was at this moment that the security policy communities on both sides of the Pacific worried seriously that the confrontation between the two countries in the economic field might spread to the security field and undermine the foundations of the alliance between them.

The 1994 North Korean nuclear crisis generated another serious concern in the minds of security thinkers and planners in both Japan and the United States for the future of their bilateral alliance. From late spring to early summer 1994, there was a real possibility of the U.S. bombing of nuclear facilities in North Korea. U.S. Secretary of Defense William Perry actually received a detailed contingency plan for such an attack.[1] If a military conflict occurred on the Korean Peninsula, it would inevitably bring up the question of how Japan should cooperate with the U.S. military operations against North Korea. Faced with this question, many security experts in the two countries worried that the U.S–Japan alliance might not work well in case of Korean contingency because Japan might not be able to cooperate with the United States in an appropriate and timely manner due to the domestic constraints, including the constitutional ban on the exercise of the right of collective self-defense. If that happened, these security experts worried at that time, the U.S. citizens would surely be enraged by the Japanese attitude and would stop seeing Japan as a responsible and trustable ally of their country, and stop supporting the continuation of the U.S.–Japan alliance.

The final report of the Advisory Group on Defense Issues (the Higuchi Commission), which was submitted to Prime Minister Tomiichi Murayama in August 1994, generated still another concern in the minds of some American security experts. In the report, titled "The Modality of the Security and Defense Capability of Japan: The Outlook for the 21st Century," the section on the promotion of multilateral security cooperation was placed before the section on enhancement of the functions of the U.S.–Japan security cooperation relationship.[2] This order of discussion, these security experts worried, might indicate Japan's intention to increase its autonomy in the security field gradually.[3] Meanwhile, in Japan, the Bush administration's two East Asian Strategic Initiative (EASI) reports of 1990 and 1992 caused some anxiety about future U.S. involvement in East Asian security.[4] The fact that the reports outlined a process for restructuring and reducing the U.S. forward presence in the region worried some U.S. watchers in Japan that the United States might be trying to gradually limit its security role in East Asia. The Japan watchers in the United States who observed such Japanese reactions to the EASI reports, in turn, worried that the Japanese might be losing trust in the U.S. commitment to defense of Japan.

Under such circumstances, the governments in Tokyo and Washington finally came to share the sense of urgency that the two countries had to recognize the importance of the security of their relationship and start the process of reevaluation and restructuring of the alliance between them as soon as possible. A series of in-depth discussion for that purpose were started between the two governments from sometime around September 1994. Since then, they have worked together to adapt the U.S.–Japan alliance to a changed international environment. What kind of roles should be assigned to the U.S.–Japan alliance in the post–Cold War world? What kind of changes should be made to the alliance so that it can fulfill such roles effectively? These have been the two central questions that the security planners in the two countries have shared.

To the first question, the two countries reached a shared conclusion in a relatively short period of time. By November 1995, when the summit meeting between Prime Minister Murayama and President Clinton was originally scheduled on an occasion of Clinton's visit to Osaka to attend the annual APEC summit, Tokyo and Washington had agreed to transform the fundamental nature of the U.S.–Japan alliance from an alliance to counter a manifest, specific security threat of the Soviet Union to an alliance to deal with the latent, unspecified sources of instability in order to buttress peace and stability in the Asia-Pacific. In other words, the two allies redefined their bilateral alliance in the post–Cold War era as a kind of international public goods that would provide regional order to the Asia-Pacific. As Clinton canceled his visit to Osaka at the last moment due to domestic reasons, the official announcement of this new rationale of the U.S.–Japan alliance had to wait until April 1996, when Prime Minister Ryutaro Hashimoto and President Clinton issued the "Japan–U.S. Joint Declaration on Security—Alliance for the 21st Century" in Tokyo.[5] Even before the issuance of the joint security declaration, however, this approach to redefine the alliance had been implicitly stated by the two governments in Pentagon's February 1995 East Asian Strategic Review (EASR, or the so-called Nye Report) and in Japan's November 1995 new National Defense Program Outline (NDPO).[6]

As for the relationship between the U.S.–Japan alliance and the emerging regional security cooperation in the Asia-Pacific, Tokyo and Washington reached a consensus that the U.S.–Japan alliance would provide the foundation on which the regional multilateral security mechanisms would be built and on which it would prosper. Admitting that multilateral security mechanisms would provide important opportunities for dialogue and cooperation among the regional states to build mutual confidence and to promote regional stability, the two governments acknowledged that such multilateral mechanisms would represent no substitute for the bilateral alliance between them. They agreed to promote trust and confidence among the regional states by multilateral security cooperation on the basis of regional order underwritten by the U.S.–Japan alliance.

Besides, by spring 1996, the two governments successfully solved the problem of the Japanese anxiety about future U.S. commitment to East Asian security and defense of Japan. The Japanese concern was largely removed by the Nye Report, which declared the U.S. commitment to maintain a stable forward presence in the region at the existing level of about 100,000 troops for the foreseeable future (i.e., for about 20 years), and repeatedly emphasized the importance of the U.S.–Japan alliance for the interest of the United States, and by the U.S.–Japan joint security declaration, in which Hashimoto and Clinton reaffirmed that the U.S.–Japan alliance "remains the cornerstone for achieving common security objectives, and for maintaining a stable and prosperous environment for the Asia-Pacific region" toward the twenty-first century.

In order to ensure that the U.S.–Japan alliance be a long-term effective regional stabilizer in the Asia-Pacific what kind of changes should be made to the alliance? As for this question, Japan and the United States had to face two kinds of tasks. First, the two countries had to establish a new framework for the U.S.–Japan security cooperation in which the two allies would share the responsibility for security problems in the region. In the traditional framework, Japan focused its security efforts on self-defense in its most narrowly defined sense and depended for almost everything else beyond self-defense on the United States, except for provision of the military bases and host-nation support (HNS). Such an attitude of Japan was largely due to the official interpretation of the constitution as prohibiting the country from exercising the right of collective self-defense. By the mid-1990s, security planners in Tokyo and Washington came to share the basic understanding that the U.S.–Japan alliance would not be an effective regional stabilizer unless this framework was replaced by a new one in which Japan would be able to cooperate more actively with the United States in case of contingencies in the areas surrounding Japan, even when no direct enemy attack on Japanese territory or territorial water took place.

Another important task for the two governments was to ensure public support to the U.S.–Japan alliance in both Japan and the United States. In the United States, as mentioned earlier, there was worry that Tokyo's failure to take prompt measures to cooperate effectively with Washington in case of contingency in the areas surrounding Japan would surely offend the U.S. citizens and undermine the domestic support for the alliance. In Japan, on the other hand, the U.S. base issue, which has always been subject to local political pressure from surrounding communities, has become even more acute since the end of the Cold War, particularly in Okinawa, where approximately 75 percent of all the U.S. bases are concentrated in less than 1 percent of Japan's total territorial land space. The strong Japanese reaction, particularly in Okinawa, to the rape of a 12-year-old schoolgirl by three U.S. marines in Okinawa in September 1995 made it clear to both Tokyo and Washington that unless they found some ways to mitigate the base issue without damaging the efficacy of the alliance, the Japanese might eventually say no to the stationing of the U.S. forces in their country and the continuation of the alliance with the United States. In addition, by the mid-1990s, there was a growing sense of dissatisfaction among the Japanese that the United States still tended to treat their country merely as a junior partner. Consequently, the Japanese desire to make the security relations with the United States a more equal one has mounted in recent years.

It is true that Tokyo and Washington has already taken several significant steps to tackle these tasks. As for the establishment of a new framework for the U.S.–Japan security cooperation in which the two allies can cooperate effectively in case of contingencies in the areas surrounding Japan, the two governments adopted the new Guidelines for U.S.–Japan Defense Cooperation in September 1997, and the Japanese Diet adopted the Contingency Laws in May 1999 and the Ship Inspection Laws in November 2000 respectively to implement the new Guidelines. At the meeting of the U.S.–Japan Security Consultative Committee (the Two-Plus-Two meeting) in New York in September 2000, the two sides finally agreed to co-establish the "coordination mechanism," which would function as a framework of mutual consultation and policy coordination between the two allies to conduct joint operations and other types of security cooperation, such as Japan's logistical support to the U.S. operations, in case of enemy attack against Japan as well as contingencies in the areas surrounding Japan. On the Okinawa base issue, in

April 1996, shortly before President Clinton's visit to Japan, Tokyo and Washington reached an agreement on the return of the Futenma Marine Corps Air Station, the largest U.S. base in Okinawa, in exchange for an alternative facility in the same prefecture. In addition, in the final report of the Special Action Committee on Okinawa (SACO) in November 1996, the United States agreed with Japan to return about 20 percent of the total land space of the U.S. military facilities in Okinawa to the original owners.

Such moves made by the two governments, however, have proven to be quite insufficient to bring about satisfactory results. As for the strengthening of the U.S.–Japan defense cooperation, the adoption of the new Guidelines was surely a significant step forward. In September 1997, however, security planners on both sides shared the understanding that the adoption represented "not the end, but the beginning," of the process to strengthen the defense cooperation between the two countries. One Pentagon official reportedly described the adoption of the new Guidelines as merely "the conclusion of the initial stage" of the U.S.–Japan security cooperation.[7] Similarly, among the foreign policy community in the United States, the revision of the Guidelines was generally received as "a small, but meaningful step" toward a deeper partnership between the two allies.[8] Three years later, a report on the future direction of the U.S.–Japan partnership by a bipartisan group of experts in the United States, which was titled "The United States and Japan: Advancing Toward a Mature Partnership" and was released in October 2000, also emphasized that the revised Guidelines "should be regarded as the floor—not the ceiling—for an expanded Japanese role in the transpacific alliance."[9] In short, the basic characteristic of the revision of the Guideline was to draw a tentative "baseline" of the strengthening of the U.S.–Japan defense cooperation, without which the U.S.–Japan alliance would not function as an effective regional stabilizer in the Asia-Pacific.[10] So far, however, there have been little prospects for the advancement of the U.S.–Japan defense cooperation beyond the provisions of the new Guidelines. The reality has been that even the implementation of the new Guidelines has proceeded rather slowly. For example, it took three years after the adoption of the new Guideline for Tokyo and Washington to establish this "coordination mechanism." As for the planning for joint operations in case of contingencies in the areas surrounding Japan, although the two sides have started discussions and consultations, little progress has been achieved as yet.

On the Okinawa base issue also progress has been slow. More than six years after the conclusion of the agreement between Tokyo and

Washington, there is still little prospect for the early reversion of the Futenma Air Station. As for the "equalization" of the U.S.–Japan alliance relations, an increasing number of officials and security experts in the United States have recognized the Japanese eagerness and irritation and have admitted the necessity to establish a "more equal partnership." Despite such rhetoric, however, no concrete steps have been taken by Washington to actually equalize the alliance.

At the last stage of the Clinton years, the U.S.–Japan security relations were in a strange stagnation. At first sight, the alliance between the two largest economic powers in the world, which went through the redefinition process in the middle to late 1990s, seemed to enter a period of smooth and stable development. In the United States, the Japan-bashing, which had been rampant in the early years of the Clinton administration, totally disappeared. To the eyes of the Americans, Japan was no longer the economic threat that it once had been when Clinton first came into office. A number of official documents and speeches by high-ranking officials repeatedly emphasized the critical importance of the alliance with Japan for the U.S. Asia-Pacific strategy. Meanwhile, in Japan, due to the major policy changes by the Social Democratic Party (formerly the Socialist Party) and the Communist Party, there was no longer any major political party that insisted on the immediate abrogation of the U.S.–Japan Security Treaty. The approval rating of the U.S.–Japan alliance among the Japanese public, which went into a nose dive after the rape of a schoolgirl by three U.S. servicemen in Okinawa in September 1995, swiftly recovered to a high level and remained stable there. Under such circumstances, Tokyo and Washington took every occasion to demonstrate that the two allies, together with South Korea, were promoting close security cooperation in order to counter the North Korean threat.

In Japan, however, since the late 1990s, the public attention has become increasingly inward-looking because of the prolonged recession. In the meantime, the confusion in Japanese politics has continued. Criticism and blame against politicians for their lack of vitality and political leadership has mounted among mass media and the general public. Considering the fact that the security relations with the United States still remains a politically sensitive issue in Japan, it is quite unrealistic to expect a remarkable progress in Tokyo's handling of the U.S.–Japan alliance under such circumstances. As for the Okinawa base issue, the public attention and media coverage of the issue has decreased to a considerable degree.

On the other side of the Pacific, general indifference to Japan has become a serious problem. Since the late 1990s, the Americans seem to have lost interest in Japan. For example, in an article titled "U.S. interest in Japan at Rock Bottom," which appeared in the *Los Angeles Times* on June 21, 2000, Jim Mann wrote that in the ongoing presidential campaign "the candidates mention Japan only slightly more often than Uzbekistan."[11] Michael J. Green contributed an article titled "The Forgotten Player" to the Summer 2000 issue of *The National Interest* and said: "today Japan rarely receives attention above the middle layers of the bureaucracy."[12] In his article published shortly after, Kurt M. Campbell pointed out the attitude in some quarters in Washington that "Japan is in the process of a long, slow decline and therefore not as important in future U.S. calculations" and warned that "[i]t would be foolhardy to underestimate the enduring dimensions of Japanese power."[13]

In the background of such serious indifference to Japan, there is a sense of contempt widely shared among the Americans for Japan's inability to carry out necessary economic reforms to overcome a prolonged economic slump as well as for the obvious incompetence of Japanese politicians. Under such circumstances, the Americans, the general public as well as political leaders in Washington, show little interest in and pay little attention to the U.S.–Japan security relations.

With such realities on both sides of the Pacific, the U.S.–Japan alliance relations at the turn of the century were, in Campbell's words, on a "bureaucratic autopilot."[14] In both Japan and the United States, due to the lack of political leadership that could point the future direction of the alliance clearly and conduct necessary alliance reforms, the alliance was in fact largely managed by mid-level professionals in two governments who shared a strong belief that the U.S.–Japan alliance represents the most important security alliance in the world and therefore should be managed well.

Thus, at the beginning of the new century and the start of the new George W. Bush, administration, Japan and the United States are still at the initial stage of the alliance reform. In order to make the U.S.–Japan alliance a long-term effective regional stabilizer in the Asia-Pacific, there remain many tasks to be done by Tokyo and Washington.

The U.S.–Japan Alliance After September 11

The U.S.–Japan alliance celebrated its fiftieth anniversary on September 8, 2001. In the commemorative conference that took place in San Francisco where the U.S.–Japan Security Treaty was originally signed 50 years before, the participants, including former Japanese Prime Minister Kiichi Miyazawa, former U.S. Secretary of State George P. Shultz, successive U.S. ambassadors to Japan and Japanese ambassadors to the United States, business leaders, and scholars from both sides of the Pacific including myself, almost unanimously praised the half century of close cooperation and friendship that has been established between the two former enemies, and urged that the two allies should strengthen their partnership in the next half century. Some American participants, however, also pointed out the fact that the U.S.–Japan alliance "has not been tested in the crucible of war"[15] and expressed concern that it is unclear what Japan would be able to do in a crisis due to domestic constraints: Japan's postwar pacifism and the consequent official interpretation of the constitution regarding Japan's right of collective self-defense.[16]

Since the end of World War II, great skepticism about the legitimacy and usefulness of military power has been widely shared among the Japanese people. They have consistently viewed anything even remotely connected with the military with a degree of wariness that borders on total rejection. There has been strong aversion to military solutions to the problems of national security and international peace, because they are seen as contradictory to the ideal of peace embodied in Japan's postwar "Peace Constitution." Because of the strong public abhorrence of anything military-related as a tool of Japan's external policy, even including policy for the defense of Japan, the security issue has been one of the most sensitive issues in postwar Japanese politics. Such a public sentiment has militated so strongly against any commitment abroad that might lead to military involvement with other nations that the Japanese government has traditionally been extremely cautious about expanding military cooperation with the United States and has been reluctant to remove the constitutional ban on the exercise of the right of collective self-defense.

For the U.S.–Japan alliance, the terrorist attacks of September 11 that occurred only three days after its fiftieth anniversary represented the first serious "test" in its history of whether it could function effectively in an actual crisis. In the wake of the incident, foreign policy and security experts in both the United States and Japan awaited Tokyo's response with significant anxiety. They knew that the Americans would be enraged at Japan if Tokyo failed to take decisive actions to help its ally. Although the U.S.–Japan Security Treaty does not obligate Japan to defend the United States when it is attacked and Japan is constitutionally banned from exercising the right of collective self-defense, Japan had to behave as a trustable ally of the United States, or it would surely invite deep disappointment and strong criticism from the American people, which would severely damage the alliance.

Many of these experts, particularly in the United States, worried about a recurrence of Tokyo's response to the Gulf Crisis, in which Japan's contribution was limited only to financial support and the sending of a small number of civilians in spite of the strong American pressure to do more, due to the public reluctance to dispatch the Self Defense Forces (SDFS) abroad. Providing some US$13 billion to support the multilateral operation against Iraq, Japan received no thanks, only strong criticism from other countries including the United States that it had not done anything more than contribute money.[17] Shortly before September 11, one of the leading foreign policy experts in Japan, Yukio Okamoto, a former diplomat who had actually handled the Japanese response to the Gulf Crisis as director of the First North American Division of the North American Bureau of the Ministry of Foreign Affairs, warned in an article titled "Won't the Same Thing Happen Again: What if the Gulf War Occurs Again?" that neither the Japanese government nor its people seemed to be ready to respond to another Gulf War in a manner that would satisfy the international community.[18]

With the strong leadership of Prime Minister Junichiro Koizumi, however, Japan acted in a timely manner with an unprecedented package of measures to support the U.S.–led war against terrorism.[19] Koizumi eloquently told his compatriots why Japan had to join the international coalition against terrorism by dispatching the SDFs, and the Japanese public accepted his bold and frank explanation. On September 19, Koizumi announced a seven-point program to respond to the crisis, including dispatch of the SDFs overseas to provide logistical support to the U.S. forces in the war against terrorism and protection of the U.S. bases in Japan by the SDFs. He submitted the bills to enable the SDFs to legally perform such functions (the so-called Anti-Terrorism Bills) to the Diet on October 5, and the Diet passed them on October 29. Such a quick deliberation by the Diet of such an important bill of a highly controversial nature was quite extraordinary, considering the fact that debates and deal-makings among political parties usually take a painfully long time in Japanese politics.

The Japanese actions satisfied the U.S. government. In his speech to the Japanese Diet on February 19, 2002, President Bush said:

> Japan and America are working to find and disrupt terrorist cells. Your diplomats helped build a worldwide coalition to defend freedom. Your Self Defense forces are providing important logistical support. And your generosity is helping to rebuild a liberated Afghanistan. Your response to the terrorist threat has demonstrated the strength of our

alliance, and the indispensable role of Japan that is global, and that begins in Asia. The success of this region is essential to the entire world, and I'm convinced the 21st century will be the Pacific century. Japan and America share a vision for the future of the Asia Pacific region as a fellowship of free Pacific nations . . . Realizing this vision—a fellowship of free Pacific nations—will require Japan and America to work more closely together than ever. Our responsibilities are clear. Fortunately, our alliance has never been stronger.[20]

The American people also appreciated the Japanese support to the United States on the war against terrorism. In a public opinion poll jointly conducted by the *Yomiuri Shinbun*, Japan's largest national daily, and the Gallup Organization in the United States, 66.3 percent of the U.S. respondents favored actions taken by the Japanese government since September 11, while only 16.9 percent answered that they did not favorably view the Japanese response. Besides, 90.6 percent of the U.S. respondents answered that they evaluated the history of the U.S.–Japan alliance during the past half century positively, and 80.5 percent of them answered that they trusted Japan.[21]

As one American expert argues, the results of Japan's extraordinary response to the September 11 terrorist attack represents "a victory for supporters of the U.S.–Japan alliance and a validation of their strategy to nudge Japan toward a greater role in regional security."[22] As another American expert points out, "[t]he war on terrorism has provided Koizumi with the incentive (and excuse) to take a major step toward becoming a 'normal' nation . . . a more equal partner to Washington and a more active participant in international security affairs."[23] It is, however, also true that the basic form of the U.S.–Japan alliance remains unchanged, despite the events since September 11. In other words, most of the tasks of alliance reform to make it an effective regional stabilizer in the Asia-Pacific, still remain to be done, although the war on terrorism has provided Tokyo and Washington with an unprecedented opportunity and incentive to achieve such reforms. The key question now is whether the two governments will be able to seize this opportunity.

Raison d'Être of the U.S.–Japan Alliance
in the Twenty-First Century[24]

As was repeatedly mentioned in the previous two sections, the essential role of the U.S.–Japan alliance after the disappearance of Soviet threat is that of "regional stabilizer" in the Asia-Pacific. There is, however, a growing, though still minority, voice among East Asians that the trend in the Asia-Pacific in the post–Cold War era is in the direction of finding alternative, multilateral means of keeping peace and stability rather than in the maintenance of the existing system. Such a voice is becoming gradually salient in Southeast Asian countries. Beijing, harboring suspicions about the purpose of the U.S.–Japan alliance in the post–Cold War era, has argued that bilateral alliances existing in the region are relics of the Cold War and should be replaced by a new multilateral regional framework based on regional security cooperation. A similar cry for multilateral peace also exists in Japan, where the division in public opinion on the propriety of the U.S.–Japan alliance as a means to achieve national security represented a serious political issue even during the Cold War. Because of the strong pacifist orientation in the postwar Japanese society, the idea of multilateral regional order has a particularly strong emotional appeal for the Japanese people and may exercise considerable influence on public attitude toward the alliance with the United States.

Are such claims valid? This section explains why it is not: it examines theoretically the limitation of multilateral security cooperation in the Asia-Pacific region and, by doing so, demonstrates why the expected development of the multilateral security cooperation in the Asia-Pacific will not decrease the importance of the U.S.–Japan alliance as a regional stabilizer.

Three Types of Multilateral Security Cooperation

To begin with, it is necessary to distinguish three different types of multilateral security arrangements: common security, collective security, and cooperative security.[25]

Common Security

The concept of common security originated in the report of the Palme Commission, entitled *Common Security: A Blueprint for Survival*, which was published when the East–West tension was high under the renewed Cold War. It emphasized the need and the common interest for both the East and the West to seek security with, rather than against, the adversary to ensure survival under strategic interdependence.

The central purpose of a common security system is to avoid a war between adversaries that neither side desires to start. The concept is predicated on the assumptions that an adversarial relationship exists among states, and that adversaries share a common interest in avoiding wars because both sides share a perception that a war between them will bring intolerable damages to both sides. The avoidance of war is best pursued by strategies of cooperation and reassurance, rather than confrontation and deterrence. The Conference for Security and Cooperation in Europe (CSCE) process during the late Cold War era represented the practical application of the concept of common security.

Collective Security

Collective security is a mechanism by which member states aim at maintaining peace among themselves by making two promises:

1   Member states are obliged to settle disputes among themselves by peaceful means, and are prohibited from using military forces against each other except in the cases of self-defense and participation in collective security actions by members as a whole to punish aggressors.

2   If any member state illegally uses military forces against another member, all the other members are obliged to take collective enforcement actions, including military actions, to punish the aggressor.

Unlike an alliance system whose central purpose is to cope with external threats, a collective security system is inward looking. Its central purpose is to deter (unspecified) would-be aggressors within the system by making it clear that any member state who conducts an act of aggression against any one member will have to confront all the members except the aggressor itself.

Cooperative Security

Cooperative security aims at stabilizing relations among states who are neither adversaries nor friends. It works best in a region where interstate relations are not characterized by obvious hostilities, at least among major powers.

In practice, the cooperative security system is inclusive in terms of its membership; like-minded as well as non-like-minded states, historical rivals, and future potential antagonists gather to form a single security system that prevents various sources of instability existing in the region from actually inviting antagonism and hostilities, to prevent existing disputes among the members from escalating into conflicts and to settle them by peaceful means, and to limit the spread of military conflicts if they occur. Unlike collective security, cooperative security does not envisage collective enforcement action by the members in case of military conflicts. Rather it attempts to build up and solidify a structure of peaceful relations among the members by measures that are neither confrontational nor coercive, such as confidence- and security-building measures and institutionalized security dialogues. In a cooperative security system, member states seek security with, rather than against, other members. It therefore emphasizes the importance of political and diplomatic, rather than military, means to achieve security. The C(O)SCE has transformed itself from a common security system to a cooperative security system with the end of the East–West confrontation.

Applicability of Multilateral Security Cooperation to the Asia-Pacific
Common Security and Collective Security
How applicable are the three types of multilateral security cooperation to the post–Cold War Asia-Pacific? First, it is obvious that common security is not suitable for this region today, because interstate relations in the Asia-Pacific are not adversarial except for the Korean subregion.

Second, there is no chance that an effective collective security system will be formed in the Asia-Pacific in the foreseeable future. A collective security system cannot function effectively to maintain peace among the member states unless at least the three conditions described in the following are simultaneously met:[26]

1 Military power enough to overwhelm any aggressor is always available for the collective security system.
2 The member states, particularly the major powers, are always willing to subordinate their national interests to the common good, defined in terms of security of all member states, and to always participate in collective enforcement actions.
3 The member states, particularly the major powers, share the same conception of peace to be defended (in other words, definition of status quo to be maintained), and agree on the criteria by which the existence of an act of aggression is determined.

There is little likelihood that even one of these conditions will be satisfied in the Asia-Pacific in the foreseeable future. The Asia-Pacific geographical expanse is extraordinarily broad, and the countries in the region are extraordinarily diverse in terms of culture, religion, political system, stage of economic development, and size of national power. Consequently, interests of the regional states are highly diverse in almost every field and sometimes highly competitive. Such diversity of interests among the regional states leads to diversity of their threat perceptions. Moreover, a number of unresolved territorial disputes still remain in the Asia-Pacific. Under such circumstances, it is difficult, if not impossible, for regional states to share the same conception of peace to be defended. It is even more unlikely that regional states are willing to relinquish their respective rights to refuse to participate in a collective security action. The establishment of an Asia-Pacific regional standing forces is out of the question. Collective security cannot be a guarantor of peace in the Asia-Pacific in the post–Cold War Asia-Pacific.

Cooperative Security

In contrast to common and collective securities, which are both inapplicable to the post–Cold War Asia-Pacific, a cooperative security system has been gradually taking shape in this region in the form of the ARF, which was established in July 1994. It can hardly be expected, however, that the ARF will become as effective a mechanism as today's OSCE in preventing military conflicts and settling disputes by peaceful means, at least in the near future. A cooperative security system cannot function effectively to maintain peace among the member states unless at least the three conditions described in the following are simultaneously met:[27]

1   There is no significant state in the region that is perceived by other regional members as a manifest, tangible security threat.

2   All significant states in the region, including the ones that are perceived by other regional members as latent security threats (i.e., countries that others perceive currently as neither friends nor enemies, but are afraid that they may turn into tangible threats in future) have intentions to participate in regional multilateral security dialogues.

3   All significant states in the region have intentions to participate in collective actions taken by the regional members.

In today's Asia-Pacific, the first of these three conditions is met. Russia, China, and Vietnam are no longer perceived by other regional members as tangible security threat as they used to be, though some still see Russia and China as latent threats. The second and the third conditions, however, are only partially met in this region. Taiwan, which is now one of the leading economies in the world, is not allowed to participate in the ARF due to strong opposition from China. Moreover, it is unlikely that China and Russia would be willing to participate in multilateral security dialogues (MSDs) if issues in which they are directly involved, such as the Taiwan Straits issue for China, become topics of discussion at the ARF. It is also quite doubtful that China would be willing to participate actively in collective actions taken by the regional members. China has insisted that the ARF should remain a forum for dialogue and exchange of views and should not aim at conflict resolution.

A radical change in the Chinese attitude cannot be expected in the near future. It is therefore unlikely that the ARF will become an effective mechanism in preventing military conflicts and settling disputes by peaceful means, although it will surely offer important opportunities for historical rivals and future potential antagonists in the region to directly exchange their views and intentions with each other.

Why the U.S.–Japan Alliance will Remain Important for Asia-Pacific Security

Based on the analyses in the first two parts of this section, it can be concluded that the Asia-Pacific has not yet obtained a framework of multilateral security cooperation that can effectively maintain regional peace by itself. But what will happen when the ARF eventually develops into an effective cooperative security mechanism? Will such a development make the U.S.–Japan alliance unnecessary for the Asia-Pacific security? In other words, can a fully developed cooperative security mechanism effectively maintain the regional peace by itself, without the help of the U.S.–Japan alliance?

The answer is no. As explained earlier, cooperative security attempts to prevent military conflicts among the regional states by measures that are neither confrontational nor coercive, and does not envisage collective enforcement actions. This means that a cooperative security system, even in a fully developed form, is not good at coping with regional military conflicts on its own once it fails to prevent them. A cooperative security system therefore must be complemented by another mechanism that can deal with military conflicts by military means. Theoretically, there are four principal candidates for such a mechanism, that is, hegemony, a concert of Great Powers, alliance, and collective security. As was demonstrated earlier, however, it is highly unlikely that an effective collective security system will be established in the Asia-Pacific in the foreseeable future. It is also highly unlikely that a powerful hegemon who possesses both capability and willingness to serve as a "regional police officer" will emerge in the region in the near future. A concert of the four Great Powers in the region, that is, the United States, Japan,

China, and Russia, may emerge only in the distant future. It can therefore be predicted that a cooperative security system, however it develops, will always go hand-in-hand with an alliance system in the foreseeable future.

In fact, the current European security situation strongly supports the validity of this prediction. Today's European security system consists of two main components that complement each other, that is, the OSCE, currently the most advanced cooperative security system in the world, and the NATO, a traditional alliance system formed in the early Cold War era. This suggests that a double-layered security system similar to the one in today's Europe will gradually take shape in the Asia-Pacific as the ARF increases its efficiency. Considering the fact that there is no prospect for a NATO-type multilateral alliance to be formed in this region in the future, it can be predicted that the double-layered Asia-Pacific security system will consist mainly of two components that complement each other, that is, the ARF as a cooperative security system that will promote mutual understanding, mutual trust, and mutual reassurance among the regional states, and the U.S.–Japan alliance as an alliance system that will secure the U.S. military commitment to the region and will prepare to cope with military conflicts if the ARF fails to prevent them. In this double-layered system, the cooperative security system and the alliance system will be mutually reinforcing, rather than mutually exclusive. For the ARF, the U.S.–Japan alliance will represent reliable insurance against failure of preventive diplomacy. Without such insurance, preventive diplomacy cannot be effective. On the other hand, for the U.S.–Japan alliance, the successful preventive diplomacy efforts by the ARF will contribute to reduce significantly the workload of the alliance partners.

The development of the ARF process may change the nature of the importance of the U.S.–Japan alliance for the region. This alliance, however, will remain essentially important for the Asia-Pacific security even after the ARF develops into an effective cooperative security mechanism.

Necessary Alliance Reforms

As the discussion in the previous section demonstrated, the further development of the multilateral security mechanisms in the Asia-Pacific in the future will not lessen the importance of the U.S.–Japan alliance as a regional stabilizer. In fact, regional multilateral security cooperation can function well only on the basis of regional order underwritten by the U.S.–Japan alliance. The U.S.–Japan alliance will provide the foundation on which the regional multilateral security mechanisms will be built and continue to prosper.

In order to guarantee that the U.S.–Japan alliance remains an effective long-term regional stabilizer in the Asia-Pacific what kinds of reform are necessary? The three key terms for the necessary reforms of the U.S.–Japan alliance are: normalization, equalization, and enlargement.

Toward a More Normal Alliance

First, it is necessary to "normalize" the U.S.–Japan alliance to a considerable degree. The U.S.–Japan alliance has lasted for almost half a century, because both sides have found it beneficial to their respective national interests. In other words, the alliance has been a reciprocal arrangement. However, the reciprocity on which the U.S.–Japan alliance is based is quite an unusual one. Usually, alliance partners promise each other to defend the other side in case of an enemy attack. In the U.S.–Japan alliance, while the United States promises to defend Japan, Japan cannot reciprocate in kind, because of its traditional policy of banning the exercise of the right of collective self-defense. Japan instead allows the United States to maintain military bases on its own soil and to station sizable military forces there. Japan also provides the United States with generous HNS— the largest among all the U.S. allies. In short, the U.S.–Japan alliance is based on asymmetrical reciprocity of "material/personnel cooperation" while ordinary alliances are based on symmetrical reciprocity of "personnel/personnel cooperation."[28] In this sense, the basic structure of the U.S.–Japan alliance has been quite an abnormal one.

This structure worked well during the Cold War years. The United States found bases in Japan indispensable for its East Asian and global strategies, while Japan, under the "peace constitution," found the U.S. military protection essential for its survival and prosperity in the face of Soviet threat. More than a decade after the end of the Cold War and at the beginning of a new century, however, it is more questionable than ever whether the alliance based on such an abnormal type of reciprocity can maintain its vitality and its effectiveness in the long term. Let me list some of the major reasons.

First, under the current structure of the alliance, without a major immediate common threat such as the Soviet Union during the Cold War, both sides tend to see that the other side is one-sidedly benefiting from the alliance at the cost of its own. For the Americans, the value of the bases in Japan has become less visible and much more difficult to understand. Consequently, the Americans now tend to see that Japan enjoys a free ride on U.S. military protection. For the Japanese, benefits of accepting the U.S. bases on its own soil have become less visible and much more difficult to understand while its costs remain visible and easy to understand. Consequently, the Japanese now tend to see that the United States enjoys free use of the military bases in Japan for its regional global strategy, with generous HNS by the Japanese government. In short, under the current structure, without a major immediate common threat, both sides easily lose sight of the reciprocal nature of the alliance arrangement.

Second, the current structure of the U.S.–Japan alliance prevents Japan from fulfilling regional and global security responsibilities that go with its economic power. This makes it difficult for Japan to become a responsible security partner of the United States. The Japanese tend to believe that their security efforts can be, and should be, focused on self-defense in its most narrowly defined sense and everything else can be left to the United States. They tend to believe that beyond self-defense, all they have to do is to provide the United States with the military bases and HNS, and a limited level of logistical and other noncombatant supports in case of contingencies. In other words, under the current alliance structure, the Japanese can dismiss most of the security problems beyond self-defense. They tend to perceive problems of war and peace beyond their territory as not their own but someone else's. Because they perceive such problems as someone else's, they do not feel responsible for them. This Japanese mentality may become a major obstacle to the maintenance of vitality and effectiveness of the U.S.–Japan alliance as a regional stabilizer.

Third, unless Japan becomes a responsible security partner, it cannot become a respected partner of the United States. As long as such a situation continues, it will surely be impossible for the two countries to establish a "special relationship" like the one between the United States and Great Britain.[29]

Fourth, the current abnormal alliance arrangement severely limits Japan's political say with the United States. Consequently, Japan tends not to be viewed by the rest of the world as being its own independent political entity. It is generally believed that Japan has little choice but to give maximum consideration to the U.S. stance on important international issues and seldom acts on its own accord. Japan's foreign policy has often been justifiably criticized as one of "taking order from the United States" or "toeing the U.S. line." The Japanese are acutely aware of and frustrated with this fact. Such a sense of frustration prevalent among the Japanese may become a serious obstacle to the maintenance of active support from the Japanese public to the maintenance of the alliance with the United States.

Fifth, under the current abnormal alliance arrangement, the scope of military cooperation between the United States and Japan in case of "contingencies in the areas surrounding Japan" will inevitably be limited. Consequently, the effectiveness and reliability of the U.S.–Japan alliance as a regional stabilizer will be limited.

In order to solve these (and other) problems to ensure the continuing vitality and effectiveness of the U.S.–Japan alliance, the alliance structure must be transformed into a more "normal" one: the U.S. bases in Japan still remain a necessary component of the U.S.–Japan alliance for it to perform the role of a regional stabilizer effectively. The "material/personnel cooperation," therefore, will remain an important part of the U.S.–Japan alliance in the future. The alliance based solely on such an abnormal type of reciprocity, however, is unlikely to maintain its vitality and its effectiveness in the long run. "Personnel/personnel cooperation" must be promoted between the two allies. In order to achieve this goal, it will be necessary for Japan to reconsider its policy with regard to collective self-defense and to make the necessary adjustments.

Toward a More Equal Partnership

To "normalize" the U.S.–Japan alliance does not necessarily mean that Japan has to become a major military power. In fact, the option to become a major military power is not at all desirable for Japan.[30]

What is important here is the record of Japan's behavior in the postwar period. Unlike a computer game, there is no reset button for international politics to undo the results of past games and start from scratch. There is no wiping the slate clean of the consequences of history. Japan has been engaging in political posturing that defies the conventional wisdom of international relations for three decades, even after it became a major economic power. As many realist scholars of international relations, such as Henry Kissinger and Kenneth Waltz, have argued, a country that has obtained economic power usually aims for military power as well. Japan, however, has never tried to pursue that path. Japan must assume responsibility for its past choices.

The current balance-of-power in East Asia, particularly among the four major powers in the region, is built upon the expectation that Japan will continue to be dependent upon the United States with respect to security to some extent and will not seek a major military power status. Japan's move toward that direction would upset the regional power balance.

History shows that a radical change in the balance-of-power often invites tensions in international relations and even war. It is therefore not a desirable option for Japan to seek a major military power status at least in the short or medium term, even if it could gradually move toward that direction in the long term. This means that Japan should remain a middle-sized power militarily and should basically maintain its traditional dependence on the U.S. alliance.

Meanwhile, as mentioned earlier, the Japanese are frustrated with the fact that their country tends not to be viewed by the rest of the world as being its own independent political entity. They want their country to become a major political power. A considerable number of Japanese doubt if that goal is achievable as long as Japan remains dependent upon the U.S. alliance for its security.

For its own national interest as well as for the sake of stability in the region and the world, Japan should not become a major military power. However, if Japan continues to be treated as a second-class political power ranking below the United States, China, and Russia because of its self-restrained military posture, the Japanese might be forced to consider ending its military dependence on the United States.

The Americans should recognize that the Japanese particularly want to be treated as an equal partner by the United States. Despite the rhetoric used by Washington, many Japanese feel that their country is still treated as a junior partner by the United States. On the condition that enough efforts are taken by Japan to become a more responsible security partner of the United States, Washington should stop treating Japan this way. The partnership between the two allies must be transformed into a more "equal" one. The United States should accept Japan's "friendly assertiveness" on the basis of Japan's own foreign policy principles and global strategy,[31] although Japan remains militarily dependent on the United States to a certain extent.

The Case for an Enlarged U.S.–Japan Alliance

As was demonstrated in the previous section, in order to secure peace and stability in the Asia-Pacific, there must be some kind of mechanism that can deal with military conflict by military means, and the U.S.–Japan alliance represents the only available basis for such a mechanism. Thus, the U.S.–Japan alliance has to be maintained as a regional stabilizer, toward a new beginning.

It is not desirable, however, that only the United States and Japan keep assuming such military roles.[32] First, there may be some countries in the region other than the United States and Japan who want to make a military contribution to the maintenance of regional peace and order.

Washington and Tokyo should be careful not to make such countries feel that they are deprived by the United States and Japan of the opportunity to make military contribution to regional peace. Second, there is the question of legitimacy. Unless Washington and Tokyo show a certain degree of readiness to share regional military roles with others, some regional members may start questioning as to whether it is legitimate for the United States and Japan to assume such roles. Third, from the standpoint of the United States and Japan, it is impractical for these two countries to continue shouldering all the military costs of the maintenance of regional peace. Even if the two governments share such a political will, the public in both countries may not support such an idea.

In order to solve these problems, Washington and Tokyo should seek the way to "enlarge" the U.S.–Japan alliance by extending it to other regional members. These members must share the basic ideals and values such as democracy and freedom with the United States and Japan, and must express a willingness to fulfill certain military responsibilities in regional security. In the "enlarged" U.S.–Japan alliance arrangement, the United States and Japan will play the central roles, but other members will be assigned limited supportive roles proportionate to their respective national powers. The enlarged U.S.–Japan alliance would make it clear to everyone, particularly to China, that its purpose would be to stabilize the region and that it would not target some specific country (or countries).

By enlarging the membership, the legitimacy of the U.S.–Japan alliance arrangement in assuming regional military roles will significantly increase. By limiting its membership to those who share the basic ideals and values with the United States and Japan, the effectiveness of the alliance will be ensured even after the enlargement. At present, possible candidates for the enlarged membership of the U.S.–Japan alliance arrangement are Australia, South Korea, Canada, and New Zealand. As democratization proceeds in East Asia, however, the membership could be expanded even further. Enlargement of the U.S.–Japan alliance could be the basis of the establishment of the NATO-type collective defense arrangement in the Asia-Pacific, which would embrace all regional members in the distant future.

Conclusion

Almost a decade after the collapse of the Soviet Union, there are still cogent reasons for the continued maintenance of the U.S.–Japan alliance toward the twenty-first century. The alliance does, and will, serve as a regional stabilizer in the Asia-Pacific without which regional multilateral security mechanisms cannot be built and continue to prosper. There exists no realistic alternative mechanism to replace the U.S.–Japan alliance at least in the foreseeable future. The U.S.–Japan alliance will serve the security interests of both countries as well as the region as a whole in the future.

This, however, is only one side of the story. There are certainly strong *demands* for the continuation of the U.S.–Japan alliance. The existence of demands, however, does not guarantee the actual *supply* of the alliance in the future. Unless the citizens of the two countries keep supporting the U.S.–Japan alliance, and unless the governments of the two countries continue their efforts in nurturing the relationship and deal seriously with the challenges that lie ahead of them, the alliance cannot be maintained. Many things have to be done for that purpose, including finding some solution to the Okinawa base issue. But the first and most pressing step that Tokyo and Washington have to take is to introduce necessary reforms in their alliance so that it can maintain its vitality and its effectiveness for a long time. Normalization, equalization, and enlargement are the three key words that should direct such efforts.

Japan's active support to the United States in the war on terrorism under the leadership of Prime Minister Koizumi has contributed to enhance the trust and the support of both the Japanese and the Americans to the alliance between their countries. In order to conserve and even strengthen such favorable public sentiments toward the alliance on both sides of the Pacific in the future, the two governments must start acting now.

Notes

1. Ashton B. Carter and William J. Perry, *Preventive Defense: A New Security Strategy for America* (Washington, D.C.: Brookings Institutions Press, 1999), pp. 128–131.
2. Advisory Group on Defense Issues, *The Modality of the Security and Defense Capability of Japan: The Outlook for the 21st Century*, August 12, 1994.
3. According to Akio Watanabe, who participated in the Higuchi Commission and drafted the final report, the commission members did not have such an intention. See Akio Watanabe, "Nichi-bei Anzenhosho Kankei no Shintenkai," *Kokusai Mondai*, No. 456 (March 1998), p. 35.
4. U.S. Department of Defense, *A Strategic Framework for the Asian Pacific Rim: Looking toward 21st Century*, April 1990; U.S. Department of Defense, *A Strategic Framework for the Asian Pacific Rim: Report to Congress 1992*, April 1992.

5. "The Japan–U.S. Joint Declaration on Security-Alliance for the 21st Century," April 17, 1996.
6. U.S. Department of Defense, *United States Security Strategy for the East Asia-Pacific Region*, February 1995; *National Defense Program Outline in and after FY 1996*, adopted by the Security Council and by the Cabinet on November 28, 1995.
7. Koji Murata, "Shin-Gaidorain Saiko," *Voice*, January 1998, p. 217; Kazuya Sakamoto, "Nichi-bei Anpo ni Okeru Sougo-sei no Katachi: Gaidorain Minaoshi ni Yosete," *Gaiko Forum*, December 1997, p. 50.
8. Hisayoshi Ina, "Beikoku Yushiki-sha ni Kiku: Ato-ha 'Nihon ga Kimeru Mondai'—Nichi-bei Domei Kankei ha Seijuku-ka no katei ni," *Gaiko Forum*, December 1997, p. 58.
9. *The United States and Japan: Advancing Toward a Mature Partnership*, INSS Special Report (Washington, D.C.: National Defense University, October 11, 2000). This report has often been referred to as the "Armitage Report" or the "Armitage-Nye Report."
10. Watanabe, "Nichi-bei Anzenhosho Kankei no Shin-tenkai," p. 30.
11. Jim Mann, "U.S. Interest in Japan at Rock Bottom," *Los Angeles Times*, June 21, 2000.
12. Michael J. Green, "The Forgotten Player (extracts)," *The National Interest*, No. 60 (Summer 2000), http://www.nationalinterest.org/issues/60/Green.html, accessed January 5, 2001.
13. Kurt M. Campbell, "Energizing the U.S.–Japan Security Partnership," *The Washington Quarterly*, Autumn 2000, pp. 127, 128.
14. Ibid., p. 125.
15. A remark by Richard Samuels, http://www.usajapan.org/home/21stCentury/html/conference/plenary3.html, accessed April 9, 2002. The conference, which was entitled "The United States and Japan: An Enduring Partnership in a Changing World," and brought together leading figures in politics and business as well as academic and cultural circles of both countries in San Francisco from September 6 to 7, 2001, was actually held to commemorate the fiftieth anniversary of the signing of the San Francisco Peace Treaty and the U.S.–Japan Security Treaty.
16. As one of the best English materials that explains Japan's postwar pacifism, see Thomas U. Berger, "From Sword to Chrysanthemum," *International Security* 17-4 (Spring 1993), pp. 119–150. In this article, Berger uses the term "anti-militarism" instead of "pacifism."
17. For the impact of the Gulf Crisis on Japanese attitude toward overseas commitments, see Matake Kamiya, "Pacifism and the Japanese Attitude Toward the United Nations," in Philippe Régnier and Daniel Warner, eds., *Japan and Multilateral Diplomacy* (Aldershot, U.K.: Ashgate, 2001), pp. 180–181.
18. Yukio Okamoto, "Mata Onaji Koto ni Nara-naika: Moshi Wangan Senso ga Mou Ichido Okottara?" *Gaiko Forum*, September 2001.
19. For a comprehensive explanation of Japan's response to the September 11 terrorist attacks by a senior official of the Ministry of Foreign Affairs, see

Yachi Shotaro, "9·11 Tero Kougeki no Keii to Nihon no Taio," *Kokusai Mondai*, No. 503 (February 2002).

20. "Remarks by the President to the Diet," Office of the Press Secretary, February 18, 2002, http://usembassy.state.gov/tokyo/wwwhus0048. html, accessed February 24, 2002.

21. *Yomiuri Shinbun*, November 30, 2001.

22. Brad Glosserman, "Making History the Hard Way," *Comparative Connections, An E-Journal on East Asian Bilateral Relations*, 4th Quarter 2001 (January 2002), http://www.csis.org/pacfor/cc/0104Qus_japan. html, accessed February 18, 2002.

23. Ralph A. Cossa, "Ushering in the Post Post-Cold War Era," *Comparative Connections: An E-Journal on East Asian Bilateral Relations*, 3rd Quarter 2001 (October 2001), http://www.csis.org/pacfor/cc/0103Qoverview. html, accessed October 14, 2001.

24. This section is based on my earlier works, Matake Kamiya, "The U.S.–Japan Alliance and Regional Security Cooperation: Toward a Double-Layered Security System," in Ralph A. Cossa, ed., *Restructuring the U.S.–Japan Alliance: Toward a More Equal Partnership* (Washington, D.C.: The CSIS Press, 1997); and Matake Kamiya, "Ajia-Taiheiyo ni Okeru Juso-teki Anzenhosho Kozo ni Mukatte: Takoku-kan Kyocho Taisei no Genkai to Nichi-bei Anpo Taisei no Yakuwari," *Kokusai Seiji* No. 115 (May 1997).

25. The definitions of common, collective, and cooperative security in this section are the author's own, but owe much to the following works: Yoshinobu Yamamoto, "Kyocho-teki Anzenhosho no Kano-sei: Kiso-teki na Kosatsu," *Kokusai Mondai* No. 425 (August 1995); Takako Ueta, "Kyocho-teki Anzenhosho toha Nani ka," *Sekai*, August 1995; Shigeru Kosai, *Kokuren no Heiwa-Iji Katsudo* (Tokyo: Yuhi-kaku, 1991), pp. 7–9; David Dewitt, "Common, Comprehensive, and Cooperative Security," *Pacific Review*, 7-1 (1994); Alan Dupont, "Concepts of Security," in Jim Rolfe, ed., *Unresolved Future: Comprehensive Security in the Asia-Pacific* (Wellington, New Zealand: Center for Strategic Studies, 1995); Olaf Palme et al., *Common Security: A Blueprint for Survival* (New York: Simon and Shuster, 1982); and Ashton B. Carter, William J. Perry, and John D. Steinbruner, *A New Concept of Cooperative Security*, Brookings Occasional Papers (Washington, D.C.: The Brookings Institution, 1992).

26. The following arguments on the necessary conditions for a functioning collective security system owe much to Hans J. Morgenthau and Kenneth W. Thompson, *Politics among Nations: The Struggle for Power and Peace*, 6th ed. (New York: Alfred A. Knopf, 1985), pp. 452–457; and Kosai, *Kokuren no Heiwa-Iji Katsudo*, pp. 34–36.

27. The following arguments on the necessary conditions for cooperative security to function effectively owe much to Masashi Nishihara, "Takoku-kan Kyocho-Shugi no Zeijaku-sei," *Boei Daigakko Kiyo, Shakai-Kagaku Bunsatsu* No. 68 (March 1994), p. 22.

28. Sakamoto, "Nichi-bei Anpo ni Okeru Sougo-sei no Katachi"; Kazuya Sakamoto, "Material/Personnel Cooperation and the Future of the

U.S.–Japan Security Treaty," paper presented at the conference on "Restructuring U.S.–Japan Security Relations," co-sponsored by the Okazaki Institute, the Policy Study Group, and the Pacific Forum CSIS, Washington, D.C., April 29–May 2, 1996.

29. *The United States and Japan: Advancing Toward a Mature Partnership*, pp. 3–4.

30. The following discussion is based on my earlier work, Matake Kamiya, "How to Gain Status on World Stage: Japan Should Become 'Militarily Middle Size, Major Political Power,'" *The Nikkei Weekly*, April 3, 2000.

31. The Japan Forum on International Affairs, *Japan's Initiative toward US, China and Russia*, the 18th Policy Recommendations of the Policy Council, drafted by Kenichi Ito, Kunihiko Ymaoka, Hiroshi Nakanishi, and Matake Kamiya, April 1999.

32. The following discussion is based on my earlier work, Matake Kamiya, "Nihon ni totte no Nichi-bei-kan Anzenhosho Kyoryoku," *Defense* No. 36 (Spring 2000).

CHAPTER 6

BEYOND THE "POST–COLD WAR"?
U.S.–JAPAN ALLIANCE AND THE FUTURE
OF ASIA-PACIFIC SECURITY

Sheila A. Smith

The U.S. and Japan have adjusted to the new security environment in the Asia-Pacific. The U.S.–Japan alliance has been revamped to bring Japan into U.S. efforts to deter and manage crises in Northeast Asia, where the tensions have been the greatest. In the decade after the end of the Cold War, the multilateral avenues for coping with key security challenges offered new opportunities for the United States and Japan to coordinate their policies toward regional security issues. The U.S.–Japan alliance has been part of the growing number of informal and formal dialogue and problem-solving initiatives that made for a full diplomatic agenda in post–Cold War Asia.

The pattern of security multilateralism that has emerged in the Asia-Pacific has been complex and has varied in intensity. The real challenge in the Asia-Pacific, and most notably in Northeast Asia, has been to devise ways in which to bring key regional states together to solve specific disputes or to prevent the eruption of subregional conflicts that might draw in the major powers. This more pragmatic, problem-solving use of multilateralism has engaged both Washington and Tokyo, and has perhaps been most visibly successful in the coordination of policies focused on the Korean peninsula. These "mini-lateral" dialogues and forums for policy coordination are, for the most part, efforts to enhance cooperation between the United States and its alliance partners, Japan and South Korea.[1] Allied cooperation and policy coordination to cope with the nuclear and missile proliferation concerns on the Korean peninsula, such as the creation of Korea Energy Development Organization (KEDO) and more recently, the formation of the Trilateral

Coordination Group (TCOG), have proceeded despite setbacks in the broader relationship between Seoul and Tokyo.

Like other U.S. alliances, the post–Cold War aim of policymakers in Washington and Tokyo has been to capitalize on and expand the institutionalized cooperation of the Cold War. In fact, the policy emphasis by both the United States and Japan has been on enhancing bilateral military planning efforts and on finding more avenues for bilateral security cooperation on a global scale. In Northeast Asia, the attempt to bring individual allies together has not produced a reconstitution of the relationships. Unfortunately, even the triangular coordination of security cooperation in Northeast Asia requires considerable effort, as Seoul, Tokyo, and Washington have at different moments sought to revamp their own policies toward North Korea. While it has served as the lynchpin or cornerstone of U.S. strategy in the region, the U.S.–Japan alliance has not been the foundation upon which broader institutions of security cooperation can be built.

More importantly, the agenda for transformation for the United States and its allies since the end of the Cold War must now accommodate the global mobilization of a "coalition against terrorism." Even before September 11, there was a growing sense that a new agenda was needed for the region, and the limits of this effort to adjust to the end of the Cold War were becoming apparent. As former Secretary of Defense William Perry argues, the last decade in the Asia-Pacific was primarily dedicated to "fine-tuning" Cold War institutions. It is more obvious today that global events are driving the policy agenda, and regional problems are being recast through the lens of a global effort at antiterrorism coalition building. This suggests new challenges for the U.S.–Japan alliance, and for the multilateral institutions that have been designed to enhance regional stability.

Looking Back: A Decade of Adjustments

Two prescriptions for change attended the end of the Cold War in Asia. The first was a desire, widely shared among the states of the region, to create a multilateral forum for security deliberations. The second was the effort, led by the United States, to adapt and accommodate its Cold War alliances to the more fluid, and more dynamic, circumstances of the post–Cold War era. Japan embraced the first goal, but took some time to begin the process of redefining its alliance with the United States. In contrast, the United States was initially nervous about the early ideas emanating from the Asia-Pacific about a new multilateralism in security affairs, fearing that this could turn into a call for a reduced U.S. presence in the region. By the end of the 1990s, however, both the United States and Japan found that these two prescriptions for change created complementary rather than conflicting avenues for enhancing regional stability.

Early in the post–Cold War era, considerable debate emerged over whether or not an institutionalized approach to confidence building would be appropriate to the region.[2] A formal confidence-building regime, such as the European Community for Security and Cooperation in Europe (CSCE), was rejected as inappropriate for Asia, and instead the ASEAN took the initiative in organizing dialogue among the diverse nations of the region to enhance confidence building and "to bring about a more predictable and constructive pattern of relations in the Asia Pacific."[3] Since its inception in 1994, the ARF has been seen as the place for creating this inclusive dialogue.[4] Yet, in keeping with the norms of ASEAN, the premise of participation is that there would be no pressures on participants to compromise their own security interests or to enter into a formal agreement that might suggest a collective security effort.[5] Moreover, China has consistently argued that the ARF stay away from any attempt to expand its agenda beyond confidence building and preventive diplomacy to include crisis management or dispute resolution.

Independently, the United States and Japan have been supportive of ASEAN's efforts to organize a regional dialogue on security. U.S. policymakers initially were dismissive of the ARF as only a "talk shop." Yet, over time, the United States has come to appreciate the value of ARF. For example, it was not at all evident in the early 1990s that China could or would be part of a regional dialogue. China has not only agreed to participate, but has engaged—if somewhat tentatively—in deliberations over a Common Code of Conduct for dispute resolution in the South China Sea.[6] The annual ARF meetings provide a venue for multilateral dialogue, but they also provide an opportunity for a variety of bilateral conversations that might otherwise be difficult to arrange. In the wake of the accidental U.S. bombing of the Chinese embassy in Belgrade in 1999, for example, the sideline meeting between the U.S. secretary of state and China's foreign minister was critical to beginning a conversation on how to repair the relationship. Furthermore, ARF discussions of nuclear proliferation in South Asia were the first opportunity to address the concerns of both nuclear and nonnuclear states in the Asia-Pacific.

Japan was an early advocate for regional security dialogue, and has consistently sought to use this forum as a means of demonstrating its commitment to multilateralism. Japanese policymakers were much less optimistic than their counterparts in Washington about the consequences of the end of the Cold War. They were considerably less sanguine about the new Russia, and while Americans were talking of "peace dividends" and celebrating the success of their Cold War competition against Moscow, there was a sense of unease among security policymakers in Tokyo. Fears that the United States would be less engaged in regional security, and perhaps less willing to attend to Japan's own security needs, were at the heart of this unease. The Japanese Ministry of Foreign Affairs cautioned Washington that there were still remnants of the Cold War in Asia, and Japan's Defense Agency advocated the need for continuing the joint exercises and studies between the United States and Japanese militaries that were the basis of military cooperation in the alliance. But Japan's security planners were also aware that the divisions created by the Cold War, on the Korean peninsula and between Mainland China and Taiwan, would continue to demand considerable policy attention.

The impetus for rethinking U.S.–Japan security cooperation in the post–Cold War era, however, came from outside the Asia-Pacific region. The Gulf War transformed the bilateral security agenda. As the United States rapidly sought to turn its Cold War alliances into a multilateral war-fighting coalition in the Middle East, Japan was caught completely off-guard. Policymakers in Tokyo were unprepared for what followed. Amidst intense international and U.S. public scrutiny of Japan's response to the Gulf War, a new agenda for the U.S.–Japan alliance emerged. The bilateral alliance—if it was to survive the end of the Cold War—had to be transformed. The U.S. government urged its counterparts in Japan to move beyond its "checkbook diplomacy" and reconsider the self-imposed restraints that kept Japan from playing a more conspicuous—and risky—role in international conflicts. In the face of the Gulf War, and growing international criticism of Japan's reluctance to act purposefully alongside other U.S. allies during Desert Storm, Japan's political leaders sought to engage the public in a debate over how to make a more visible "contribution" to global security. The answer was to allow Japan's SDF to participate in UN-sponsored peacekeeping activities. A new law, passed in 1992, provided the framework for dispatching the SDF and other government agency officials to UN peacekeeping operations on a case-by-case basis. The first test case was the UN Transitional Authority in Cambodia (UNTAC), and a Japanese UN official, Akashi Yasushi, was designated as its head. For its part, the Japanese government sent SDF engineers, police officers, and other officials abroad in its first attempt to demonstrate Japan's engagement in peacekeeping.

It was against this backdrop of change—both in the global security dialogue and in Japan's own domestic debate over its responsibility to contribute to resolving international disputes—that the United States and Japan sought to revamp their bilateral security coordination in the first half of the decade. But it was the increasing instability in the Asia-Pacific region that provided the concrete focus for redefining the way that the United States and Japanese militaries would cooperate in the post–Cold War era. A nuclear crisis on the Korean peninsula in 1994 gave security planners in Washington a new sense of urgency in defining the role of U.S. forces deployed in Asia. The United States decided to shelve its old plan for reorganizing its forces in the Asia-Pacific, a plan that was created when the outlook for post–Cold War Asia seemed more favorable to U.S. interests.[7] Instead, a Department of Defense policy review (referred to as the "Nye initiative") concluded in 1995 that the United States would maintain its military presence in the region at around 100,000 and unambiguously articulated the need for more rather than less security cooperation with key U.S. allies, Japan and the ROK.[8] Concern that the U.S. public would be unforgiving of Japan's hesitancy to use its military should a regional crisis require U.S. military action, coupled with the Japanese government's inability to clarify its response to U.S. planners looking at a potential outbreak of conflict in Korea in 1994, made the task of focusing on Japan's ability to act alongside U.S. forces in case of a crisis the focal point of the U.S.–Japan security dialogue. For U.S. planners, the highest priority in the U.S.–Japan alliance was to encourage Japan to remove the political obstacles to contingency planning for regional crises.

Likewise, Tokyo policymakers also initiated a national policy review that sought to contend with the end of the Cold War and the new peacekeeping mission for the SDF that emerged after the Gulf War. The first task was to revise Japan's outdated statement of its security goals. The National Defense Program Outline (NDPO), originally drafted in the mid-1970s, was based on Cold War contingency planning, and it called for the SDF to prepare for a "limited and small-scale invasion" of Japan, a scenario that many in Japan's defense community thought was inappropriate even for the Cold War. Japan's political leaders, as well as its defense experts, agreed that the time had come to consider its security interests more broadly. The new NDPO not only incorporated Japan's decision to participate in UN-sponsored peacekeeping efforts, but also defined the effort to create a regional security dialogue as a priority for Japan. Consultations between policymakers in Washington and Tokyo were close during these respective national policy reviews, and modifications in language and tone were made to ensure that the two allies were communicating a similar message. The message was that the bilateral alliances with the United States were still key to providing deterrence and thus key to the stability of the region. Fears by some in the United States that Japan's enthusiasm for multilateral initiatives would lead to undermining the bilateral U.S.–Japan relationship were gradually assuaged, and Prime Minister Hashimoto and President Clinton issued a Joint Security Declaration in 1996. This became the basis for a bilateral policy review that created new Guidelines for U.S.–Japan Defense Cooperation.

The new Guidelines had to contend with two very specific scenarios of crisis in Northeast Asia. The fear of nuclear proliferation on the Korean peninsula, and growing tensions between the People's Republic of China (PRC) and Taiwan, brought the possibility of military confrontation in the region sharply into focus. From the U.S. vantage point these crises revealed key problems in alliance preparedness.[9] With growing fears of instability in these two familiar flashpoints, policymakers in Washington and Tokyo sought to direct the attention of Japan's politicians to the problems that would confront U.S. planners if Japan was unprepared to respond in a crisis. Ultimately, these bilateral Guidelines for the alliance became the basis for drafting new legislation in Japan, legislation that would allow for greater Japanese participation and support for U.S. forces in the region should a conflict develop.[10] The Japanese government's position that it was now prepared to consider joint operations with the United States on a "situational" basis removed the geographic constraints on coordinating contingency planning between the United States and Japanese security policymakers. In theory, this opened up the possibility that Japan would act in concert with the United States beyond Northeast Asia.

Regional reaction to this expansion of the operational goals of the U.S.–Japan alliance was relatively muted compared with the past, suggesting a new willingness to accommodate Japan's desire to shore up its alliance with the United States.[11] ASEAN clearly supported the maintenance of the U.S.–Japan alliance, and in Northeast Asia, there was a quiet but important emphasis on maintaining the status quo. Even China came to acknowledge that the existence of the alliance was positive for regional stability. In fact, many of the states that had been nervous about Japan's military role in the region quietly advocated a more forthright agenda for Tokyo and Washington. Those who had been most likely to accuse Japan of "militarist" activities in the past were in quiet ways helping Japan shore up its relationship with Washington.

Singapore had allowed for Japanese minesweepers to call on their way to clean-up operations after the Gulf War. Seoul was busy pursuing closer security ties with Tokyo, and the Kim Dae-jung visit to Japan in 1998 seemed to propel the troubled Japan–ROK relationship beyond their "quasi-alliance" during the Cold War.[12] Only China openly chastised Japan for its new role in the alliance, but here too the new regional mood of confidence building had made consultations by Japan's foreign policy and defense policymakers with their counterparts in Beijing part of the process leading up to the adoption of the new Guidelines legislation.

The coincidence of enhancing crisis management within the U.S.–Japan alliance and of expanding multilateral avenues for deliberating key security concerns within Northeast Asia undoubtedly facilitated a more accepting regional response to the changes in Japan's security planning. During the Cold War, repeated efforts by Japan's leaders to convince the states of the region that Japan had abandoned its ambition to be a military power seemed to fall on deaf ears. The post–Cold War effort at region-wide institution building provided a new context for Japan to provide evidence of its commitment to transparency in its security policymaking. For example, in the ARF, the attendant meetings of senior military officials have been particularly advantageous to Japan's effort to demonstrate this commitment to transparency. Bringing the SDF into greater contact with its counterparts in the region, and most specifically getting them to focus on the goal and mechanisms for confidence building has been important both at home, and around the region. The increasing role played by Japan's military in dialogues on regional security has provided an opportunity to demonstrate that the SDF—perhaps even more than their civilian counterparts—can be a force for advocating that Japan collaborates with its neighbors as well as the United States in its pursuit of security.

The Limits of the "Post–Cold War" Agenda

The post–Cold War decade in the Asia-Pacific region can be characterized by the creation and coexistence of a variety of security dialogues and institutions of cooperation. In the ARF, the aim was to create a dialogue that incorporates as many states of the region as possible, and over the years, membership in the ARF has expanded to include 24 countries.[13] The agenda is to develop common understandings, and thus to develop norms that will shape the way the states of the region seek to resolve their disputes. The "minilaterals" around the region have sought to focus on specific problems, and the most successful of these have been those related to the Korean peninsula where interests diverge and where the potential for conflict is the highest. There have also been a series of bilateral dialogues around the region that have strengthened defense cooperation between the countries of the region and the United States.[14]

Security cooperation between the United States and its allies is an integral part of the fabric of regional security relations, but these relationships are only one part of the overall complexion of regional security dynamics. A multilateral U.S. vision for the region, the Southeast Asia Treaty Organization (SEATO), was rejected early in the postwar period partly because of sensitivities to Japan, but also partly because there was a desire within Southeast Asia to limit external influence over regional affairs. The ANZUS pact was the only multilateral security alliance that included the United States, but it has not emerged from the Cold War fully intact. Northeast Asia, Japan, and South Korea, despite their common goals and interdependent security, have sought their security in bilateral alliances with the United States. In so far as the United States and Japan have embraced the region's desire for more multilateral avenues for considering common security problems, the U.S.–Japan alliance has served as a vehicle for coordinating policies, and for advocating the need for transparency and for finding shared solutions to common security challenges.

Yet, there are limits to this post–Cold War agenda. The United States and Japan have been more successful at the task of "fine-tuning" their alliance than they have in devising new avenues for regional cooperation. Several factors account for this. One is the continuing concern over the balance-of-power in the region, and as one of the region's major powers, Japan's own ambitions within the region will continue to be the subject of much speculation. Sensitivities run particularly high in Northeast Asia. This of course harks back to the region's pre–World War II history, but it is also related to the uncertainties currently confronting China, the two Koreas, and Japan. Korean unification, whether sooner or later, softer or harder, could dramatically alter the international relations of Northeast Asia, and could also have broad-ranging implications for domestic societies. China's own future is viewed today with some optimism, given its economic vitality and its leadership's seemingly resolute commitment to continuing on the path of economic reform. Here too there are uncertainties, however, and the future of China is a topic of great concern to all of its neighbors.

Thus, there continues to be a preference for bilateral security arrangements with the United States. Even during the Cold War, there was little motivation for translating bilateral cooperation into a broader regional coalition, and this has to do with the specific defense concerns of individual allies more than with history. In the wake of the Cold War, bilateral security cooperation with the United States is accepted in the region as the norm, as old antagonisms have given way to the new realities of day-to-day defense planning. Japan's own reticence to assume defense responsibilities beyond its own territory throughout the Cold War made security cooperation with other U.S. allies unthinkable, but there are more consultations on security issues between Japan and other U.S. allies today. The end of the Cold War created opportunities for consultations, but only in a few instances, such as the intermittent cooperation between Tokyo and Seoul, for formal military cooperation between U.S. allies in the region.

Another factor that is often overlooked these days is the continued resonance in the Asia-Pacific of the notion of regional institutions crafted and led by the countries of Asia. This vision has deep historical roots, and there continues to be a strong desire for regional institutions that reflect regional aspirations. On the one hand, postcolonial Asia has wanted to create its own institutions for the management of regional affairs. But on the other, there has been a realistic assessment of the need to ensure the balance-of-power. When Gorbachev advocated a multilateral institution that would focus on the future of regional security, the United States dismissed it as a challenge to its role in the region. China too has more recently argued for an Asia without "foreign troops," a reference to Beijing's interest in seeing post–Cold War Asia be rid of U.S. bases. But the aim of creating a multilateral institution designed by Asian states and responsive to Asia's needs, was a goal that was widely embraced by the countries of the region.

Thus, a competing location for regional security multilateralism was found in ASEAN.[15] ASEAN's own success in creating a subregional security community, and in developing a complex series of dialogues between ASEAN and the other powers of the region, made it an obvious candidate for attending to the newly emerging interest in a region-wide security dialogue. China's comfort with the ASEAN, as well as ASEAN's established relationships with the United States and Japan, made ASEAN an attractive host for what became the ARF. The demonstrated success of this alternative center of regional diplomatic activity during the Cold War, and its central place in post–Cold War multilateralism in the region makes it unlikely that the U.S. alliances will take a leading role in defining the future of security cooperation in the Asia-Pacific.

Another factor that must be considered when evaluating the impact of the U.S.–Japan alliance on regional security has to do with the way in which Japan and the United States have defined the terms of their security cooperation. Throughout the Cold War, Washington has steadily encouraged Tokyo to enhance its military capability and to take a larger military role in the alliance, and Tokyo has resisted because of the postwar constitution and the strength of popular support for its limitations on Japan's military. Instead, the Japanese government offered to improve the infrastructure on U.S. bases and to extend its contributions to HNS. When Japan's economy began to outpace that of the United States in the last decade of the Cold War, even this alternative arrangement for offsetting the U.S. "burden" for defense assistance to Japan seemed inadequate. Moreover, Japan's economic contribution to shared goals began to be defined globally, rather than in terms of the more geographically rooted demands of Northeast Asian security trends. In other words, the United States and Japan chose to negotiate the terms of their alliance by enhancing the role that Japan plays worldwide. Alternative mechanisms for demonstrating Japan's commitment to assisting the United States in contributing to global security were found. Japan vastly increased its Overseas Development Aid (ODA), and began to direct economic assistance to key states in unstable regions around the globe. Japan demonstrated its shared security commitments with the United States by economic means, and on a global scale.

The Gulf War severely tested this formula for resolving the demands for "burden-sharing." The U.S.–Japan formula for balancing burdens in the bilateral relationship was unique among U.S. alliances during the Cold War, and by the end of the Cold War it has resulted in a search for ways in which Japan could contribute via economic means to a common agenda. Washington and Tokyo sought global opportunities for allied cooperation rather than regional ones. But Japan's hesitancy to use its military came under fire during Desert Storm. This war, far removed from the dynamics of Asia-Pacific international relations, was the impetus for renegotiating the goals of the U.S.–Japan alliance in the post–Cold War decade. Moreover, the tensions generated between the United States and Japan during the Gulf War set the stage for the changes that were to come a year or two later when proliferation concerns arose on the Korean peninsula. But it is important to remember that it is Washington that wants to see Japan's military "flying the flag" in the case of a potential military clash on the Korean peninsula, not Seoul or Beijing. The imagery of the Gulf War was powerful and vivid: Japan must be willing to shed blood, to risk the lives of its citizens, if it is to demonstrate that it is a "true ally" of the United States.

Today, the attacks on the United States on September 11 have provided another example of this effort to demonstrate visibly Japan's willingness to risk its military in support of the United States. Washington and Tokyo have again demonstrated the post–Cold War utility of their alliance on the global—rather than on the regional—stage. The legacy of the Gulf War on Japanese thinking about the use of their military to support U.S. military operations in Desert Storm was obvious. Prime Minister Koizumi and his Cabinet quickly advocated the dispatch of Japan's Maritime Self Defense Force to the Indian Ocean in support of U.S. operations in Afghanistan, and also initiated a diplomatic offensive that supported U.S. coalition building for the "war on terrorism."[16] Legislation approving Japanese military and intelligence support for the U.S. "war on terrorism" passed the Diet in record time, and made it possible for the Japanese prime minister to visit Washington and New York within weeks of the attack. In the months to follow, Japan emerged as a U.S. partner in the sponsorship of postwar reconstruction in Afghanistan.[17]

Finally, Japan's bilateral relations with its two neighbors, South Korea and China, will be key to any attempt to avert or reduce tensions in Northeast Asia. The increased number of venues for policy "problem-solving" in security affairs of the region has not prevented a sharp downward turn in Tokyo's diplomatic relations with both states. And here it is perhaps important to recognize the limits not only on the U.S.–Japan alliance, but also to consider the limits of governments in determining the tone and tenor of interstate relations. Most volatile have been Japan's relations with South Korea. Security cooperation between Tokyo and Seoul emerged as a result of North Korea behavior, and subsequent efforts by Washington to ensure that policies toward the North were coordinated between Seoul, Tokyo, and Washington. Japan–South Korean relations were at a high point in 1998, when President Kim Dae-jung visited Tokyo and promised a new forwarding-looking era for Japan–Korean relations. But within a few years, the relationship sunk to a new low point. In April 2001, Seoul "temporarily" recalled its ambassador from Tokyo in response to the issuance of a new controversial Japanese textbook. Some semblance of cordiality in the relationship was resumed when Prime Minister Koizumi vigorously sought to emphasize the importance of Japan's relations with South Korea. Tokyo agreed to form a bilateral commission to study the textbook issue. As cosponsors of the Soccer World Cup in May 2002, Japan and South Korea needed to coordinate their security precautions, and the events of September 11 created a catalyst for closer dialogue on antiterrorist measures. Strenuous efforts on both sides were needed to get the relationship back on a more stable footing, and it was clear from the complex events of 2001 that security cooperation could easily fall victim to broader currents within that relationship.

Likewise, the downward spiral of Japan's relations with Beijing recently emphasizes the complexities of that relationship. In 2001 alone, Tokyo and Beijing clashed over history textbooks, the issuance of a visa for Taiwan's former president, Lee Teng-hui, the imposition of safeguards on Chinese agricultural products, Chinese maritime research ships, Prime Minister Koizumi's Yasukuni Shrine visit, and the decision to cut ODA to China by 10 percent. While these difficulties coincided with the election of Prime Minister Koizumi, they cannot be attributed solely to his efforts to demonstrate his conservative credentials at home. Like South Korea, China was unhappy with the new textbook and with his Yasukuni Shrine visit in August 2001, issues that evoke the charge of insensitivity to Chinese war memory. His effort to repair the damage during his visit to China later that year included an official visit to China's war memorial, and a statement of renewed Japanese commitment to avoid the mistakes of the past.

But of note in this litany of bilateral stresses are the new issues that complicate the relationship. Trade disputes and rising economic competition between Japan and China within the Asia-Pacific region are feeding speculation that the two countries will undoubtedly clash more forcefully in the future. Japan's own economic stagnation also plays into a sense of urgency in Tokyo. Cutbacks in ODA are being made across the board, but China has long been the recipient of large lump sum aid payments. Now Japan has announced that it will review individual projects on an annual basis, and that it will be more interested in financing projects that will have an impact on the environment, on human resource development, and on China's WTO accession. Japan's finance minister was quoted in the Japanese press as defending this change in policy by saying he was not quite sure why Japan should give aid to a country that is aiming missiles at Japan. More recently, Tokyo and Beijing have had to negotiate difficult terrain over the sinking of the suspected North Korea ship, and by the arrest by Chinese police of North Korean defectors in the Japanese Consulate office in Shenyang. Today, the issues that complicate the Sino-Japanese relationship cannot be attributed to events of the past. Rather, they are intimately related to the changing economic and political currents of the region. Japan's economic stake in China remains very high, and it is likely that the two countries will continue to negotiate their way out of difficulties. But it is a fragile relationship, one that is bound up in anticipation of a changing Asia and of a latent competition that needs to be managed carefully.

This is the basis upon which the United States and Japan must think about the alliance's future in the region. For the United States and its allies, the post–Cold War decade meant reviewing and revising the mechanisms for security cooperation. But it also meant a broader rethinking of the dynamics of regional international politics, and of the value of Cold War institutions. Washington continues to see its alliances in Asia as the primary vehicle for security relations with the region.[18] Japan continues to see its security alliance with the United States as the pillar of its foreign policy, but also seeks to encourage the development and strengthening of regional multilateral initiatives, especially the ARF. In this respect, Japan has acted much like other states in the region. The post–Cold War era preferences of individual states in the Asia-Pacific were to enhance defense preparations, including greater security cooperation with neighbors and allies, while at the same time developing regional dialogue and confidence building.

Looking Forward: September 11 and the Post–Cold War Agenda

The dynamics of Asia-Pacific security are clearly not separate from broader global trends. There is a tendency at times to see the Asia-Pacific as a place unto its own, with its own particular dynamics. The rise of Chinese power continues to conjure up images of a balance-of-power Asia, much like that of the first half of the twentieth century. But the material power of the countries of Asia has been transformed, and while the relations between major powers—China, Japan, the United States— may be critical to finding solutions to regional problems, it is no longer possible to think of regional political dynamics solely in terms of major power interactions. Moreover, the dynamics of regional interactions are not the only factor shaping the choices of individual states. Relations with states outside the region provide important avenues for complementing the balancing act of diplomacy within. The Asia-Pacific does have its own security realities, but they are not impervious to global events. This has been made very clear by the impact of September 11, and the events that followed.

It is too early to tell, however, if September 11 will be the beginning of a process of realignment in the priorities of the states of the region. But it does seem that the rather vague post–Cold War phase of adjusting regional security relationships has come to an end. It is a good moment to look back, and assess this "post–Cold War" effort to define a security policy agenda for the region. For Washington and Tokyo, the policy responses were two-fold: strengthen the mechanisms for alliance cooperation developed over the course of the Cold War, and support efforts to repair the relationships that were fraught with tension. Redefining alliance goals was driven in part by the internal dynamics of the bilateral alliance, in part by a series of events that tested the ability of political leaders to cope with crisis. Erasing the silences on security issues among and between key Asian states was as important, and here Japan's relationship with its neighbors was one of the focal points of regional attention.

Some basic understandings were reconfirmed. In the Asia-Pacific, the U.S.–Japan alliance has contributed to reassuring Japan's neighbors of its continued commitment to cooperating with the United States in providing for its own national security. Japan continues to insist that regional security be sought collectively, and in its enthusiasm for participation in the ARF and other regional efforts to enhance confidence building, it has found new opportunities for communicating its postwar goal of resolving disputes in cooperation with other states of the region. Closer to home, Japan must also find a way of creating more stable and predictable relationships with its neighbors in Northeast Asia.

Despite these efforts, however, domestic political change in the region has complicated diplomatic efforts. Japan's own political congestion has frustrated many. As politicians maneuver for power, there is increasing evidence that the Japanese public is now uneasy. There is greater willingness to reward strident stances on foreign policy, and less sympathy for the complaints lodged by South Korea and China about Japan's attitudes toward its history. South Koreans remain fearful that the United States will mishandle the opportunity for engagement with the North, and while the government-to-government coordination of policy toward the North remains close, public perceptions of U.S. goals and intentions are less than generous. China's behavior is also driven by the massive political and economic transformation that is underway. The Taiwan issue easily translates into a "nationalist" cause. The Belgrade bombing of the Chinese embassy and the spy plane incident have done much to give credence to the argument that the United States is hostile to China.

While these sensitivities are not new, it is the anticipation of potential change—the new environment of uncertainty—that magnifies them. It is important to remember that alliances are designed to mitigate security dilemmas, and thus they will be successful first and foremost when they help ensure the security of their members. In moments of transformation, however, there is also a need to be aware of the potential for creating new security dilemmas. In the Asia-Pacific, the United States has concentrated appropriately on the demands of Northeast

Asia, and specifically, has sought to find a way to cooperate with Japan and South Korea in contending with the often unpredictable and dangerous regime in Pyongyang. There has been a more problematic U.S. goal, and that has been the push to build a missile defense system and to deploy this in Northeast Asia. China has been concerned about both efforts, but while there has been considerable attention to China's concerns on the Korean peninsula, there has been a tendency to take a more unilateralist stance on missile defense. The Bush administration's goal of pursuing missile defense technology, and of abandoning the Anti-Ballistic Missile (ABM) treaty, has consequences beyond Asia, but in its application to Northeast Asia, Japan will be hard-pressed to endorse this agenda.[19]

There are signs too that Japan will need to pay close attention to how its policies affect its neighbors Northeast Asia. Attitudes within Japan toward security issues are changing, and at the same time, there is a growing public frustration with Japan's political leadership. The United States is anxious to see Japan ease its restrictions on its military, at least in so far as it leads to a greater Japanese role in support of shared regional and global crises. The way in which Japan "normalizes" its approach to the use of military force will, undoubtedly, be of concern to its neighbors. South Korea and China are more prone to viewing these changes in the context of broader social changes in Japan than Washington. By the end of the 1990s, a new appreciation within Japan for the dangers of the post–Cold War world complicated efforts to coordinate policies between Seoul, Tokyo, and Washington. In the wake of the *Taepodong* missile, public and government attention in Japan has focused on fishing vessels from North Korea that freely come and go along the coast of the Sea of Japan. Concern over Japan's own border security led to the creation of new rules of engagement for the Maritime Self Defense Force (MSDF) in defense of Japanese waters and territory, and the MSDF fired warning shots for the first time across the bow of "suspicious ships" in 1999.[20] Public concern about the activities of North Korean ships in and around Japan has bolstered the Japanese government's efforts to deal more effectively with these intrusions, and when a ship tried to outrun Japan's Coast Guard last December, it was pursued out of Japanese waters, fired upon and it sank. Diplomatically, the Chinese and Japanese governments have handled this carefully, perhaps because of the post–September 11 concern about terrorism. What caused the ship to sink remains under investigation, as does the identity of those on board, but Japan has insisted that the ship be raised and that the details of its activities be publicized. This use of force by Japan in what turned out to be China's exclusive economic zone creates new questions about the norms that will govern maritime activities in the East and South China Seas.[21]

What has perhaps not been fully appreciated in Washington is the impact of post–Cold War events on the public in Japan. There is a new consensus within Japan, one that has developed alongside the effort to enhance U.S.–Japan alliance cooperation, that national security deserves more forceful attention. For the bulk of the Cold War, the Japanese public had little engagement in security issues, and when there was public attention, it was critical of the alliance and of the U.S. conduct of the Cold War. Issues such as nuclear threat, proliferation, or the development of WMD were of little interest, and there was little appreciation among the Japanese public that these impinged upon Japan's security. North Korea's missile, however, struck a deep chord of insecurity among the Japanese public, and revealed how easily public threat perceptions could diverge from the perceptions of the security policy elite. Long accustomed to downplaying the SDF's capabilities, the Japanese government was ill-prepared to reassure its citizens that their security was adequate. While the U.S. and Japanese governments share a common understanding of the need for a combined response in case of a conflict on the Korean peninsula, or even in the less likely case of a cross-straits clash between Beijing and Taiwan, the Japanese public's response to the joint management of a crisis will be less predictable, and potentially more volatile.

The attacks of September 11 have created a more profound sense of public vulnerability in the United States, also. The Bush administration's initial framing of the coalition that conducts the "war on terrorism" was unequivocal—countries around the globe were either "with us, or against us." The speed and substance of Japan's response clearly demonstrated that it was supportive of U.S. goals. But Japan is one of many, and there is little public attention given in the U.S. media to its contributions.[22] The post–Cold War task of fine-tuning U.S. alliances seems to be giving way to a new, and much more difficult agenda. The United States seeks to create "coalitions of the willing," as it pursues terrorists and the states that harbor them. Unlike in the past, Washington has clearly decided that it is willing to consider preemptive strikes against threats to global stability from terrorists and the states that sponsor terrorism. For now, Iraq seems to be the primary target of possible military action, but it is possible that North Korea, as one member of the "axis of evil," could also be added to that list. The U.S. public will be even more sensitive to the behavior of U.S. allies in the wake of September 11, and this suggests yet again a new agenda for the

United States and Japan, one that must go beyond the revised Guidelines for Defense Cooperation that were crafted with such care in the 1990s.[23] As in the past, the United States and Japanese alliance will need the support of its respective publics, and the public estimation of the utility of the alliance will depend upon their own sense of security.

The role of the U.S. military, globally and within the Asia-Pacific, will continue to be a critical factor in thinking about regional security dynamics. Given continuing public sensitivities to its presence in Asia, the U.S. military can easily become a target of criticism. The value of its presence for regional stability needs to be demonstrated, not assumed. Here again, the strategic goals articulated by policymakers may not always address the concerns about the social consequences of the U.S. military presence in the region. Even in Japan, where the public supports the alliance and values its importance to regional stability, there continues to be some frustration over the management of the U.S. military. The lack of a comfortable resolution of the base issue in Okinawa means that public irritation there continues to fester, and a series of new crimes committed by U.S. military personnel have prompted calls for a revision of the Status of Forces Agreement (SOFA). Moreover, the sinking of the *Ehime Maru* by the *USS Greenville* in February 2001 reinforced the Japanese public's perception of a U.S. military that disregards public safety, and that retains a privileged status in the U.S.–Japan relationship—beyond the reach of accountability to Japanese citizens. The U.S. Navy went to considerable lengths to address public outrage over the accident, but like the incidence of crime by U.S. military personnel in Japan, the accident revealed yet again that the Japanese public's views of the U.S. military are linked to a broader dissatisfaction with the role of Japan's own politicians in defending Japanese interests—including citizen interests—in the alliance.

And it is the privileges accorded to the U.S. military that is at the heart of domestic reaction to the alliance these days in Japan. Should this be coupled with a broader regional debate about U.S. unilateralist behavior, or about the conduct of the U.S. military in the region, it could prove to be a potent source of tension within the alliance. This desire for more accountability by the United States regarding its military objectives is shared around the region. U.S.–Chinese antagonism over the downing of a Chinese fighter jet, and the detention of crew of the U.S. intelligence-gathering aircraft, revealed yet again the sensitivities of the post–Cold War U.S. presence in the region. The idea that U.S. forces belong in the region is not a comfortable one for many, and this holds equally true with the societies allied with the United States as with those who are not.

And finally, the dynamics of Asia's regional security can no longer be considered without reflection on the longer-term domestic political changes currently underway throughout the region.[24] Domestic politics are increasingly seen as a significant determinant of how relations between states will be managed. The regional security agenda has been full of cases of conflict or crisis that can be traced to the more complex and longer-term transformations taking place within Asia. The highly charged issue of the cross-straits relationship between the PRC and Taiwan invokes complex domestic political relationships in both countries. Taiwan's transition from a single-party system to a more competitive political process remains a delicate issue for the region, particularly for policymakers in the United States and Japan.[25] Enthusiasm for democratization has been uneven in Asia, but the need to establish reliable mechanisms for leadership transitions, to consider the social impact of economic growth—and then economic crisis, and in many cases, to manage ethnic diversity has made for complex demands on governments throughout the region. On top of these longer-term domestic transformations, the events of September 11 have created new dilemmas for the governments of the region, particularly those in Southeast Asia. National responses to the September 11 attacks have varied, but the leaders of the Philippines, Indonesia, and Malaysia all issued their support of U.S. efforts to eradicate terrorism. Within these countries, however, there is considerable divergence of opinion. For those with large Muslim populations, such as Indonesia, the U.S. "war on terrorism" created a wave of criticism against the United States for its treatment of Muslims within the country after the attacks. Prime Minister Mahathir of Malaysia has also drawn strong criticism from Muslim groups for his willingness to go along with the United States. Less criticism is evident in the Philippines, which has a much smaller Muslim population, but President Arroyo's willingness to allow the U.S. military to help the Philippine government to assist with operations against the Abu Sayyaf guerrillas has angered those who fought to get rid of U.S. military presence in their country a decade or so ago.[26]

More so than in the past, regional institutions will need to take a more active role in designing a security agenda that accommodates these domestic currents of change. While the governments of Asia have supported the U.S. aim of eradicating terrorism,[27] there are other issues that are as likely to shape the regional agenda. The impact of the Asian Financial Crisis, perhaps more than events in North Korea or the attacks on September 11, weighs heavily on regional leaders. The ASEAN Plus Three's (ASEAN members plus China, South Korea, and Japan) focus on Northeast Asian relations is a new and important indicator of a different kind of emphasis for easing tensions and expanding avenues of cooperation. A new vision, prepared by its East Asia Vision Group in October 2001, suggests that the key to confidence building in Northeast Asia is in the creation of a regional community. This community-building goal incorporates not just the security relations among the states, but focuses on building trust through enhanced economic, social, environmental, and cultural cooperation.[28] This new discussion on Northeast Asian community building was prompted first and foremost by the impact of the Asian Financial Crisis, and the prescriptions included in the vision statement include trade, financial, and development policy coordination.

New ideas about how to reduce uncertainty in the region are emerging from within the Asia-Pacific, and most of these see economic goals as key to the region's future. As important as the ARF has been to beginning a regional security dialogue, it is only one of many efforts to identify shared goals. The idea that regional peace can only be achieved through the pursuit of prosperity continues to animate regional discussions, and in a region that was once admired globally for its economic achievements, many see economic and social interdependence as the route to developing real confidence and trust.

Conclusion

The Asia-Pacific has had a full agenda related to building confidence, to expanding dialogue activities, and to repairing relationships susceptible to tension and confrontation. Concern about the real potential for the eruption of military conflict in key areas—such as the Korean peninsula or across the Taiwan straits—was at the root of these efforts. This is in part due to the divisions created by the Cold War, but much of this high level of diplomatic activity also suggests the high level of uncertainty that pervades regional international relations in its wake. In the face of uncertainty, old relationships and patterns of interaction produce the comfort of familiarity. Nowhere has this been more evident over the past decade than in the U.S.–Japan relationship.

A new perspective on the U.S.–Japan alliance and its relationship to regional security trends is needed, however. The United States and Japan have expended limited effort, and have had only minimal success in using their alliance relationship to effect broader changes within the Asia-Pacific region. Washington and Tokyo have spent much of their security policy effort on the task of "normalizing" Japan's military preparations as a means of strengthening their security relationship.

Far less policy attention has been exerted on considering how to craft a common approach to developing a regional vision.

There is little evidence that the underlying balance-of-power in the region will change any time soon. The United States and Japan have advocated the need to strengthen their alliance. China's rising power is, of course, often noted, but the ability of China to transform the region continues to be an anticipated event rather than an accomplished fact. Moreover, China in recent years has exhibited an interest in being part of the process of managing regional security dynamics, and this belies the more dire predictions that it will seek to change or challenge the status quo radically. What we need today as we seek to consider what might be ahead for the United States and Japan, and how the U.S.–Japan alliance affects regional security, is a greater understanding of the dynamics that have been at play since the Cold War ended.

Two factors will undoubtedly continue to be important. The first is that while the region has its own balance—or subregional balances—of power, regional security relations cannot be fully understood without reference to global currents. It was the positive experience of Europe's multilateralism in the wake of the Cold War that prompted much of the debate over the need for a similar security institution in Asia. The form may have been different, but the example set in Europe and the role that multilateral institutions played in paving the way for a regional dialogue after the Berlin Wall came down is key to understanding the prescription for post–Cold War Asia.

Global transformations are particularly important also for viewing the role played by the U.S.–Japan alliance. Since the end of the Cold War, key moments of transformation have generated from beyond the Asia-Pacific context—and thus the alliance relationship has evolved in ways that often seem to have little bearing on the immediate realities of Northeast Asia. Japan has clearly sought to provide for its own security in conjunction with—not isolated from—U.S. priorities, and this has put pressure on Tokyo to remove constraints on its military. While this new emphasis on assisting the United States has not removed all constraints on Japan's use of force, Washington's emphasis on "normalizing" Japan complicates assessments of the ultimate impact the alliance has on the region. Instead, it has been Tokyo's efforts to create more transparency in its security policymaking and to emphasize the SDF role in regional security dialogue that has offered the most reassurance to Japan's neighbors about its ultimate intentions.

The second key to the future of regional stability will be in the management of domestic social, political, and economic transformations.

The diversity of the Asia-Pacific societies is the most frequently cited characteristic of the region, and this still holds today. Economic disparity and the often-volatile process of democratization make for a powerful set of social conditions. In the aftermath of September 11, there is also a growing awareness in the United States of the complex vulnerabilities that attend the process of globalization. Current regional support for the goal of eradicating terrorism is based on a shared condemnation for the indiscriminate use of violence. Governments around the region have indicated this publicly, and regional institutions have echoed Asia's support for a collective, global response. The United States, and Japan will need to demonstrate that they too are committed to a collective and global response, and that the new multilateral institutions of the Asia-Pacific will be an important place for developing regional support and cooperation.

Notes

1. Recent meetings between Japan's Prime Minister Koizumi with Australia present another effort to expand security cooperation and dialogue among U.S. allies. Prime Minister Howard suggested the possibility of a new "defense triangle" between the U.S., Japan, and Australia. Koizumi agreed to begin consultations between the two countries, including annual security meetings. Issues of common concern include piracy, crisis management, and the longer-term question of China's role in the region.
2. There was quite a variation in views on what sort of framework for multilateralism would suit the Asia-Pacific in the early 1990s. Proposals for "common security," "cooperative security," and a "regional security dialogue" were put forth by the former Soviet Union and Australia, by Canada, and by ASEAN and Japan, respectively. For a clarification of the content of these proposals, see David Dewitt, "Common, Comprehensive and Cooperative Security," in *Pacific Review*, Vol. 7, No. 1 (1994). See also Amitav Acharya, *Constructing a Security Community in Southeast Asia: ASEAN and the Problem of Regional Order* (London: Routledge, 2001).
3. The 27 ASEAN Ministerial Meeting in 1994 produced the conclusion that an ARF could become an effective consultative Asia-Pacific Forum for promoting open dialogue on political and security cooperation in the region.
4. The objectives of the ARF were outlined in the First ARF Chairman's Statement (1994): (a) to foster constructive dialogue and consultation on political and security issues of common interest and concern; and (b) to make significant contributions to efforts toward confidence building and preventive diplomacy in the Asia-Pacific region.
5. For a full discussion of ASEAN's efforts to translate its own norms or "ASEAN Way" beyond its original security community, see Amitav Acharya, *Constructing a Security Community in Southeast Asia* particularly chapters 5 and 6.

6. China has been drafting its version of a Code of Conduct, as has the ASEAN nations. See www.aseansec.org for text. For a broad discussion of the history of this process, and the more recent impact of the U.S. Navy EP-3 collision with a Chinese fighter jet on confidence building in the South China Sea, see Scott Snyder, Brad Glosserman, and Ralph A. Cossa, "Confidence Building Measures in the South China Sea," *Issues & Insights*, No. 2-01, Pacific Forum CSIS, Honolulu, Hawaii.

7. *A New Strategic Framework for the Asia-Pacific*, 1988, Department of Defense.

8. *US Strategic Security for the East Asia-Pacific Region* in East Asia Strategy Report—EASR (Department of Defense, 1995).

9. Japan and the United States had very little in the way of joint contingency plans for the alliance during the Cold War. While the possibility of military contingencies in Asia—most obviously the Korean peninsula and Taiwan—had been at the forefront of the security dialogue during the Cold War, Japan's own internal constraints on allowing its military to plan joint operations kept the two allies from preparing contingency plans. In 1978, the two governments concluded their first Guidelines for U.S.–Japan Defense Cooperation, a policy exercise that brought the SDF and U.S. militaries together formally for the first time to identify ways in which they should develop their capability to act jointly to defend Japan. The new Guidelines for Defense Cooperation crafted after the Cold War sought to identify ways in which the two militaries might act jointly in case of regional crises. For a review of Cold War military cooperation, see Sheila A. Smith, "The Evolution of Military Cooperation in the U.S.–Japan Alliance," in Michael J. Green and Patrick M. Cronin, *The U.S.–Japan Alliance: Past, Present and Future* (New York: Council on Foreign Relations, 1999).

10. The New Guidelines for U.S.–Japan Defense Cooperation, adopted on September 23, 1997, can be found at http://www.jda.go.jp.

11. Equally important was the changing perceptions within Japan about the function of the U.S.–Japan alliance. By the mid-1990s, a broad political consensus had emerged on the need to pursue greater security cooperation with the United States, and when polled, the otherwise hesitant Japanese public agreed that Japan's security relationship with the United States contributes to regional security. *Yomiuri*/Gallop Survey conducted December 22–25, 2000 revealed that 62.1% of respondents answered positively when asked if the U.S.–Japan security treaty contributed to the stability of the Asia-Pacific region.

12. See Victor Cha, *Alignment Despite Antagonism: The United States–Korea–Japan Security Triangle* (Stanford: Stanford University Press, 1999).

13. The current participants in the ARF are as follows: Australia, Brunei Darussalam, Cambodia, Canada, China, EU, India, Indonesia, Japan, DPRK, ROK, Laos, Malaysia, Myanmar, Mongolia, New Zealand, Papua New Guinea, Philippines, Russian Federation, Singapore, Thailand, United States, and Vietnam.

14. In addition to its allies, the United States has bilateral military exercises, and training programs, with many of the states of the region, including Indonesia, and Malaysia. Moreover, Singapore, Indonesia, and Brunei have

agreed to allow visits to their countries by U.S. ships. In the wake of September 11, Indonesia states that it will allow the transit of "foreign warships" through its waters, and even China has allowed U.S. warships to call in Hong Kong.

15. It is important to remember that ASEAN was created shortly after the failure of the U.S. initiative to create SEATO, its vision of a regional security organization similar to NATO in Europe, and ASEAN's identity is intimately related to its efforts to ensure that the region's problems are addressed and resolved by the countries of the region.

16. Japan's immediate response to the events of September 11 included: drafting of an antiterrorism special measures law (which passed the Diet on October 29), refugee assistance, emergency measures to assist Pakistan (and those Afghan refugees in Pakistan), including debt rescheduling, emergency aid assistance to Tajikistan (and Afghan refugees there), ending of sanctions against India and Pakistan imposed in response to nuclear testing, measures to cut off terrorists' funds, and $10 million contribution to the New York State World Trade Center Relief Fund and Twin Towers Fund. For updates on Japan's efforts see http://www.mofa.go.jp.

17. The Japanese government has cochaired meetings with the United States on planning for Afghanistan postwar reconstruction, and has offered to provide reconstruction assistance of up to 500 million dollars over two and a half years at the International Conference on Reconstruction Assistance to Afghanistan in January 2002. Most recently, the Japanese government has dedicated 2.7 million dollars to the Ump's efforts to facilitate an Emergency Loya Jirga, including transportation costs for Emergency Loya Jirga Special Commission members and international observers and the procurement of equipment and materials necessary for monitoring of the regional election process.

18. For an articulate argument in support of this approach, see Ralph A. Cossa, "US Asia Policy: Does an Alliance-Based Policy Still Make Sense?" *Issues & Insights*, No. 3-01, Pacific Forum, CSIS, Honolulu, Hawaii, September 2001.

19. In fact, Japan's Defense Agency has already signaled its reticence to move beyond the research and development phase of a Theater Missile Defense (TMD) program.

20. Not only Japan's navy, but also its Ground Self Defense Force (GSDF) has been tasked with dealing with potential North Korean activities in and around Japan. Last year, the GSDF announced the formation of an urban guerrilla unit, designed to contend with potential guerrilla and spy activities by North Korea.

21. For an assessment of how the use of force today in and around the East and South China Seas could have a significant impact on the development of international legal norms regarding maritime activitiles, see Mark J. Valencia and Ji Guoxing, "The 'North Korean' Ship and U.S. Spy Plane Incidents: Similarities, Differences and Lessons Learned," *Asian Survey*, Vol. 42, No. 5 (September/October 2002).

22. The U.S. Department of Defense created a list of those countries that provided assistance to the United States in the wake of September 11. Unfortunately, Japan's name was left off that list. For Japanese diplomats,

this was a repeat of their experience during the Gulf War when Kuwait did not include them on their thank you list after Desert Storm. The Pentagon, after being admonished by Japan, apologized for its oversight.

23. The Japanese government has submitted new "emergency" legislation that is designed to facilitate crisis management, and to clarify steps that will be taken in case of war. Yet, this legislation continues to focus on a conventional attack against Japan, and is inadequate for thinking about Japan's new threat environment.

24. To get a better sense of how domestic political change has and continues to affect regional security relations, see Muthiah Alagappa ed., *Asian Security Practice: Material and Ideational Influences* (Stanford: Stanford University Press, 1998), particularly chapter 19.

25. For a thorough discussion of the links between domestic political change in Taiwan and the cross-straits relationship, see Muthiah Alagappa, ed., *Taiwan's Presidential Politics: Democratization and Cross-Strait Relations in the Twenty-First Century* (New York: M.E. Sharpe, 2001).

26. Immediately after the September 11 attacks, the Philippine government proposed the creation of a tri-national committee with Malaysia and Indonesia to represent Asia in the "global anti-terrorist coalition" being organized by the United States. See *Manila Times*, September 20, 2001.

27. In the aftermath of September 11, overall support for the United States around Asia was impressive. China's quick expression of support, along with the cooperation of the major Muslim states in the region, suggested that antiterrorism could provide a new common cause between the United States and the states of Asia. But it is also important to note that this is seen as a global cause, one that should be spearheaded by the UN, and through cooperative means. See e.g. the statement issued on October 18, 2001 in Shanghai at the APEC meeting. The key points of the APEC leaders' consensus included a strong condemnation of terrorism in all forms, a call for the full implementation of all antiterrorist international covenants adopted by the UN Security Council, and a call for greater international cooperation and a strengthening of the role of the UN and its Security Council (as reported in the *BBC*, October 18, 2001).

28. See *Towards an East Asian Community: Region of Peace, Prosperity and Progress*, prepared by the East Asia Vision Group of the ASEAN Plus Three, October 31, 2001.

CHAPTER 7

MULTILATERAL SECURITY IN ASIA AND THE U.S.–JAPAN ALLIANCE

Victor D. Cha

There is a basic puzzle with regard to multilateral security and the U.S.–Japan alliance. Both the United States and Japan generally agree on the tenets of multilateralism in Asia. They agree that multilateral security should be inclusive rather than exclusive. They agree that such institutions and practices should be seen as a complement to, and not a replacement of, the bilateral alliance (or for that matter global multilateral institutions).[1] They also value the basic norms of multilateralism (e.g., preservation of national sovereignty).[2] This general convergence of views should provide the permissive conditions for multilateralism to thrive in the region; however, the empirical record shows otherwise, raising a host of unanswered questions. Why is it that has multilateral and/or regional security been relatively ineffective in East Asia? Why is it that in spite of general agreement on multilateral principles and norms, the participation in such institutions remain problematic for the alliance. Why do some see multilateral institutions as a threat to the alliance? Why do others see multilateralism as impeded by the alliance? And why do yet others see it as irrelevant to the alliance?

This chapter tries to address this puzzle. It presents two arguments. First, advocates of multilateral security in Asia face "twin dilemmas of appeal" vis-à-vis the U.S.–Japan alliance: an asymmetry of need, and functional redundancy. In short, multilateral security dialogues (MSD)—as they are currently constituted—are ineffective and do not resonate loudly within the U.S.–Japan context because: (1) MSDs need the alliance more than the alliance needs the MSDs; and (2) the MSDs duplicate rather than complement security functions that are already provided by the alliance.

Second, I argue that there are three ways in which MSD-advocates can mute these twin dilemmas of appeal and create greater complementarity between the needs of the alliance and the needs of MSDs. These have to do with broadening the underlying security conceptions operative among MSDs; creating "binding and reinforcing" rationales for MSD participation by Japan and the United States; and utilizing MSD participation as a means to facilitate "minilateral" security dialogues.

Understanding how to create better convergence between bilateralism and multilateralism in Asia is important because it avoids pitting an old system of managing security against the new. In other words, it is incumbent on the U.S.–Japan alliance (and more generally the traditional American network of bilateral alliances established since the Cold War) to cope with, rather than reject or ignore, the newer attempts at indigenous and multilateral regional security initiatives and institutions. These two variables, more than any other (barring major war), will determine the future security landscape of the region. Therefore, I seek to show how these two pieces fit together and what their potential points of conflict are. More importantly, I try to show how the two can be mutually reinforcing and what are the potential divisions of labor between MSDs and U.S.–Japan alliance commitments.

The Underwhelming Record of Multilateral Security in Asia

Unlike Europe, the history of security multilateralism in Asia has been unimpressive. There are no comparable institutions like NATO and the Warsaw Pact. States instead chose paths of security self-reliance, neutralism, or bilateralism (largely with the United States, but also with China or the Soviet Union). Attempts at constructing institutions did exist but these were largely subregional rather than region-wide (e.g., SEATO [1954], ANZUS [1951], and FPDA [1971] and met with limited success).[3] Efforts at a region-wide "PATO" equivalent to NATO failed miserably despite a compelling Cold War security environment and established venues for dialogue.[4] While more recent institutions at official and track 2 levels have been more successful (e.g., ARF, APEC, CSCAP, NEACD, ASEM), they differ fundamentally from these predecessors, exhibiting a "softer"quality not extending beyond dialogue and transparency-building.[5] The most advanced of these at the region-wide level is the ARF, formed in July 1994 and meeting annually with regard to cooperative security dialogue and preventive diplomacy.[6]

The absence of a NATO-type organization in Asia stems from a variety of factors. First, geography mattered. Unlike Europe, Asia was both a maritime and land theater without the same sort of clearly identifiable geographical boundaries that divided contiguous Europe. Moreover, the two poles that defined NATO and The Warsaw Pact membership were never as clear in Asia. On the one hand, Asia's balance-of-power was always complicated by a third pole in China whose geostrategic leanings varied throughout the Cold War. On the other hand, residual mistrust and animosity among Asian nations toward Japan ensured that any leadership role for this key power in a NATO-type organization would be politically impossible. These disparate perceptions of external threat did not constitute ideal conditions for collective or multilateral security. Furthermore, any enthusiasm in the region for such institutions was dampened by domestic factors. Postcolonial nation building made anathema the notion of submitting newfound sovereignty to a larger external entity (moreover, in many of these cases, the primary threat to security was internal rather than external). Initial choices by the United States were also important. The priority in American postwar planning was Europe. The United States put the best minds, political focus, and economic resources into creating a new set of institutions in Europe to ensure peace and economic recovery.[7] In Asia, however, the policy was more ad hoc and reactive (with the exception of Japan's occupation) with the priority on managing a process of decolonization in the context of the Cold War. Another factor often unobserved for the absence of multilateral security in Asia is the region's peace. This is not to deny that wars occurred in Asia in the post-1945 era and during the Cold War, but they were never on a scale that commanded a bold push for multilateralism or regional security models.[8]

"Ain't Broke, Don't Fix it"

The weakness of multilateral security in the region has not been helped by American and Japanese attitudes. Traditionally, both powers have been conspicuously ambivalent and even outright opposed to such initiatives. U.S. disinterest particularly at the end of the Cold War stemmed from a combination of a "ain't broke, don't fix it" mentality and initial concerns that such regional initiatives were meant to undermine U.S. leadership. Whether these initiatives took the form of Mahathir's EAEC or less radical alternatives (i.e., APEC proposals by Australia), the United States was decidedly ambivalent. In November 1990 Secretary of State James Baker criticized the notion of regional security dialogues replacing the American "hub and spokes" network of bilateral alliances in Asia, which had been at the center of Asian security and prosperity for four decades.[9] Statements by then assistant secretary for East Asia Richard Solomon in October 1990 typified the attitude:

> ... the nature of the security challenges we anticipate in the years ahead—do not easily lend themselves to region-wide solutions. When we look at the key determinants of stability in Asia . . . it is difficult to see how a Helsinki-type institution would be an appropriate forum for enhancing security or promoting conflict resolution.[10]

This gave way (post-1991) to grudging acceptance that MSDs could complement (but not replace) the U.S.-based bilateral architecture.[11] However, at the same time that American acceptance of a role for regional security grew, the rhetoric remained somewhat ambivalent for an alternative reason: if the United States were now *too* enthusiastic about multilateral security, this might be interpreted in the region as the pretext for American withdrawal.

Japan's interest in regional security has been traditionally even less enthusiastic than that of the United States. In theory such an attitude was derived directly from the Yoshida doctrine that emphasized security bilateralism with the United States. In practice as well, the alliance provided all that Japan needed in security and economic goods thereby obviating any pressing need for alternative multilateral or bilateral partners. The cost of this dependence was the persistent Japanese fear of becoming entrapped in military contingencies or political situations in which Japan did not share or only partially shared American interests, but this was acceptable.[12]

Japanese disinterest in multilateral security also stemmed from an acute sensitivity to the region's lingering past suspicions. Any multilateral security architecture would by definition require a larger Japanese leadership role that would be deemed unacceptable by many in the region. For example, discussions of a Northeast Asian NATO equivalent ("PATO") in the 1960s could not advance past popular opposition and suspicion that this might spark a renewal of Japanese dominance in the region. Such proposals fell on deaf ears at home as Japan experienced a postwar aversion to Asia and focused on the West (with World War II symbolizing Japan's expulsion from Asia). Japanese attempts at a larger political and economic role in Southeast Asia in the 1970s and in the 1980s in the form of Prime Minister Ohira's Pan-Pacific Cooperation Concept also met with fiercely negative reactions (e.g., riots in Southeast Asia against Tanaka in 1974). Part of the problem in this regard stemmed from perceived zero-sum trade-offs of U.S. and Japanese leadership roles in the region. In other words, from the perspective of potential participants in MSDs, any enhancement of the Japanese role by definition meant a reduction in the American role and therefore looked like the United States was "handing off" the region to Japan.[13]

This is not to deny that Japanese participation and enthusiasm for multilateralism exists today. But participation, at least initially, to a large extent reflected reactive rather than proactive thinking. In other words, Japanese participation in multilateral exercises like RIMPAC, or the extension of sealane defense to 1000 nautical miles (1981) only came with intense U.S. pressure.[14] More recent enthusiasm is a result of generational changes in the political leadership in Japan. China's rise in the region also made Tokyo's participation in multilateral institutions more attractive as a means of checking and restraining Beijing's influence.[15] Most importantly, international criticism of Japanese passiveness during the Gulf War provided the impetus for a more proactive Japanese interest in multilateral security. A bold manifestation of this was the 1991 Nakayama proposal for more open discussions of Japan's role in regional security (i.e., historical impediments to such a role) and for discussions on regional security structures.[16]

Twin Dilemmas of Appeal

From the region's perspective, MSDs face twin dilemmas of appeal with regard to the U.S.–Japan alliance. Japanese and American receptiveness to multilateral security has grown in recent years relative to the initial skepticism that pervaded the Cold War and early post–Cold War years.[17] In spite of this recent turn in attitudes, a symmetry of needs between the alliance and multilateralism has not been achieved. In the simplest of terms, the region still needs the alliance more than the alliance has traditionally needed the region. This observation is most apparent in the inability of MSDs to thrive (at least in Northeast Asia) without avid support from Washington and Tokyo. The bilateral alliance, by contrast, arguably does not require MSDs to remain resilient.

Advocates of regionalism might point to the region's record of MSDs, finding examples of functionally based groupings facilitated by middle and smaller powers in the region. However, without the support of the two most important economic and security powers in the region, these have been ineffective at best and irrelevant at worst. Many have argued that APEC—hardly an irrelevant institution—was founded and developed by powers in Asia like Australia and ASEAN despite

American passiveness and Japanese reluctance,[18] but in actuality, Washington and Tokyo's tacit support (and lack of resistance) were indispensable, some have argued, to APEC's success.[19]

In a similar vein, the other major example of multilateralism in the region, the ARF, was linked in no small part to active initiatives by the Japanese government. The origins of the group date back to the July 1991 ASEAN Post-Ministerial Conference (PMC) where the Japanese government first proposed the formation of a security dialogue mechanism based on ASEAN. Although the reaction to the Japanese proposal was not fully welcoming, ASEAN members were motivated by Japanese initiatives and at the ASEAN summit in January 1992 agreed to strengthen political and security dialogue through the ASEAN PMC. The following July, 1993, the ASEAN PMC eventually created the ARF including China and Russia. Japan also played a quiet but critical role in subsequent ARF meetings to expand discussions about confidence-building beyond Southeast Asia including Northeast Asia.[20]

The region faces an additional dilemma deriving from the first one. The multilateral security groupings often seek to appeal to the alliance on as many levels as possible to elicit U.S. and Japanese participation. These levels have ranged traditionally (i.e., during the Cold War) from "hard" security issues (e.g., PATO proposals) to transparency-building, CBMs, and preventive diplomacy. However, many of these appeals for participation are redundant—their purpose duplicates what the United States and Japan already can deal with either in a bilateral context or in a global multilateral one. Or, participation in such institutions provides little value added in terms of resolving salient security problems. For example, the three traits often trumpeted as virtues of MSDs,[21] do not necessarily offer the alliance better options or alternatives when it comes to dealing with traditional security issues like North Korean missiles, Taiwan straits, or proliferation. The Democratic People's Republic of Korea (DPRK) may now be in the ARF, but the United States and Japan still deal with DPRK security problems in the bilateral context or trilaterally with the ROK. The net assessment is unfavorable to MSD participation: MSDs offer the alliance little marginal security and more marginal entanglement.

Creating Complementarity

From the region's perspective, the challenge then is to conceive of ways to resolve the twin dilemmas of MSD's appeal to the alliance, and create greater complementarity between the needs of the alliance and multilateral security.

Defining Security Broadly

One way of doing this is to narrow the "overlap" between multilateralism and bilateralism in the region. This entails a circumscribing of the "traditional/military" security roles played by multilateral institutions and broadening the focus on nontraditional or "new" security issues.[22] Setting collective security or collective defense as the conceptual endpoint of MSDs in the region is a self-defeating exercise. Conceptually and historically, the conditions necessary for success are highly restrictive (i.e., well-defined threat/purpose; no free-riding; security as indivisible; aversion to war; etc.).[23] In addition, the region faces further obstacles in the form of historical distrust (vis-à-vis Japan), ambiguities with regard to membership (e.g., is China in or out?), and outstanding territorial disputes.[24] And perhaps most important, neither the United States nor Japan see such organizations as providing military security and protection of sovereignty more effectively than their current bilateral arrangements.

Having the MSDs appeal to the alliance on broader, nonmilitary security issues offers better promise. First, as in the case of the CSCE, issues in "baskets" 2 and 3 (i.e., cooperation in the field of economics, science, technology, environment, and humanitarian issues) are easier and prior to those in basket 1. Second, in Asia there are a host of problems including piracy, environmental degradation, human rights, refugees, maritime safety, narcotics trafficking, disease, and terrorism that are considered salient nonmilitary security issues.[25] Third, the transnational nature of these problems makes them not easily resolvable through the mere application of resources within the bilateral alliance. Rather, the problems are more effectively addressed through the United States and Japan acting in larger coordinated regional efforts. Fourth, because such MSDs focus on nontraditional security issues outside the alliance's purview, they are not only helpful, but are also nonthreatening to the alliance.

In July 1999 at the ASEAN PMC, Secretary Albright explained how the United States considered one of the most important functions for multilateralism in Asia to be the prevention of transnational crime, maritime piracy, and the illegal trafficking of women and children. Devised at the Clinton–Miyazawa summit in 1993, the U.S.–Japan Common Agenda is a distinct document in the alliance (despite its relative obscurity today) because of its vision that allied cooperation should not be limited to just bilateral security but should extend over a wide range of global issues including climate change, disease prevention, science and technology research, HIV, women in development, and natural disaster relief.[26] These views were reaffirmed in part at the

George W. Bush–Junichiro Koizumi summit in June 2001 with Japan's stated intention to complement U.S. contributions of $200 million to the Global Health Fund.[27] The absolute sums of money in this instance are not as important as the message: the U.S.–Japan alliance supports multilateral initiatives that complement and validate what the alliance stands for. In a similar vein, a variety of binational commissions have advocated joint U.S.–Japan action vis-à-vis human security issues through the UN and other international organizations. Such joint action not only enables the two countries to deal with certain problems that are not as easily addressable in bilateral or unilateral contexts, but they also offer important symbols and validation of the common values and principles that reinforce the bilateral alliance.[28]

These sorts of statements are indicative of the two necessary preconditions for greater complementarity between multilateralism and bilateralism. The United States and Japan must perceive MSDs as the appropriate venue for dealing with larger nontraditional and transnational problems. At the same time, Washington and Tokyo must agree that the definition of their bilateral security extends beyond the mutual defense treaty to encompass these larger issues. In short, the United States and Japan must see MSDs as the best instrument for dealing with nonmilitary security problems, yet also see the alliance's scope as not exclusive of such problems. If both conditions exist, then the alliance will value its participation in MSDs.

Creating Convergence: "Gulliver" Incentives for Multilateralism[29]

From the American Perspective: Amplifying and Legitimizing Japan

Equally important to the resolution of the twin dilemmas is tying participation in MSDs in positive ways with the continued resiliency of the U.S.–Japan alliance. Bilateral efforts at strengthening the alliance— starting from the 1978 Defense Guidelines through the Reagan years to the recent revision of the Guidelines—have focused primarily on ensuring that the necessary understandings, division of responsibilities, and legislation were in place; this would enable the alliance to function in a military contingency. Since then, alliance watchers have talked about an "upgrading" of the alliance pursuant to the Guidelines Revision and missile defense cooperation. As the Armitage/INSS report put it, the future of the U.S.–Japan alliance should take the Guidelines as the "floor, not ceiling" of defense cooperation.[30] There are, however, two prerequisites to such an upgradation of the alliance.

From Washington's perspective, a key component for upgrading the alliance is Japan's enhancement of its military capabilities (within the alliance). Whether this takes the form of independent intelligence-gathering capabilities, full participation in peacekeeping and humanitarian relief missions, greater "jointness" in U.S.–Japan training, or exercising the right of collective self-defense,[31] any of these enhancements are not possible as long as Japan suffers a "legitimacy deficit" in the region. One source of the legitimacy deficit is external. Memories of World War II still inform the region's distrust of Japan. This collective historical memory translates into a reluctance to accept a larger Japanese military presence and political leadership role.[32] The other constraint is internal. Overdependency on the United States as an economic and security patron afforded Japan certain luxuries relative to other countries in Asia, however it also created a postwar generation of relatively passive and reactive Japanese leadership, unwilling to take on a larger role.

Thus the United States faces a delicate problem in its desire to see an upgraded U.S.–Japan alliance. It seeks to promote a more active Japanese military and political role as the alliance moves beyond "burden-sharing" to "power-sharing," yet at the same time, it needs to mute the regional security dilemmas bound to emerge from this more active role. This is where MSDs can be useful. Integrating Japan as much as possible in multilateral regional institutions can strengthen its political ties with the region, reduce suspicions, and legitimize its role as a leader. As some have argued with regard to Europe, a parallel experience was evident with Germany. Its deep integration in a network of postwar institutions created transparency, familiarity, and dialogue habits that loosened many of the insecurity spirals that might have otherwise accompanied German unification at the end of the Cold War. In a similar form of institutional "family therapy" others who were formerly fearful of Japan, would benefit and grow accustomed to its leadership role through participation in these institutions.[33] For example, at ARF meetings, Japan has tried to play the role of mediator between ASEAN and non-ASEAN countries. At the fourth meeting of the ARF in 1997, Japan was able to explain the major points of the new U.S.–Japan Defense Guidelines to the region. At the fifth ARF meeting in 1998, the region was able to hear Japan outline its policy of assistance in the face of the economic crisis and plans for rejuvenating the Japanese economy.[34] "Enmeshing Japan" thereby creates regional legitimation of Japan's enhanced presence. While this accomplishment is itself valuable, what is additionally useful from the American perspective is that such a leadership legitimation for Japan is ultimately good for *bilateral* alliance robustness.

Japanese MSD participation also addresses the internal constraints on Japanese leadership. Practitioners of the alliance observe that one of the new variables, distinct from the Cold War era, that drives the future of the alliance is growing domestic sentiment for a "normal" Japanese diplomatic role in world affairs.[35] As one scholar put it, the younger generation chafe at Japan's "high aspirations but low status" predicament, and grow frustrated at the desire to be a major player while remaining a middle, dependent power.[36] They abhor being considered a "non-factor" with regard to issues in Korea (i.e., four-party talks) when their security is directly tied to peninsular peace. Widespread humiliation during the Gulf War as well as in the aftermath of the South Asian nuclear tests (i.e., being shunted aside by the nuclear powers in responding to these developments despite Japan's record as a prominent advocate of nonproliferation) feed the reservoir of discontent among a younger, brash, and more confident generation. This dynamic sounds typical of virtually any country, but one of the concerns expressed by experts given Japan's unique postwar history of acute dependency and its longer history of rapid swings in foreign policy behavior is an adverse reaction. Prolonged periods of frustration and stasis could facilitate the rise of a leadership that advocates cutting down Japan's dependencies and striking out on its own as the solution.[37]

Multilateralism can preempt such reactions. Encouraging Japanese participation in regional groupings becomes the cathartic means by which Japan expresses its new role and identity among a younger generation of leadership. On the one hand, it gives Japan the practice and confidence to surmount the insecurities of the postwar generation. On the other hand, it offers a release valve by which to deflate any pent-up frustrations and inclinations toward more radical reactions. Although there is a disgruntled minority in Japan who oppose Japan's high proportion of UN contributions, the overall trend in Japan for an expanded diplomatic role is unmistakable across the political spectrum.[38] To restate, the argument is not merely for greater Japanese participation in MSDs; instead it is that the United States should encourage Japanese *multilateralism* for the *bilateral* alliance's resiliency. In this sense, as Ikenberry has argued, multilateral institutions serve multiple functions: (1) they legitimize the region's view of a larger Japanese leadership role; (2) they bolster Tokyo's confidence to assume this new identity; and (3) they implicitly bind and preempt frustrated negative reactions that might send Japan astray. Moreover, all of these functions are necessary prerequisites to any "bilateral upgrading" of the alliance.

From Japan's Perspective: Binding America

From Japan's perspective, there are equally strong rationales for linking American MSD participation to the bilateral alliance's resiliency. For Tokyo, the key concern with regard to the alliance's future is not just Japan-passing as Michael Green and others have argued, but more generally, American unilateralism. As the Armitage/INSS Report notes, concerns abound in Tokyo that the United States is becoming increasingly arrogant and unable to recognize (or even worse, chooses not to recognize) that its prescriptions are not universally applicable.[39] Ambassador Hisashi Owada argues that while the United States practiced unilateral globalism after World War II in terms of providing security, aid for development, and so on it is now pursuing "global unilateralism" where it acts without concern for others.[40] In a different but related way, some see America's overwhelming power at the end of the Cold War as creating dual incentives for the rest of the world akin to Microsoft's relationship with the market: everyone uses and benefits from its operating system, but they also feel the need to make sure that this overwhelming dominance is somehow checked and restrained.[41]

Thus for Japan, one of the keys to future bilateral alliance resiliency is to avoid and discourage American unilateralism. Japanese encouragement of American participation in MSDs is a means by which Japan can mute these unilateral tendencies. Tokyo's support of American active membership in all regional groupings has the effect of amplifying the voices of all other members who share the table with the United States. Despite its overwhelming power, the United States must respect and listen to its colleagues with an attention that would not be the case without the MSD institution.[42] "Enmeshing America" in MSDs therefore not only prevents rash behavior, but also reassures Tokyo and the region that the United States is acting in good faith and is cognizant of others.

This dynamic was somewhat evident, for example, in Tokyo's views on APEC. Although Australia and ASEAN took the public lead, behind the scenes Japan, strongly encouraged American involvement primarily for binding rationales. American involvement in APEC would undercut any tendencies toward unilateralism at the end of the Cold War; and help ameliorate trade frictions in the bilateral alliance.[43] Similar thinking underlay Japanese enthusiasm for U.S. participation in the ARF. As one foreign ministry official wrote, "[A] major goal for Japan [in the ARF] was to ensure constructive engagement of the major powers around the Asia-Pacific region. In order to keep the US engaged in the region, development of concrete discussions regarding cooperation and burden-sharing through debate at ARF (sic) would be extremely important."[44] More recently, one of the successes of U.S. policy on North Korea has been the establishment of TCOG among Seoul, Tokyo, and Washington. The value of this institution for Japan stems in good part from the fact that American participation in this group assures Tokyo that the United States will not move unilaterally on policy toward the DPRK.[45] Indeed, with the change of administrations in Washington and uncertainty regarding future changes in U.S. policy, Seoul and Tokyo's heightened focus on convening TCOG as soon as possible (March 26, 2001 meeting) reflected the value of the institution's binding and transparency-building functions.

From the region's perspective therefore, the need is to create "Gulliver" mentalities in the United States and Japan. Each sees their respective interests vis-à-vis the bilateral alliance served by encouraging the *other* to participate in multilateral institutions. As Ikenberry has argued, MSDs become somewhat like mutually binding institutions. They keep the United States engaged, "honest," and non-unilateral; and they legitimize a larger Japanese leadership role beneficial to the alliance (and to those in Japan who seek a more proactive foreign policy).

Traditional Security-Enhancing Mechanisms

As noted earlier, the appeal of MSDs to the U.S.–Japan alliance is most promising on broader, nonmilitary security issues rather than traditional "hard" security problems. Implicit in this view is that the U.S.–Japan alliance may value mutual participation in MSDs not just for tangible reasons (i.e., whatever particular issue the MSD is organized around), but also for less tangible ones having to do with mutually binding and evolving the bilateral alliance.

In addition to these important binding functions, this argument is not meant to imply that MSDs serve no useful purpose for the United States and Japan on traditional security issues. The effects of MSD participation are less direct but not less useful in at least two dimensions of traditional security issues. First, Japanese and American participation in MSDs along with other regional allies and competitors can provide an arena in which interaction can help mute security dilemmas over things that make the bilateral alliance threatening to others. For example, one area where such dialogues might prove useful is in the issue of missile defense.[46] Deployment of a U.S.–Japan-based TMD system (Navy theater) raises Chinese concerns about a potential Japanese role in Taiwan's defense (i.e., if the United States were to respond to Chinese missile coercion against Taipei).[47] Trilateral dialogue among Washington, Beijing, and Tokyo would be ideal, but in the absence of this, participation by the three in MSDs provides a useful venue in which the sides can gain greater transparency on each other's intentions. Participation in such MSDs also enable security experts from Beijing and Tokyo to continue small-scale and nonofficial initiatives on missile defense. On the Chinese side, for instance, these talks give voice to expert groups that understand Japan's need for some form of missile defense to defend against North Korean missiles. These experts could engage those on the Japanese side who understand Beijing's trepidations regarding Japan's potential engagement in a Taiwan straits crisis (and for this reason have called, e.g., for explicit Japanese statements that Japanese cooperation in U.S.-based missile defense should not be construed as part and parcel of the revised U.S.–Japan Defense Guidelines).[48]

Second, multilateral security participation could be sold to the United States as a way to facilitate "minilaterals." This term refers to a form of security cooperation in the region that has emerged largely in the post–Cold War era. Minilaterals have three general traits: (1) they are small in terms of number of participants relative to multilateral security (usually three to four parties); (2) they are ad hoc in formation, usually formed for a temporary period of time and disbanded without an institutional legacy; and (3) they usually deal with real or traditional security issues. As the 1998 EASR described, these dialogues are functional, temporary, and U.S.-based: "[They] are intended to be overlapping and interlocking, complementing each other to develop an informal security framework for promoting understanding and mutual confidence, and facilitating bilateral ties between participants."[49] The most well-known example of a minilateral at the official level is U.S.–Japan–South Korean trilateral coordination on North Korea nuclear proliferation (the institutional product of which is the Korea Energy Development Organization [KEDO]). Other minilaterals include unofficial dialogue among the United States, Japan, and Russia, prior to the historic November 1997 Japan–Russia summit; the four-party talks among the United States, China, and the two Koreas; and proposed discussions between the United States, Japan, and China on the revision of the U.S.–Japan Defense Guidelines.

Despite U.S. acceptance of multilateral initiatives in the region, many critics would argue that the genuine U.S. interest in multilaterals to deal with the harder security issues does not extend beyond these minilateral groupings. These groupings have the advantage of being small in number, more focused, and more U.S.-centric than the larger multilateral groupings. Yet even in this regard, multilateral dialogues can provide a ready venue in which the United States could seek to "peel off" key participants and facilitate or enable the creation of smaller minilateral groupings.

Conclusion and Implications: A Spectrum of Security

Four general conclusions emerge from my analysis of the relationship between multilateralism and bilateralism in Asia. First, one can envision a spectrum of security in Asia, defined by three axes: multilateralism, minilateralism, and bilateralism:

Multilateral security dialogues	Minilateral security	Bilateral alliances
5+ participants	3–4 participants	2 participants
New security issues	Traditional security issues	Traditional security
(environment, transnational	harder to address through	
crime, maritime piracy)	unilateral or bilateral channels	

Second, while the value-added of participation in MSDs is that they enable participants to deal with new security issues that are difficult to address outside a region-wide context, I have argued that U.S. and Japanese participation in MSDs indeed have *second-order traditional* security effects. In particular, such participation in MSDs offer a means by which Washington and Tokyo can enhance the resiliency of their bilateral alliance. Through encouraging its ally's participation in these institutions, Japan and the United States are each able to alleviate its own concerns about its counterpart. In Japan's case, American participation helps to prevent and remind the United States about the ill-effects of unilateralism. In America's case, Japanese participation helps promote a larger leadership role for Japan in the region, which is a necessary precondition for any "upgrading" of the bilateral alliance's political and security functions.

Third, at a functional level, if policymakers agree that there are synergies in multilateralism and bilateralism that are beneficial to the alliance (rather than seeing the former as undercutting or distracting to the latter), then a premium must be placed on coordination between these two tracks. For example, prior to major multilateral meetings, the United States and Japan through bilateral institutions (greatly enabled by those set up at the Bush–Koizumi June 2001 summit) could coordinate agendas and present united views in these larger fora. Efforts at U.S.–Japan coordination (bilateral arms control commission) prior to the Geneva Disarmament convention offer working precedents in this vein.

Fourth, at a conceptual level, this chapter has shown how multilateral institutions can have effects that go beyond merely the functional and transparency-enhancing characteristics normally associated with them in the international relations literature. In supporting the resiliency of the U.S.–Japan alliance, multilateral institutions perform a variety of different functions. They legitimize Japanese power by facilitating a new Japanese leadership role in the region. They also mute "negative" Japanese power by directing pent-up frustrations for a more proactive Japan among younger generations in the direction of the MSDs and the bilateral alliance rather than in the direction of hyper-self-help reactions. These institutions also bind U.S. power by creating not only greater accountability to the region of any tendencies for American unilateralism, but also by tying these to the resilience of the bilateral alliance.

Notes

1. For the now classic statement, see Joseph Nye, "The Case for Deep Engagement," *Foreign Affairs* 74.4 (1995); also see *United States Security Strategy for the East Asia-Pacific Region* 1998 (Department of Defense, Office of International Security Affairs, November 1998).

2. These are: the preservation of national sovereignty; the principle of noninterference in domestic affairs; pursuit of prosperity through markets; economic interdependence to enhance security; peaceful resolution of disputes; and adherence to global multilateralism. See Stuart Harris, "Asian Multilateral Institutions and Their Response to the Asian Economic Crisis," *Pacific Review* 13.3 (2000), p. 502.

3. The Southeast Asian Treaty Organization was established at the Manila Conference of 1954 largely on the model of NATO, but failed because members found internal subversion rather than compelling external threats to be their primary security concerns. The Australia–New Zealand–U.S. Pact formed in 1951 as an extension of the U.S.–Australia treaty (the U.S.–New Zealand axis dissolved in 1986). The Five Power Defense Arrangement was established in 1971 among Britain, Australia, New Zealand, Malaysia, and Singapore. Its function was consultative based on historical legacies of the Commonwealth rather than any overt security purpose; see Leszek Buszynski, *SEATO: The Failure of an Alliance Strategy* (Singapore: Singapore University Press, 1983); Chin Kin Wah, "The Five Power Defence Arrangement: Twenty Years After," *Pacific Review* 4.3 (1991); and Michael Yahuda, *International Politics in the Asia-Pacific* (London: Routledge, 1996).

4. For example, the Vietnam War Allies Conference met regularly in Saigon in the late 1960s and early 1970s providing a ready venue for multilateral security discussions on larger Cold War issues and strategy beyond Indochina,

but nothing came of this. The Asia and Pacific Council (ASPAC) was established in 1966 as a forum for cooperation among Asian states on cultural and economic issues. Members included Australia, Taiwan, South Korea, Malaysia, New Zealand, Philippines, Thailand, South Vietnam, and Japan. Proposals in the early 1970s were floated by various countries (e.g., South Korea in 1970) to devise a new ASPAC charter based on collective self-defense with region-wide membership (including Laos, Indonesia, and Singapore), but these failed in part because of lack of support for a active Japanese leadership role in the group. For other studies of Northeast Asian regionalism focusing more on economics and the Russian Far East, see Gilbert Rozman, "Flawed Regionalism: Reconceptualizing Northeast Asia in the 1990s," *The Pacific Review* 11.1 (1998), pp. 1–27.

5. Higher degrees of institutionalization exist among the original ASEAN nations including proposals for national defense manufacturer associations, C-130 flight training centers, F-16 joint training bases, etc.

6. The ARF was formed pursuant to meetings of the ASEAN Post-Ministerial Conference (PMC) in 1993.

7. G. John Ikenberry, *After Victory* (Princeton: Princeton University Press, 2000), chapter 6.

8. The region's relative peace in spite of the levels of historical enmity and armaments is often a factor overlooked in many IR analyses foreboding of Asia's impending conflicts. In the former vein, see e.g. Kurt Campbell, "The Challenges Ahead for US Policy in Asia," presentation at the FPRI Asia Study Group, March 30, 2001. In the latter vein, see Aaron Friedberg, "Ripe for Rivalry," *International Security* (Winter 1993/94); Richard Betts, "Wealth, Power and Instability," *International Security* (Winter 1993/94); Kent Calder, *Pacific Defense* (New York: Murrow, 1996); Paul Bracken, *Fire in the East* (New York: HarperCollins, 1999); and Michael Klare, "The Next Great Arms Race," *Foreign Affairs* 72.3 (Summer 1993).

9. See *Australian Financial Review* May 2, 1991 ("Security, in Letter and Spirit").

10. Cited in Paul Midford, "Japan's Leadership Role in East Asian Security Multilateralism," *Pacific Review* 13.3 (2000), p. 372.

11. See James Baker, "America in Asia: Emerging Architecture for a Pacific Community," *Foreign Affairs* 70.5 (1991/92); and Baker in *New York Times* July 25, 1991.

12. See John Welfield, *An Empire in Eclipse* (London: Athlone, 1988).

13. Japanese disinterest also traditionally stemmed from the implications that multilateral participation would have on outstanding territorial issues. With its fair share of territorial disputes in the region, Japan was concerned that certain proposals for multilateralism entailed a de facto ratification of the territorial status quo, which worked against Japanese interests. For this reason, Tokyo opposed Soviet proposals in 1986 for a region-wide CSCE-type grouping in Asia as this might reinforce the status quo and Moscow's possession of the northern territories.

14. For a concise and enjoyable exposition on changes in the terminology that defined the U.S.–Japan relationship (e.g., "burden-sharing," "division of

roles," "level playing field"), see Mike M. Mochizuki, "US–Japan Relations in an Era of Globalization," *Sigur Center Asia Papers* (Elliott School of International Affairs, George Washington University, 1999).

15. For this point as tied to larger shifts in Japan toward a more strategically oriented rather than economic-based foreign policy, see Michael Green and Benjamin Self, "Japan's Changing China Policy: From Commercial Liberalism to Reluctant Realism," *Survival* 38.2 (Summer 1996).

16. Foreign Minister Taro Nakayama's proposal called for: (1) an MSD component within the ASEAN post-ministerial conference (PMC); (2) a Senior Officials Meeting (SOM); and (3) discussions of the region's concerns about Japanese remilitarization. This was Japan's first regional security initiative, largely emerging out of the fiasco of Japanese participation in the Gulf War. The proposal itself did not meet with popular acceptance (including opposition from the United States), but was an important impetus to the eventual thriving of the ARF (see Midford, 2000).

17. This was manifest in the context of the bilateral alliance in the April 1996 U.S.–Japan Defense Guidelines revision, which emphasized a larger Japanese regional security role (see Rajan Menon, "The Once and Future Superpower," *Bulletin of Atomic Scientists* (January/February 1997), pp. 29–34.

18. For example, see Miles Kahler, "Institution Building in the Pacific," in *Pacific Cooperation* ed. Andrew Mack and John Ravenhill (Boulder, CO: Westview, 1995).

19. For the argument, see Yoichi Funabashi, *Asia-Pacific Fusion: Japan's Role in APEC* (Washington DC: IIE, 1995), esp. pp. 192–195; and Ellis Krauss, "Japan, the US, and the Emergence of Multilateralism in Asia," *Pacific Review* 13.3 (2000), pp. 473–494. Both argue that Australian Premier Bob Hawke's ideas on an East Asian financial grouping was based on thinking and ideas that came out of MITI and the Reagan–Takeshita summit in 1988.

20. See Kohno, "In Search of Proactive Diplomacy," p. 30.

21. These are: (1) not a substitute for global multilateral institutions; (2) weighted toward semi-official/track 2 dialogues rather than formal ones; and (3) open regionalism and inclusive memberships, including China and North Korea (see Harris, "Asian Multilateral Institutions,").

22. This is a process that is already underway in Asia. One analytical distinction deserves mention here. The discussion of MSDs and transnational, lower-tier security issues has largely been in the context of making multilateral security more viable—i.e., such issues are considered easier ones around which to organize regional security than a NATO-type agenda. I focus more on how an MSD-focus on these lower-tier security issues makes MSDs more appealing to the U.S.–Japan alliance because it fulfills functional needs that the alliance cannot. Thus I do not disagree with the first argument but seek to complement it.

23. See Robert Jervis, "From Balance to Concert," *World Politics* 38.1 (October 1985); Charles Kupchan and C. Kupchan, "Concerts, Collective Security, and the Future of Europe," *International Security* 16.1 (Summer 1991); and Mira Sucharov and Victor Cha, "Collective Security Systems," in

Encyclopedia of Violence, Peace and Conflict (Academic Press, 1999), pp. 343–353.

24. The last factor in particular is problematic for a collective security institution as the implicit assumption for participation is that all members are satisfied with the territorial status quo.

25. See William Carpenter and David Wiencek eds., *Asian Security Handbook* (New York: M.E. Sharpe, 2000), esp. the contributions in part II; Tetsuya Nishimoto, "Problems in Managing the Japan–US Security Treaty After the Guidelines," unpublished paper presented at the Atlantic Council meeting on the U.S.–Japan alliance, Tokyo, Japan March 2001; and Bonnie Jenkins, "Prospects for a Conventional Arms Reduction Treaty and Confidence-Building Measures in Northeast Asia," *INSS Occasional Paper* 34, August 2000 (USAF Institute for National Security Studies, Colorado).

26. See Masaharu Kohno, "In Search of Proactive Diplomacy: Increasing Japan's International Role in the 1990s (with Cambodia and the ASEAN Regional Forum as Case Studies)," *CNAPS Working Paper*, Fall 1999 (Brookings Institution).

27. "Partnership for Security and Prosperity," June 30, 2001 (accessed July 13, 2001).

28. For example, see East Asian Institute, Columbia University and Japan Institute of International Affairs, *Strengthening the United Nations' Capability for Ensuring Human Rights and Environmental Protection* (May 2000).

29. See usage of the term in Krauss, "Japan, the US and the Emergence of Multilateralism in Asia."

30. "The United States and Japan: Advancing Toward a Mature Partnership," *INSS Special Report* (October 11, 2000); Michael Green, "The Forgotten Player," *The National Interest* (Summer 2000); Yoichi Funabashi, "Tokyo's Temperance," *Washington Quarterly* (Summer 2000); and James Auer, "US–Japan Defense Ties: Excellence over Arrogance," *Japan Digest*, October 13, 2000.

31. See "The United States and Japan," *INSS Special Report*, pp. 3–5.

32. For example, revision of the U.S.–Japan Defense Guidelines in 1996 added further clarity to Japan's role and responsibilities in the event of a Korean contingency. Objectively speaking, this had a positive impact on South Korean security and U.S.–Japan–South Korea policy coordination, yet the popular reaction, expressed through the voicebox of history, was highly negative, accusing Japan of renewed militarization (see Ilpyong J. Kim, "Korea's Relations with China and Japan in the Post–Cold War Era," *International Journal of Korean Studies* 2.1 (Fall/Winter 1998), pp. 27–44.

33. The term is Friedberg's, "Ripe for Rivalry", p. 11.

34. Kohno, "In Search of Proactive Diplomacy," pp. 30–31.

35. Kurt Campbell, "Energizing the US–Japan Security Partnership," *Washington Quarterly* (Autumn 2000), p. 128; Green, "The Forgotten Player," pp. 43–46.

36. Matake Kamiya, "How to Gain Status on World Stage," *Nikkei Weekly*, April 3, 2000.

37. For example, one of the reasons Shintaro Ishihara won the election as governor was not necessarily because the public agreed with his views, but because he was seen as someone who could shake things up. The point is that the potential for adverse directions are real in Japan and (as discussed later), multilateralism provides a means of closing off such negative paths. For the classic "pendulum" statement on Japan's foreign policy, see Robert Scalapino, ed., *The Foreign Policy of Modern Japan* (Berkeley: University of California, 1977).

38. Kohno, "In Search of Proactive Diplomacy," p. 35.

39. *INSS*, "The United States and Japan," p. 2.

40. See Samuel Huntington, "The Lonely Superpower," *Foreign Affairs* 78.2 (March/April 1999), p. 42; also see Funabashi, "Tokyo's Temperance," pp. 135–144.

41. See Kurt Campbell, "The Challenges Ahead for US Policy in Asia," March 30, 2001, FPRI fpri@fpri.org.

42. On the amplification effects of institutions, see Ikenberry, "Institutions, Strategic Restraint, and the Persistence of American Postwar Order," *International Security*, Vol. 23, No. 3 (Winter 1998/99), pp. 1–35.

43. See Krauss, "Japan, the US and the Emergence of Multilateralism," p. 483; and Funabashi, *Asia-Pacific Fusion.* Similarly, the United States wanted Japanese involvement in APEC to give Tokyo a larger leadership role in the region.

44. Kohno, "In Search of Proactive Diplomacy," p. 29.

45. For similar observations, see John Ikenberry, "Getting Hegemony Right," *The National Interest* 63 (Spring 2001), p. 124.

46. Campbell, "Energizing the US–Japan Security Partnership," p. 130.

47. A full discussion of missile defense is beyond the scope of this chapter. For an excellent overview, see Michael Green and Toby Dalton, *Asian Reactions to US Missile Defense* NBR Analysis 11.3 (November 2000). For additional observations on the political "cascade effects" of missile defense, see Victor Cha, "Title: 'Second Nuclear Age: Proliferation Pessimists versus sober optimism in South Asia and East Asia' *Journal of Strategic Studies*, Vol. 24, No. 4, 2001, pp. 79–120."

48. See Kori Urayama, "Chinese Perspectives on Theater Missile Defense," *Asian Survey* 40.4, pp. 599–621.

49. *East Asian Strategy Review 1998*, p. 43. Also see Sheila Smith's chapter in this volume for additional information.

SECTION 3
NEW DIMENSIONS TO ALLIANCE COOPERATION

CHAPTER 8

THE "REVOLUTION IN MILITARY AFFAIRS" AND SECURITY IN ASIA

Michael O'Hanlon

Much of the American and international defense community is now taken up with the idea that a historically significant revolution in military affairs (RMA) is underway—quite possibly rivaling the change in warfare that occurred just before, during, and just after World War II. If true, the claim could have many implications for the U.S.–Japan alliance. It could reduce the importance of American bases in Japan, fundamentally affect the dynamics of future U.S.–PRC military competition in uncertain but potentially quite momentous ways, make it hard for Japan to keep up technologically with the American military given Japan's much smaller defense budget, and shift both countries' defense priorities even further toward high technology (and away from manpower and ground forces) than they have already been shifted in recent decades. Such shifts could have broad implications for the alliance as a whole, with the most likely net effect being a weakening of its robustness and a diminution of its importance in the years ahead.

This chapter considers several dimensions of the RMA issue of particular relevance for East Asia, and thus of particular interest for this book's central focus on the future of the U.S.–Japan alliance. Some of the questions are broad; others are more specific. In the first category, it is important to ask at the outset if the RMA hypothesis is basically correct. The chapter next explores whether technology trends will likely complicate allied relations and interoperability efforts by making it difficult for U.S. security partners to keep up with the U.S. armed forces. A final big question is whether trends in military technology, tactics, and strategy will allow—or even require—the United States to scale back its overseas presence in the region. In terms of more practical and immediate issues, the chapter also asks if trends in military technology are likely to make Theater Missile Defense (TMD) a promising endeavor, and if new technology—as well as innovative applications of existing capabilities and concepts—will allow the United States to reduce the Marine Corps presence on Okinawa without harming combat capabilities, deterrence, or forward engagement.

In answering these questions, this chapter raises serious questions about whether an RMA is underway, but does not rule out the possibility of such a revolution. It suggests that TMD, and national missile defense (NMD) for that matter as well, will become moderately effective against low-technology missile powers such as North Korea, but that TMD and NMD will remain very difficult against more advanced and wealthier countries such as China. It further argues that the so-called RMA should not prevent allied militaries such as Japan's from being compatible and interoperable with U.S. armed forces, provided that the allies make wise decisions about how to spend their defense resources. Finally, it shows that forward presence will remain quite important—but that it should nonetheless be possible to reduce the number of Marines on Okinawa by at least 50 percent. Part of the purpose in reducing these U.S. forces and bases would be to ensure that Japanese domestic politics will continue to support even more important U.S. bases, such as the Navy and Air Force facilities at Yokosuka, Atsugi, Kadena, Sasebo, and elsewhere. On the whole, therefore, this chapter is somewhat skeptical of the RMA hypothesis and even more skeptical that trends in military technology and tactics will necessarily weaken the U.S.–Japan alliance. For the purposes of this book, this is good news, even if those favoring an RMA may find such a message objectionable.

The Contemporary Revolution in Military Affairs Debate

Due to the excellent performance of American high-technology weapons in the 1991 Persian Gulf War, as well as the phenomenal pace of innovation in the modern computer industry, many defense analysts have posited that an RMA is either imminent or already underway. The RMA thesis holds that further advances in precision munitions, real-time data dissemination, and other modern technologies, together with associated changes in warfighting organizations and doctrines, can help transform the nature of future war and with it the size and structure of the U.S. military. RMA proponents believe that military technology, and the resultant potential for radically new types of warfighting tactics and strategies, is advancing at a rate unrivaled since the 1920s through 1940s, when blitzkrieg, aircraft carriers, large-scale amphibious and airborne assault, ballistic missiles, strategic bombing, and nuclear weapons were developed.

In the abstract, it is unobjectionable to favor innovation. But the prescriptions of some RMA proponents would have major opportunity costs. RMA proponents tend to argue that more budgetary resources should be devoted to innovation—research and development (R&D), procurement of new hardware, frequent experiments with new technology—and, to the extent necessary, less money to military operations, training, and readiness. To free up funds for an RMA transformation strategy, some would reduce U.S. global engagement and weaken the military's deterrent posture.[1] For example, in its 1997 report, the National Defense Panel (NDP) dismissed the current two-war framework as obsolete (without suggesting what should replace it, however). The NDP also suggested that U.S. military retrenchment from forward presence and peacekeeping operations might be needed simply to free up money to promote the so-called RMA.[2] These suggestions, if adopted, would have important effects on U.S. security policy; they should not be accepted simply on the basis of vague impressions that an RMA may be achievable.

Some have argued that a radical transformation of the U.S. military will save money.[3] But that argument is unconvincing, at least for the short to medium term. Transformation means accelerating replacement of existing equipment, and while it is theoretically possible that doing so could produce smaller, less expensive units wielding highly advanced and effective weaponry, there is little practical evidence that such an outcome is achievable in the near future.

Given the budgetary and opportunity costs associated with rapidly pursuing an RMA, and the popularity of the RMA concept in the contemporary defense debate, some caution is in order. Before developing a modernization agenda, it is worth remembering what can go wrong with a rush to transform and what innovations can occur even if no RMA is formally declared or pursued.

History tells us that radical military transformations only make sense when technology and new concepts and tactics are ripe. At other times, targeted modernizations together with vigorous research, development, and experimentation make more sense. A good analogy is the period of the 1920s, when major military vehicles and systems such as the tank and airplane were not yet ready for large-scale purchase. In addition, advanced operational concepts such as blitzkrieg and carrier aviation had not yet been fully developed in a manner that could guide hardware acquisition or the reshaping of military organizations. As such, research, prototyping, and experimentation were the proper elements of a wise innovation and acquisition strategy. In the 1930s, new operational concepts were better understood, technologies better developed, and geostrategic circumstances more foreboding. Under these circumstances, large-scale modernization made sense, and those countries that did not conduct it tended to perform badly in the early phases of World War II. Because most RMA proponents cannot clearly specify what a near-term transformation should consist of, I am inclined to liken today's situation to the 1920s rather than to the 1930s.

The simple fact that an electronics revolution has been underway does not mean that a military revolution is now appropriate or necessary. Military technology has advanced steadily and impressively throughout the twentieth century, including its latter half. Helicopters radically reshaped many battlefield operations after World War II. ICBMs and space-launch vehicles followed. Satellite communications were first used militarily in 1965 in Vietnam, where aircraft-delivered, precision-guided munitions also made their debut in the early 1970s. Air defense and anti-tank missiles played major roles in the 1973 Arab–Israeli War. Stealth fighters were designed in the late 1970s.[4] Infrared sensors and night-vision technologies made their debut in this period as well. It is far from obvious that military technology is now poised to advance even more quickly than it has in the last half century. Yet RMA proponents assert that it will when they call for a radical transformation strategy for current U.S. armed forces. No such DoD-wide transformation strategies were necessary to bring satellites, stealth, precision-guided munitions, advanced jet engines, night-vision equipment, or other remarkable new capabilities into the force in past decades.[5] We did not need to declare an RMA to make revolutionary changes in various areas of military technology.

RMA proponents are certainly right to believe that a successful military must always be changing. But the post–World War II U.S. military has already taken that adage to heart. The status quo in defense circles does not mean standing still; it means taking a balanced approach to modernization that has served the country remarkably well for decades. Indeed it brought on the very technologies displayed in Desert Storm that have given rise to the belief that an RMA may be underway.[6] It is not clear that we need to accelerate the pace of innovation now.

Moreover, radical innovation is not always good. If the wrong ideas are adopted, transforming a force can make it worse. For example, in the world wars, militaries overestimated the likely effects of artillery as well as aerial and battleship bombardment against prepared defensive positions, meaning that their infantry forces proved much more vulnerable than expected when they assaulted enemy lines.[7] Britain's radically new all-tank units were inflexible, making them less successful than Germany's integrated mechanized divisions in World War II. Strategic aerial bombardment did not achieve nearly the results that had been expected of it; airpower was much more effective as close-air support for armored formations in blitzkrieg operations.[8] Later on, the U.S. Army's Pentomic division concept, intended to employ tactical nuclear weapons, was adopted for a time and then abandoned in 1961.[9]

But these are only historical arguments, uninformed by the realities of today's world. Current trends in defense technology, and the potential for corresponding innovations in tactics and doctrine, are what will really determine the prospects for a near-term RMA. These trends suggest that the technological case for a patient, targeted approach is much more compelling than that for a radical remaking of the U.S. armed forces more generally.

One type of evidence to support this argument is that despite their haste to push the revolution along, radical RMA promoters tend to lack clear and specific proposals for how to do so. In that light, even if they are right that an RMA may be within reach sometime in the foreseeable future, they may be quite wrong about what should be done about it in the near future. In practical terms, there is a major distinction between the early stages of a possible RMA and the later stages. As Stephen Rosen writes: "The general lesson for students or advocates of innovation may well be that it is wrong to focus on budgets when trying to understand or promote innovation. Bringing innovations to fruition will often be expensive. Aircraft carriers, fleets of helicopters, and ICBM forces were not cheap. But *initiating* an innovation and bringing it to the point where it provides a strategically useful option has been accomplished when money was tight . . . Rather than money, talented military personnel, time, and information have been the key resources for innovation."

Some individuals feel that these arguments notwithstanding, the United States really has no choice but to rebuild its equipment inventories and combat units from first principles. They believe that future adversaries will make greater use of sea mines, cruise and ballistic missiles, chemical or biological weapons, and other means to attempt to deny the U.S. military the ability to build up forces and operate from large, fixed infrastructures as in Desert Storm. As a result, they consider major changes in the way U.S. armed forces deploy and fight to be essential. However, many of the solutions to these problems are not in the realm of advanced weaponry. True, long-range strike platforms, missile defenses, short-takeoff aircraft, and other such advanced technologies may be part of the appropriate response. But so might more minesweepers, smaller roll-on/roll-off transport vessels useful in shallow ports, concrete bunkers for deployed aircraft, and other relatively low-tech approaches to hardening and dispersing supplies and infrastructure. The military services already are biased in favor of procuring advanced weaponry at the expense of equally important but less advanced hardware. By emphasizing modernistic and futuristic technology, the most ambitious RMA concepts could reinforce this existing tendency, quite possibly to the nation's detriment.

Most centrally, one should be skeptical about the RMA hypothesis because many of its key technical underpinnings have not been well established and may not be valid. Proponents of the RMA concept often make passing mention of Mores "law"—the trend for the number of transistors that can fit on a semiconductor chip to double every 18 to 24 months—and then extrapolate such a radical rate of progress to much different realms of technology. For example, in its 1997 report the NDP wrote: "The rapid rate of new and improved technologies—a new cycle about every eighteen months—is a defining characteristic of this era of change and will have an indelible influence on new strategies, operational concepts, and tactics that our military employs." However, conflating progress in computers with progress in other major areas of technology is unjustified. To the extent RMA believers hinge most of their argument on advances in modern electronics and computers, they are at least proceeding from a solid foundation. When they expect comparably radical progress in land vehicles, ships, aircraft, rockets, explosives, and energy sources—as many do, either explicitly or implicitly—they are probably mistaken, at least in the early years of the twenty-first century.

A survey that I carried out in 1998 and 1999 suggested that progress in these latter areas of technology is, and will likely remain, modest in the years ahead. As such, the case for aggressively modernizing electronics, munitions, sensors, and communications systems is much more compelling than that for replacing the main vehicles and large weaponry of the armed forces.

Policymakers must also pay close attention to trends in technology because they could increase vulnerabilities. They could make surprise attack easier, at least if a country is not prepared for the possibility of such an attack; they can also increase the vulnerability of domestic societies to WMD on the one hand and cyberwarfare on the other. Whether or not an RMA is happening, important changes are in the works—as indeed they always have been during the history of modern warfare.

The RMA and Theater Missile Defense

How do trends in technology affect the crucial debate over TMD? In short, TMD is likely to improve quite a bit over the next five to ten years. But it will have major limitations even in 2010 and beyond. Technology will help attackers as well as defenders—and in the missile arena, attackers also have a natural advantage due to the speed and range of the weapons in question.

North Korea remains the most important potential threat justifying TMD in East Asia. While all hope for a continuation and acceleration of the promising process of détente on the peninsula, security planners and officials cannot yet assume that the process will continue. It has not to date resulted in any diminution of the existing North Korean conventional or missile threats. Engagement makes good sense—and perhaps should even include more substantial incentives for Pyongyang. But at the same time, deterrence should be sustained. Given how much North Korea has increased its missile threat to Japan over the last decade, particularly with its NoDong missile, it is only appropriate that Tokyo as well as Washington take steps to defend their territories, populations, and forces against such weapons.

Chinese scholars and officials frequently question whether the United States and Japan really should fear a North Korean missile attack. In my view, the clear answer is yes. That is not to say that North Korea will irrationally launch a volley of missiles. But it could well strike in the context of possible war on the peninsula, a scenario that has become less likely in recent years but that is hardly implausible.

The United States lost 28 soldiers to a single SCUD missile during the Persian Gulf War, defending oil supplies on which both the United States and Japan depend. And that missile carried only a conventional warhead. Moreover, North Korea's missile capabilities are superior to that of Iraq's.

In the unlikely but hardly inconceivable event of another Korean War, a North Korea armed with missiles and WMD could be extremely dangerous. It might well threaten to use conventionally tipped warheads against parts of Japan hosting U.S. bases, in an early effort to dissuade Tokyo from supporting the war effort. Even if that attempt fails, North Korea might again rattle its missile saber later in the war. For example, if U.S. and South Korean forces decided to respond to a North Korean attack with a counteroffensive to overthrow the regime in Pyongyang, North Korean leaders might be sorely tempted to threaten missile strikes against U.S. or Japanese targets as a deterrent. It is even possible that

North Korea might actually launch such missiles—and under such circumstances, the missiles might even carry nuclear, biological, or chemical warheads atop them. Such actions would not necessarily be irrational under such extreme circumstances; if North Korean leaders believed that they were about to be overthrown in a conflict, they might consider such threats—and even such attacks—their last hope of convincing the invading powers to stop their invasion and negotiate terms. Or if Kim Jong-Il had lost power to one or more internal commanders with a visceral hatred of Japan or the United States, these rogue leaders might be tempted to launch attacks simply for vengeance's sake. Most Chinese officials and scholars do not find these arguments persuasive but it is easier to trivialize threatened attacks when one is not the potential victim.

There may also be some situations in which limited defense against possible Chinese missile strikes would make sense. In particular, defenses for U.S. military forces and Japanese bases against conventionally armed missile attacks may be important in a future war over Taiwan. If, despite the best efforts of all parties to prevent conflict, war should occur between China and Taiwan, the United States might be drawn into it. In that event, China might fire missiles against U.S. ships, aircraft, and regional bases—possibly including those on Japan. Tokyo might elect for that reason not to allow American combat operations to proceed from Japanese bases. But, as we all recall from the ambiguous nature of the 1997 Defense Cooperation Guidelines, Japan might also wish to support a U.S. military role, depending on the circumstances. So Japan should probably preserve all options, and acquire TMD to improve its defensibility in any such scenario.

Nonetheless, Japan and the United States need to be realistic in their expectations about how effective TMD might be. If China really wanted to strike the Japanese homeland with missiles, it could probably do so, despite the best efforts of advanced TMD systems.

Decoys could fool systems such as the Clinton NMD system and Navy Theater Wide (NTW); saturation attacks could overwhelm defenses in any one part of Japan; short-range missiles or depressed-energy missiles could underfly defenses like NTW. China, with its extensive resource base and technological capabilities, could almost certainly take advantage of these options to defeat TMD and NMD. So TMD makes sense for complicating China's attack options, for possibly stopping a limited missile attack, and for reducing the number of warheads that might get through to Japan in a larger attack. But it almost certainly will not be able to provide robust, leakproof protection of the Japanese islands and U.S. bases on those islands.

These sorts of considerations, by the way, also argue in favor of boost-phase NMD for the United States (rather than the exoatmospheric system proposed and developed by the Clinton administration). Boost-phase defense attempts to destroy an enemy missile early in its flight, while it presents a hot and large target, and before it has had the opportunity to release decoys. Such boost-phase defenses, based on land, at sea, or in the air (during crises or wartime in that latter event), are more technologically promising than midcourse interceptors. They are also more likely to be consistent with good relations with China, since they could not shoot down ICBMs launched from China's interior.

What would China really do about deployments of TMD and NMD? It depends. If leaders in Beijing were only moderately upset, they might simply increase and upgrade their missile force somewhat—a plan they may have anyway. This reaction might ensue if Japan and the United States deployed TMD and NMD—but focused the TMD on limited strikes, most probably from North Korea—and if Washington restrained transfers of advanced TMD to Taiwan while also focusing on boost-phase NMD for its own territorial defense. If Beijing felt that Tokyo and Washington had fundamentally ignored its security interests, however, it might take steps with more serious consequences. Those steps could include everything from selling more sophisticated missile technology to North Korea, such as decoys that could fool missile defenses, to suspending cooperation with Japan and the United States and South Korea in their efforts to make peace on the peninsula, to resuming nuclear testing, to becoming more aggressive toward Taiwan. Some of these latter steps might leave the United States and Japan less secure and less well off than if they had never deployed missile defenses in the first place.

In short, Tokyo and Washington should avoid the dangerous and futile illusion that they can achieve reliable and robust TMD against a Chinese threat. They should pursue limited TMD (and NMD, for the United States), regardless of Beijing's objections, but be realistic in their expectations and be careful not to antagonize China so much that they worsen their own security. With their aspirations limited in these ways, China would perhaps object, but would probably stop short of resorting to extreme responses. Limited missile defense is the best way to balance various types of security concerns, and to recognize the potential as well as the limitations of technology, for the East Asia region.

With regard to Taiwan, against which China already has 300 missiles deployed in its southeastern coastal regions, a balanced strategy is also required. Both China and Taiwan need to be reassured—and both also need to be constrained. China should not be given free rein to threaten the people of Taiwan with missiles, for if it gains confidence that it is in a dominant position, it may become impatient about timetables for reunification. By the same token, Taiwanese leaders should not be led to believe that they have defenses large and capable enough to thwart any Chinese attack—such confidence could increase the chances of them taking steps toward declaring independence, thereby provoking war. Creating a reliable defense for Taiwan will prove impossible in any event, since China can build decoys and increase the size of its missile force. So Washington should help Taiwan improve its TMD, but not so much as to encourage an arms race. Specifically, U.S. TMD sales to Taiwan should be significant but restrained, especially if China agrees to slow its missile buildup near Taiwan.

American Allies and the RMA

Turning to another important issue in the RMA debate, some have claimed that trends in technology are making the United States even more militarily dominant than before. They worry that the U.S. armed forces may become so technologically advanced that meaningful alliance operations become impossible. Communications and reconnaissance systems may fail to be interoperable, and other problems may arise as the United States simply fights on a different plane than what any of its allies can reach. This concern is real, but often overstated. If allies are wise in how they spend their defense resources, they should be able to keep up with the United States—or at least not fall more than a half step behind.

To see why this debate is so important, it is necessary to take a broad strategic and historical perspective. Since 1990, the United States has often been described as the sole surviving superpower. This nickname is particularly apt in the realm of conventional military operations. The degree of U.S. supremacy is remarkable, not just one order above any other countries but two full and discernible steps. Not only does the United States spend five times more on its military than any other country and wield correspondingly larger military capabilities than any other country with an advanced modern military but it also actually spends its money better, producing a far more potent bang for the buck than any of its major NATO allies or Japan. Among the capabilities it possesses that most other countries do not even own in proportionate terms are long-range strategic transport, mobile logistics, advanced precision-guided weaponry, stealth technology, and global satellite surveillance and communications systems.[10]

This situation, even if it is convenient for America's allies and desirable to some in Washington who enjoy the influence it accords the United States, is very unhealthy for the Western alliance. Even if some policymakers might like to preserve this global correlation of forces, most of the American people and most of the rest of the world seem unlikely to tolerate such an approach.[11] It would reduce the prospects that U.S.-led operations will receive enough international backing to gain strong legitimacy in the eyes of the global community—making it harder not only to solicit participation from other countries' armed forces but even access to their overseas bases (which, as argued later, will remain very important). It would also risk a situation in which, after suffering substantial losses in a future war in defense of common Western interests, the American people become fed up with allies they see as free-riding and force U.S. leaders to abdicate the U.S. leadership role—perhaps pulling out of major alliances and focusing thereafter only on North America's security. Such a backlash may not even require a major war. If the United States continues to spend a considerably higher percent of its GDP on defense than most of its allies, and experiences a protracted economic downturn, isolationist sentiments could arise even if no Americans come home in body bags.

Either way, both U.S. global leadership and the Western alliance system could be seriously weakened. Some may believe the twenty-first-century world will be a sufficiently safe place that this would not matter. But few analysts and statesmen expected the twentieth century to be particularly conflict-ridden or bloody, yet they were proven wrong. International relations tend to be very dangerous when they lack a clear security anchor in the form of a strong global power or a strong global alliance system; it would be irresponsible to base policy on optimistic assumptions about the obsolescence of war.[12]

The RMA debate risks making this problem worse. Rather than seek to redress these imbalances in deployable military power, allies may decide it is pointless to try to keep up with the United States. For example, in the words of a Dutch general, "Looking at the development of Army XXI in the U.S., I wonder whether the other NATO countries are able to keep up with our ally";[13] a British officer stated, "digitization might make coalition warfare all the more difficult."[14] Lawrence Freedman worries about the possibility of a two-tier alliance in which the United States may wish to—or at least be seen as wishing to—provide high-tech capabilities while its allies perform more mundane tasks such as peace operations because they may not be able to keep up with enough technology to be part of the U.S.-led RMA.[15]

American officials share some of these concerns. On a trip to Australia in 1998, Secretary of Defense William Cohen suggested that at least that particular U.S. ally was in danger of falling so far behind American forces technologically as to reduce its ability to participate usefully in coalition operations.[16] And Under Secretary of Defense Jacques Gansler and Joint Chiefs Chairman Henry Shelton commissioned a Defense Science Board study on the issue of U.S.-led coalition operations out of a concern that advanced technologies could make them more difficult.[17]

However, there is no good military or economic reason that advanced technology should make coalition operations more difficult. If one discards the sweeping theoretical language that has characterized much of the RMA debate to date and focuses on specific technologies, it is possible to see why.

Future battlefield integration and interoperability will depend on having computers and communications systems that can talk to each other across national lines. That is admittedly a challenge. But it is hardly a new one for the alliance—or even for the U.S. military itself.[18]

The technology gap does not need to widen, even if allied defense budgets stagnate and even if the United States continues to be at the vanguard of developing sophisticated new computers, communications, and other high-tech electronics-based systems. By coordinating their purchases of computers and communications systems, the allies can work together very effectively on the future battlefield. Admittedly, that is easier said than done given the existing political challenges. But it is hardly impossible.

Once they are developed in research labs and test ranges, the prices of purchasing technologies key to creating a "system of systems" should generally be modest. Innovations in electronics at the turn of the century are characterized as much by declining price as by increasing capacity and power. Improvements to munitions, avionics, computers, communications systems, and other electronics can be made at relatively low costs.[19]

On top of these reassuring considerations, there is no reason to think that most allied military forces need to be anywhere near their present size. If Europe and Japan need to cut force structure to afford modernization, they can certainly do so.[20]

If it were so hard and expensive to keep up with trends in high technology, the U.S. Marine Corps would surely be shut out of the action. Admittedly, it has direct access to various U.S. military satellites, strategic transport, and other critical enabling technologies that it does not have to pay for. In this regard, it is like a U.S. ally that assumes it would generally fight only as part of a U.S.-led coalition. But its funds are very modest. At $10 billion a year, with only about $1 billion typically for procurement, it has a budget only one-third to one-fourth the size of several large U.S. allies including Japan.[21]

Thus, U.S. allies can certainly afford the next wave of defense modernization. Smaller allies may have to tolerate a certain partial dependence on the United States for research and development and key enabling technologies like satellites—just as the Marine Corps depends on the rest of DoD itself. Larger allies, or groups of small allies acting together, would not even need to accept these constraints on their independent capabilities.

To see just how affordable the so-called RMA should be for major U.S. allies, consider the following shopping basket of "RMA" technologies. They include most of the types of advanced sensors, computing and communications grids, and precision firepower needed to rapidly detect, target, and destroy military assets on the future battlefield. It is admittedly not a comprehensive list, but it is nevertheless a rather extensive one. In fact, it may even provide more land-attack capability than Japan would want in the foreseeable future, given the anxieties that such capabilities could cause in Northeast Asia. Nonetheless, it would be affordable for Japan or another of the United States' larger allies.

1 Advanced radios, computers, and identification-friend-or-foe devices for all major vehicles and aircraft in three modern divisions.
2 Advanced radios, avionics, datalinks, and helmet-mounted displays in three air wings.
3 A dozen ground stations, some fixed and some mobile, to integrate and disseminate data and commands, with electronics and computers similar to those of the Joint STARS aircraft.
4 A fleet of 50 unmanned aerial vehicles of various sizes, ranges, and payloads similar to those operated by the United States in the early twenty-first century.
5 1,000 cruise missiles.
6 5,000 short-range munitions including an assortment of laser-guided bombs, Maverick, and Hellfire-like ordnance.
7 500 advanced air-to-air missiles, a mix of beyond-visual-range radar-homing missiles and short-range infrared missiles;
8 A squadron of stealth aircraft to map out an enemy's radar defenses and lead any attack, particularly in its first days.
9 Several batteries of TMD radars and missiles.

This system of systems would be remarkably affordable. In rough numbers, the respective costs would be perhaps $3 billion for the Army radios and small computers, $1 billion for the ground stations, $1 billion for the UAVs, $2 billion for the cruise missiles, $500 million for the smaller air-to-ground munitions, $500 million for the advanced air-to-air missiles, $2 billion for the computers, avionics, radios, datalinks, and helmet-mounted displays for aircraft, $2.5 billion to acquire the stealth aircraft, and $2–4 billion for missile defenses—a total investment of around $15 billion.[22] That is hardly an inexpensive price tag. But it is the equivalent of less than two years of procurement spending for a major European country or Japan. Averaged out over a decade, it would cost perhaps 15 percent of the weapons acquisition budget of such a country. Generally speaking, there would be few if any additional operating costs, since these systems would replace existing assets rather than require formation of additional units.

Admittedly, this list of technologies does not push all types of possible military innovation equally rapidly. It focuses on information warfare, not stealth or speed. Pursuing stealth across the board would admittedly be extremely costly. Not only combat aircraft, but also transport helicopters, ships, and armored vehicles, might have to be designed and built from scratch to fully profit from abilities to reduce radar, acoustic, and other signatures. In addition, other areas of technological progress, such as advanced engines and armor, could be pursued even if they did not promise revolutionary results.

However, these types of improvements are not at the core of the current electronics-led defense modernization wave. They are generally either areas where technological progress, albeit impressive, is clearly modest and evolutionary in pace, or where radical improvements in capability are unlikely to be necessary for countries likely to play a supporting role in a U.S.-led operation. For example, the allied forces do not generally need to purchase large numbers of stealthy ships or stealthy air-assault helicopters if U.S. naval and air assault forces would take the lead at establishing a beachhead and opening a logistics line in a theater like the Persian Gulf. Even if they wished to be capable of acting without the United States, advanced stealth technologies would be most sorely missed only against the most advanced foes. And the allies could acquire such systems in modest numbers, as recommended here, without inordinate budgetary challenge.

The main point is this: even without increasing their defense budgets, major U.S. allies can be very capable of twenty-first-century military operations. If they are wise about how they structure their militaries and their defense budgets, and if the United States tries to be a fair-minded and cooperative ally as well, the so-called RMA should not worsen allied military cooperation in future operations.

The RMA and U.S. Overseas Military Presence

One of the most common arguments made by RMA proponents is that technology may offer a way to scale back U.S. global military presence substantially—if not right away, then certainly within the first decade or two of the twenty-first century. It is a refrain heard from bomber advocates, the U.S. Air Force from time to time, and some regional security experts who have begun trying to apply the RMA concept to theaters such as the Asia-Pacific.[23]

Although reduced by more than 50 percent from Cold War levels, U.S. forces based or deployed abroad number 250,000 uniformed personnel. Forward-deployed forces now constitute just over a sixth of the 1.4 million active-duty force, down from a quarter of the total in Cold War times. But many of the remaining deployments are particularly demanding. Troops in Korea and Bosnia, half of the Marines on Okinawa, Air Force pilots in Saudi Arabia, and of course Navy sailors and Marines at sea are unescorted by their families. Forces on Okinawa are much less welcome than they once were locally; Air Force units in Saudi Arabia suffered a deadly attack against their barracks in 1996 and remain a focal point for terrorists; the tragic accident in which a Marine aircraft sent 20 tourists plummeting to their deaths strained the U.S.–Italy relationship as well.

How much nicer it would be if U.S. troops could stay at home until called upon in a crisis or conflict. Then, according to RMA believers, they could lash out rapidly, intercontinentally, and lethally, from U.S. bases with spacepower, long-range airpower, and other twenty-first-century gadgetry.

Alas, this image of future warfare succumbs to the most unrealistic elements of the RMA vision while failing to pay heed to real-world technical constraints. Among the enduring realities it overlooks are the following.

1 Most airplanes will remain short range given the realities of aerodynamics and engine technology.
2 Ground forces may become somewhat lighter, but they will hardly be light; they will continue to depend on motorized and armored vehicles powered by fuel-intensive internal combustion engines.

3 Long-range sensors will remain of limited value against a number of types of militarily relevant assets, including most WMD and small arms.

4 Ships will get faster but remain fairly slow, requiring many days or weeks to cross oceans.

5 Finally, it will remain very difficult to seize ports, airfields, and other fixed infrastructure held by an enemy.

These ideas are developed further in the following.

Air Superiority

Let us first consider the air superiority mission. Even if bombers operating out of U.S. bases are someday able to provide much of the air-to-ground punch in future conflicts, other aircrafts will be needed to patrol the skies. And those aircrafts will need dependable bases in the actual theater of combat.

The kinds of new aerial vehicles being researched today will not allow the United States to establish and maintain air superiority out of bases on its own territory. Unmanned aerial vehicles are primarily short range; jet engine technology is not advancing enough to make intercontinental flights quick or fuel-efficient; extremely fast hypersonic vehicles, if they can be built at all, will be very expensive and specialized in their purposes.

Why will air superiority still be needed in 2010, 2020, and beyond? For one thing, just to make good use of stealthy ground-attack aircraft like the B-2. The B-2 is not invisible or invulnerable—it is just hard to see on radar. It is somewhat harder than most airplanes to detect by visual or infrared techniques, but not truly stealthy in these regards. If an enemy knew that the chief threat to its forces were the stealth bomber, it could elect to move only during the daytime when its own fighters could visually detect and target the B-2, digging in and camouflaging its assets at night. Since most countries prefer to fight during the day anyhow, that would be no great handicap. Given the B-2's inability to outfly even unsophisticated fighters, it would fare poorly if unescorted under those circumstances.

In fact, B-2 bombers might even need fighter escort at night against a moderately sophisticated enemy. When the B-2s used their radars to search for targets, they would give away hints of information about their locations. If an enemy had numerous radar sensors with real-time data links between them, it could sometimes locate the B-2 through a triangulation technique (by measuring the times of arrival of a given search beam at different points and inferring the aircraft's position from the differences in those times).[24]

What if missiles launched from arsenal ships were used instead of B-2s? These futuristic vessels would have little superstructure to give away their locations, sit low in the water, require only small crews, and carry perhaps 500 medium-range missiles. The missiles would each hold ten or more submunitions to destroy armored targets as well as other enemy assets.

To be effective, however, arsenal ships would have to be based in the right part of the world when a conflict broke out. They would also need targeting data to know where to fire their missiles—and that might itself require airpower to obtain, since imaging satellites may prove vulnerable to antisatellite weapons against a relatively advanced adversary. Also, the arsenal ships would only be as good as the submunitions they delivered. We do not yet know how well new classes of submunitions will work against a foe using dispersal, decoys, camouflage, jammers, and other techniques to defend itself.

Finally, air superiority would also be needed to protect any U.S. and allied ground forces that were needed in a counterinvasion or similar operation. And it is straightforward to see why, even in an era of fancier and faster and more brilliant munitions and computer networks, ground forces will still be important in war.

The Continued Relevance of Ground Forces

In future warfare, the United States will need to retain the capability to seize and hold territory. It may have to overthrow an extremist enemy regime developing nuclear weapons, committing genocide, or otherwise causing an acute international crisis. Or a friendly country may be attacked out of the blue and be defeated before U.S. forces could respond, making it necessary for U.S. armed forces to evict the aggressor from the territory it had conquered.

To do these things, ground troops will continue to be needed. Long-range reconnaissance assets will continue to have trouble finding enemy forces that have hunkered down or are mixed in with civilian populations. They will be especially challenged to locate critical military assets like mortars, man-portable antitank and antiair weapons, rocket-propelled grenades, soldiers themselves, underground bunkers and communications facilities, and well-concealed WMD.

The reasons are not hard to understand. All sensors have limitations—and to a large extent they are limitations imposed by the basic and immutable laws of physics, not simply the temporary state of current technology. Visible-light and infrared detectors cannot see through heavy clouds. Radars tend not to have excellent resolution. None of these sensors can penetrate metal, water, or most kinds of soil very far. Most X-ray and particle-beam sensors have very short ranges.

Improvements are underway. But to take one example, even if good foliage-penetrating radar is developed, it will have a hard time seeing through tree trunks, a very difficult if not impossible time discriminating camouflaged heavy equipment from trucks and other civilian vehicles, and an impossible time seeing inside normal vehicles.

Other new sensors and weapons are also being designed for close-in infantry operations. Robotics may allow individual soldiers to investigate areas behind or within nearby buildings without exposing themselves to fire. New handheld weapons with miniaturized mortar rounds may allow these soldiers to shoot around trees or city corners by sending one of these rounds to a very precise location before detonating it. Acoustic or infrared sensors may allow troops to see through walls or pick up the precise location of an enemy sniper from the report of his weapon.

However, these sensors and weapons will remain short range. They will not be able to peer or fire through thick layers of concrete or soil. They will not have magical powers to tell good guys from bad guys or divine the unspoken intents and plans of the enemy.

Future ground forces may be able to carry less heavy weaponry with them in the future, calling in precision-fire support when needed, as a 1996 Defense Science Board summer study suggested. In fact, greater battlefield dispersion and use of long-range power would continue longstanding trends. As Trevoy Dupuy has estimated, a force of 100,000 soldiers tended to fight over an area of about 20 square kilometers in Napoleonic times, 250 square kilometers in World War I, 2,750 square kilometers in World War II, and 3,500 square kilometers in the 1973 Arab–Israeli War. However, significant constraints will remain. Even hypersonic missiles would generally take tens of seconds or minutes to deliver their ordnance—a time lag that will not always be acceptable against enemy forces that are able to move and take shelter. Moreover, such missiles and their submunitions will be of limited utility in heavy forest or urban environments. So ground forces will need to carry a certain amount of weaponry with them, as well as a certain amount of armor and organic mobility for self-defense purposes. They will therefore continue to require large and heavy logistics tails.

The only way to move such heavy ground force formations is, and will remain, sealift. That implies a need for protected areas, preferably developed ports, to unload equipment. It also means that moving large forces from the United States will take time. Even if technological break-throughs are achieved, ships will do well to sail at 40 or 50 knots in contrast to today's speeds of 20 to 30 knots. So ground forces that need to be on hand early in a fight will have to be based in the region, or at least have most of their equipment stored there.

If ports are to be needed, it is much better to control them in advance than to conduct a forced-entry operation to secure them. Amphibious warfare and air assault have always been tough, and are unlikely to get any easier. Enemies will retain a range of weapons from mines to anti-ship cruise missiles to submarines, to impede the use of seacoast that they control. In fact, their ability to use such weapons against us will probably improve at least as fast as our ability to counter such challenges, a point emphasized by Andrew Krepinevich of the Center for Strategic and Budgetary Assessments. U.S. adversaries could also disseminate chemical or biological weapons in areas they control. We do not want to have to fight ashore in such places—meaning that unless our allies are strong enough to hold ports and airfields, some permanent U.S. troop presence will remain well advised to protect infrastructure needed to deploy large numbers of reinforcements.

The Marines on Okinawa

The 20,000 U.S. Marines on Okinawa in Japan, though a capable military force for certain missions, now appear to be causing serious strains in the bilateral alliance. Innovative use of both old technologies, such as storage ships, and new technologies, such as advanced precision munitions, can make this possible. One need not support the RMA hypothesis to rethink certain specific ways in which the United States maintains forward presence today. RMA or not, trends in technology—together with creative strategic thinking—can and should help reduce the U.S. military footprint on Okinawa.

It is possible to bring home about three-fourths of the 20,000 Marines in Japan today, and return control of major training ranges and most other Marine bases on Okinawa to Japan. Of the 15,000 Marines who would leave the island, they could come home or redeploy to a place such as Australia.

The Marines who remained would be important. They would include those who manned the thirty-first Marine Expeditionary Unit (MEU), which conducts routine ocean patrols in the vicinity using the three troop ships based in Sasebo, Japan. They would also include those maintaining equipment and staging facilities on the island.

If the decision to make this change was made within the next few years, it could also permit Japan to save the money that would otherwise have been spent replacing the Marine Corps Futenma Air Station—and perhaps devote some of it to other alliance priorities, like TMD. Under the proposal outlined here, that station would no longer be needed. The modest number of flights needed routinely for the thirty-first MEU could be conducted out of the Air Force's Kadena base; in a crisis or conflict, Naha International Airport could be made available as a staging base for a larger Marine operation in the region if Tokyo supported it.

Mostly because of the Marine presence, U.S. military bases continue to cover 18 percent of Okinawa's territory. That number is due to decline to about 16 percent if and when the Futenma Marine air base is relocated and other changes agreed to in 1996 are instituted. But it will still be down only modestly from the 21 percent figure at the time of the island's reversion to Japan in 1972. Okinawa has as many people as the state of Hawaii on less than one-tenth the land and is densely populated even by Japanese standards. Given the huge benefits that the United States gains from having navy and air force bases in Japan, it is prudent to protect those assets (which require much less land than Marine training facilities) and stop putting the health of the alliance at risk over the less-than-critical Marine Corps presence.[25]

This approach would also have Japan purchase equipment and storage facilities to keep as much Marine equipment on Okinawa in the future as is there now. The keys technologically would be to make greater use of old-fashioned technologies such as storage ships, as well as new technologies such as advanced munitions. By basing and stockpiling such assets in Japan, the United States could actually improve its rapid-response capabilities for combat operations in Asia with one-fourth as many Marines as it now has on Okinawa.

The main concrete downside for U.S. planners would be budgetary: if they were returned stateside, or to a less cash-rich country than Japan (like Australia and perhaps also South Korea), the United States would lose the HNS payments for these Marines and see their annual cost go up by about $300 million to $500 million.[26]

Some U.S. policymakers would be even more troubled by the symbolism of retrenching the U.S. military presence in Japan and East Asia more generally. Having declared in the Defense Department's 1995 report on the East Asia-Pacific region that U.S. forces in the region would remain roughly 100,000 strong, and reiterated that position in 1996 and 1997, they are unwilling to back away from the figure. Any consideration of redeploying the Marines to a place like Australia, which would preserve the total number of U.S. troops in the region, has apparently been ruled out in light of the continued North Korean military threat and tension between Taiwan and the PRC. Whether or not counterbalancing military steps could be taken to compensate for the redeployment of the Marines, officials worry about causing even the appearance of a weakening of U.S. commitment to the region or northeast Asian subregion.

But it is not worth jeopardizing the strength of the U.S.–Japan alliance for HNS payments worth 0.1 or 0.2 percent of the American defense budget. Moreover, if the United States and Japan made it clear that they were taking steps that not only compensated for the redeployment of the Marines, but actually improved the alliance's rapid reaction capabilities through better use of prepositioned ships and supplies, they should be able to demonstrate that the alliance had not been weakened.

Conclusion

This chapter suggests that the RMA, even if realized, should not prohibit allies such as Japan from keeping up with American military technology and power. It further argues that technology changes will not themselves permit a radical reduction in U.S. forces abroad, though selective reductions in the Okinawa Marine presence should be possible. Finally, it argues that TMD has a certain place in the region, but that it is much more likely to work well against North Korean attack or perhaps a limited PRC attack—and not against a full-fledged concerted strike by China.

The overall message of this chapter is both sobering and reassuring. Trends in technology are not going to radically change the nature of statecraft. The U.S.–Japan alliance as well as U.S. military presence in Japan will remain important. Policymakers in Tokyo and Washington will still have to make strategic choices in the future similar to those they have made—or avoided making—in the past. And this book's policy agenda will be neither precluded, nor greatly facilitated, by new types of weaponry. Although a wide range of new problems and opportunities will arise, the basic character of security policy will not change because of technology trends in the early decades of the twenty-first century.

Notes

1. For an argument in favor of taking a large part of the active force structure "off line" so as to devote it to experimentation and acceleration of the RMA, see James R. Blaker, "The American RMA Force: An Alternative to the QDR,"

Strategic Review, Vol. 25, No. 3 (Summer 1997), pp. 21–30; for a similar but more general argument, see also Richard K. Betts, *Military Readiness: Concepts, Choices, Consequences* (Washington, D.C.: Brookings Institution Press, 1995), pp. 35–84. For the view of a conservative critic of the RMA concept, see Frederick W. Kagan, "Wishful Thinking on War," *Weekly Standard* (December 15, 1997), pp. 27–29. Kagan argues that the country may need to spend more on technology—but must not do so at the expense of its present engagement and deterrence strategies.

2. National Defense Panel, *Transforming Defense: National Security in the 21st Century* (Arlington, VA.: Department of Defense, December 1997), pp. vii, 2, 23, 49, 59, 79–86.

3. See, most notably, Admiral William A. Owens with Ed Offley, *Lifting the Fog of War* (New York: Farrar, Straus, and Giroux, 2000).

4. Lawrence Freedman, *The Revolution in Strategic Affairs*, Adelphi Paper 318 (New York: Oxford University Press, 1998), p. 21.

5. Martin Van Creveld, *Technology and War: From 2000 B.C. to the Present* (New York: The Free Press, 1989). Trevor Dupuy uses yet another categorization scheme, different from those of Krepinevich, Van Creveld, and others, to understand the history of military innovation. He groups all progress since 1800 together under the title of "The Age of Technological Change." See Trevor N. Dupuy, *The Evolution of Weapons and Warfare* (Fairfax, VA: HERO Books, 1984).

6. For sound warnings about both dismissing the RMA and jumping on the bandwagon too enthusiastically, see Colin S. Gray, *The American Revolution in Military Affairs: An Interim Assessment* (Camberley, England: Strategic and Combat Studies Institute, 1997), pp. 5–7, 33–34; for a reminder that militaries must always be innovating and changing, see Jonathan Shimshoni, "Technology, Military Advantage, and World War I: A Case for Military Entrepreneurship," *International Security*, Vol. 15, No. 3 (Winter 1990/91), pp. 213–215.

7. John Keegan, *The First World War* (New York: Alfred A. Knopf, 1999), p. 20; Dan Goure, "Is There a Military-Technical Revolution in America's Future?" *Washington Quarterly* (Autumn 1993), p. 185; and Dupuy, *The Evolution of Weapons and Warfare*, pp. 218–220, 258–266.

8. Robert Pape, *Bombing to Win: Air Power and Coercion in War* (Ithaca, New York: Cornell University Press, 1996), pp. 87–136, 254–313; and Brian Bond and Williamson Murray, "British Armed Forces, 1918–1939," in Allan R. Millet and Williamson Murray, eds., *Military Effectiveness*, Vol. II (Boston: Unwin Hyman, 1988).

9. Stephen Biddle, "Assessing Theories of Future Warfare," Paper Presented to the 1997 Annual Meeting of the American Political Science Association, Washington, D.C., August 1997, pp. 37–38; Andrew J. Bacevich, *The Pentomic Era: The U.S. Army between Korea and Vietnam* (Washington, D.C.: National Defense University Press, 1986); John Keegan, *A History of Warfare* (New York: Vintage Books, 1993), pp. 362–379; Van Creveld, *Technology and War*, pp. 193–195; and Stephen Peter Rosen, *Winning the Next War: Innovation and the Modern Military* (Ithaca, NY: Cornell University Press, 1991), pp. 13–18, 37–38.

10. An earlier version of this argument appeared in the Spring 1999 issue of *National Security Studies Quarterly*.

11. Richard N. Haass, *The Reluctant Sheriff* (New York: Council on Foreign Relations, 1997), pp. 54–55.

12. See Kenneth N. Waltz, *Theory of International Politics* (Reading, MA: Addison-Wesley, 1979), pp. 129–193; Robert Gilpin, *War and Change in World Politics* (Cambridge, United Kingdom: Cambridge University Press, 1981), pp. 231–244; Aaron L. Friedberg, "Ripe for Rivalry: Prospects for Peace in a Multipolar Asia," *International Security*, Vol. 18, No. 3 (Winter 1993/94), pp. 5–10; Donald Kagan, "Locarno's Lessons for NATO," *Wall Street Journal*, October 28, 1997, p. 22.

13. "US Forces' Digital Revolution Threat to Interoperability," *Jane's Defence Weekly*, June 11, 1997, p. 17.

14. "Task Force XXI Portends Future Interoperability Problems with Allies," *Inside the Pentagon*, April 10, 1997, p. 24.

15. Lawrence Freedman, *The Revolution in Strategic Affairs*, International Institute for Strategic Studies, Adelphi Paper 318 (New York: Oxford University Press, 1998), pp. 70–75.

16. Greg Sherman, "U.S. Warns of Risk to Defence Ties," *The Australian*, July 31, 1998.

17. Bryan Bender, "US Worried By Coalition 'Technology Gap,'" *Jane's Defence Weekly*, July 29, 1998, p. 8.

18. Paul B. Stares, *Command Performance: The Neglected Dimension of European Security* (Washington, D.C.: Brookings, 1991), pp. 194–205.

19. Minor procurement also includes trucks, satellites, radars, and a host of other systems, some of them RMA-related and some not. See Lane Pierrot and others, "The Costs of the Administration's Plan for the Air Force Through the Year 2010," CBO Memorandum, Congressional Budget Office, Washington, D.C., November 1994, pp. 23–24; and Frances Lussier, "The Costs of the Administration's Plan for the Army Through the Year 2010," CBO Memorandum, Congressional Budget Office, Washington, D.C., November 1994, p. 11.

20. International Institute for Strategic Studies, *The Military Balance 1997/98* (Oxford: Oxford University Press, 1997), pp. 293–294.

21. U.S. Marine Corps, *Concepts and Issues 97* (Washington, D.C.: Department of Defense, 1997), pp. 20–25, 134; International Institute for Strategic Studies, *The Military Balance 1997/98*, pp. 293–294.

22. For documentation of these costs, see David E. Mosher, "The Grand Plans," *IEEE Spectrum*, Vol. 34, No. 9 (September 1997), pp. 28–39 (on TMDs); Michael O'Hanlon, *How to be a Cheap Hawk: The 1999 and 2000 Defense Budgets* (Brookings, 1998), pp. 132–134 (on munitions and Joint STARS); Donald Stevens et al., *The Next-Generation Attack Fighter* (Santa Monica, CA: RAND Corporation, 1997), p. 70 (on the costs of partially stealthy aircraft); Michael Miller et al., "Costs of Operation Desert Shield," CBO Staff Memorandum, Congressional Budget Office, Washington, D.C., January 1991, p. 17 (on munitions); David Mosher and Michael O'Hanlon, *The START Treaty and Beyond* (Washington, D.C.: Congressional Budget Office, October 1991), p. 139 (on cruise missiles);

Mark Hanna, "Task Force XXI: The Army's Digital Experiment," *Strategic Forum*, no. 119 (July 1997), pp. 1–4 (on communications and computers); David Pugliese, "Software, Computers to Lead Canadian CF-18 Upgrades," *Defense News* (January 11, 1999), p. 8; Brooks Tigner, "NATO Likely Will Adopt U.S. Tank ID System," *Defense News* (January 5–11, 1998), p. 3 (on IFF technologies); Defense Airborne Reconnaissance Office, "UAV Annual Report, FY 1996," Department of Defense, November 1996 (on UAVs); "USAF to Upgrade F-16C/D Avionics," *Aviation Week and Space Technology* (July 6, 1998), p. 59.

23. See Paul Dibb, "The Revolution in Military Affairs and Asian Security," *Survival*, Vol. 39, No. 4 (Winter 1997–98), p. 106; Rebecca Grant, ed., *Origins of the Deep Attack Weapons Mix Study* (Arlington, VA: IRIS Independent Research, 1997), p. 16; James R. Blaker, "Understanding the Revolution in Military Affairs: A Guide to America's 21st Century Defense," defense working paper #3, Progressive Policy Institute, Washington, D.C., January 1997, pp. 24–26; Christopher J. Bowie, *Untying the Bloody Scarf* (Arlington, VA.: IRIS Independent Research, 1998), p. 17; Charles M. Perry, Robert L. Pfaltzgraff, Jr., and Joseph C. Conway, *Long-Range Bombers and the Role of Airpower in the New Century* (Cambridge, MA: Institute for Foreign Policy Analysis, 1995), pp. ix–xxii.

24. See Robert Wall, "U.S. Seeks Innovative Ways to Counter Air Defenses," *Aviation Week and Space Technology* (July 20, 1998), p. 54; Beth M. Kaspar, "Advanced Tactical Targeting Technology," DARPA Tech '97 Systems and Technology Symposium, Kansas City, Missouri, September 1997.

25. For a fuller description of the relative benefits of the different types of bases the U.S. military possesses in Japan, see Michael O'Hanlon, "Restructuring U.S. Forces and Bases in Japan," in Mike Mochizuki, ed., *Toward a True Alliance: Restructuring U.S.-Japan Security Relations* (Brookings, 1997), pp. 149–178.

26. See Mochizuki, ed., *Toward a True Alliance*, pp. 24–28, 138–143, 149–178.

CHAPTER 9

BALLISTIC MISSILE DEFENSE AND THE U.S.–JAPAN ALLIANCE

Umemoto Tetsuya

Japan has embarked on the course of acquiring a ballistic missile defense (BMD) capability in cooperation with the United States. In December 1998, Tokyo announced its decision to participate in technical research for the NTW defense program. The NTW system, which will be mounted on Aegis cruisers/destroyers, represents the U.S. Navy's candidate for "upper-tier" defenses intended to engage incoming theater ballistic missiles in high altitudes. The development of NTW will proceed as the Sea-Based Midcourse Program under the Bush administration. For "lower-tier," or low-altitude intercept, the Defense Agency of Japan is apparently considering introduction of the Patriot Advanced Capability (PAC)-3, which is being developed for the U.S. Army to engage short-range missiles, although no formal decision has been made yet.[1]

So far, Japan's involvement in BMD is fairly cautious, and it will probably be more than a decade, if at all, before Japan arms itself with defensive systems in upper-tier configurations. The Japanese have agreed to share in the work on the nose cone, second-stage rocket engine, kinetic warhead, and infrared seeker for the NTW interceptor. The money appropriated for the joint research, however, has been relatively small though rapidly increasing: 0.96 billion yen in FY1999, 2.05 billion yen in FY2000, and 3.70 billion yen in FY2001. At the end of the research phase, which is expected to last a few more years, Tokyo will review the results and decide whether to proceed to development. For production and deployment, a separate review and decision will be required at the conclusion of the development stage. Such a deliberate approach by the Japanese government as well as the timelines for NTW development in the United States all but guarantees that Japan would not obtain sea-based systems for upper-tier intercept before 2010.[2]

It is not too early, however, for the Japanese and the Americans to give a serious thought to the implications of Tokyo's BMD undertakings for the bilateral alliance. For one thing, Washington has begun to alter the context for the development of defensive systems to be loaded on Aegis vessels. The Bush administration has made known its policy of merging the TMD program to protect overseas U.S. troops as well as America's allies and friends and the NMD scheme designed to repel ballistic missile attack against the territory of the United States. While the NTW system has heretofore been associated solely with TMD missions, the Sea-Based Midcourse Program also aims for the protection of the U.S. homeland. Moreover, the Pentagon is planning to achieve some Aegis-based contingency capabilities for territorial defense, which might include the intercept of enemy ballistic missiles in the boost phase, within several years.[3]

Further, BMD activities of Japan and the United States have already caused diplomatic repercussions in the Asia-Pacific region. Russia and China have staunchly opposed the creation of an antimissile shield over the territory of the United States, although their reaction to the U.S. decision to withdraw from the Anti-Ballistic Missile (ABM) Treaty in December 2001 was remarkably mild. The Chinese spearhead the protest against the U.S.–Japan collaboration in defense against theater ballistic missiles, which has also been denounced by the North Koreans. While not objecting to the NTW research per se, South Korea may nevertheless be wary of an enlargement of Japanese military capability as well as the possibility of BMD further complicating its troubled relationship with the North. Taiwan hopes that introduction of antimissile systems by the United States and Japan, together with its own defensive efforts, would frustrate Beijing's annexation bid.[4]

Whether Tokyo will carry its BMD cooperation with Washington into the development and deployment stages would (and should) be determined ultimately by the anticipated impact of its decisions on the security of Japan. In order to enhance Japanese security, antimissile systems operated by the SDFs of Japan should be able to make at least some contribution to countering ballistic missile threats that might realistically arise. At the same time, defensive undertakings must not provoke potential adversaries into substantially raising their ballistic missile and other types of military threats to the Japanese archipelago. Finally, the process of bilateral collaboration in missile defense should not create unnecessary frictions in the overall alliance tie, because, regardless of the outcome of such collaboration, that tie would remain indispensable to Japan in dealing with ballistic missile and other military threats. In other words, if Japanese participation in BMD is to be encouraged, at least these three requirements would have to be met.

Whether and how Japan and the United States can indeed meet those requirements will constitute the main theme of this chapter. The first section will examine the strategic significance of hypothetical Japanese defenses in relation to hypothetical ballistic missile threats, with Russia, China, and North Korea designated as potential adversaries for the sake of argument. Provision of reassurance for the Japanese public in the face of such threats will be shown to represent one of the most prominent functions that Japan's antimissile capability could perform. The second section will explore ways to make Tokyo's missile defense activities compatible with reduction of ballistic missile threats from the potential adversaries. Promises of, and limitations to, attempts to involve Moscow, Beijing, and Pyongyang in strengthened global nonproliferation regimes or in arms-control and confidence-building processes within the region will be pointed out. The third section will address questions of alliance management so that BMD cooperation might bolster, rather than vitiate, the U.S.–Japan security relationship in general. Discussion will range from the confidence in U.S. extended deterrence to the interpretation of the Japanese constitution to the exchange of military technologies.

Strategic Significance

A hypothetical Japanese BMD capability could be relied upon to intercept a fairly small number—a few tens, for illustrative purposes—of theater ballistic missiles and, perhaps, a handful of long-range missiles. As explained in the following, deployment of such defenses, in combination with the U.S. nuclear guarantee, would go a long way to reassure the Japanese populace in a crisis about deterrence and defense against ballistic missile attack by China or North Korea as well as defense against accidental or unauthorized launch of ballistic missiles from the territory of the former Soviet Union.

Main assumptions from which to draw these statements about the strategic significance of Japanese BMD are the following. First, Japan would arm itself with upper-tier defenses similar to NTW mounted on several Aegis destroyers, in addition to lower-tier systems like the PAC-3 fired from a few dozen batteries on the ground. Second, the deployment of the upper-tier interceptors would take place in roughly ten to fifteen years from now, while the lower-tier defenses could be fielded much earlier. Third, the political orientation of Russia, China, and North Korea as potential adversaries, as well as their military posture with regard to ballistic missiles and weapons of mass destruction (WMD) deliverable thereby, would essentially represent an extension of the present trends. Fourth, the United States would acquire defensive capabilities against theater ballistic missiles as they become available, at the same time continuing its pursuit of homeland defense against long-range missiles.

While opinions may diverge as to the plausibility of the first, second, and fourth premises mentioned here, the third would represent by far the most controversial assumption, given the great uncertainties about developments within, and external relations of, those regional powers. Some supposition is needed, however, concerning the origin and character of ballistic missile threats. Extending the current political and military tendencies for more than a decade, that is, until Japan had its antimissile systems in place, is admittedly risky, but it will at least yield a baseline prediction to which revisions can be made as the situation unfolds. Moreover, the present frequently determines the tone of debates about the future, as exemplified by the Chinese preoccupation with the impact of prospective Japanese and U.S. defenses on their existing military and national strategies. Looking at the future as a projection of the present will make it easier to join such debates.

Russia

Russia will continue to be a major nuclear-armed power, but its intercontinental ballistic missile (ICBM) and submarine launched ballistic missile (SLBM) arsenals are expected to shrink considerably in the next decade. As long as it adheres to the 1987 treaty to eliminate the intermediate nuclear forces (INFs), Russia will have neither intermediate-range ballistic missiles (IRBMs) nor medium-range ballistic missiles (MRBMs). According to a unilateral declaration by Moscow, tactical nuclear weapons for short-range ballistic missiles (SRBMs) have also been withdrawn, although questions remain as to the accuracy of that declaration.[5]

On the other hand, erection of an antimissile shield by the United States over its territory would give Russia incentives to slow down reductions of its ICBM and SLBM forces.[6] Moscow might also decide to renounce the INF Treaty, thereby legitimizing reintroduction of IRBMs and MRBMs, largely out of concern that China might substantially increase its ballistic missile capabilities in response to U.S. deployment of homeland defenses. Moreover, the weakness of their conventional forces has apparently led the Russians to rediscover the value of tactical nuclear weapons, some of which would be delivered by SRBMs.

Since the end of the Cold War, the possibility of a confrontation in which Moscow might contemplate missile strike on Japan has receded into the background. Geared to theater ballistic missiles, Japan's hypothetical BMD would at least initially have little prospect of countering a salvo of Russian ICBMs or SLBMs. Only with substantial upgrades in the interceptor, and only if they could get cuing information from radars and satellites being developed effectively as part of the U.S. territorial defense program, would the odds of their upper-tier elements shooting down long-range missiles improve.[7] Even then, the Russians would have more than enough ICBMs and SLBMs to overwhelm the Japanese defenses, not to mention sophisticated countermeasures that they could equip their missile warheads with to increase the chances of penetration. The antimissile systems of Japan, therefore, would not count very much in relation to Russia's offensive forces, except in an unlikely situation in which Moscow reintroduced IRBMs, MRBMs, or nuclear SRBMs and began to plan a limited assault with those missiles.

On the other hand, the danger of an accidental or unauthorized launch of ballistic missiles from Russia and other parts of what used to be the Soviet Union is real and likely to remain for some time. Japan's BMD capabilities could be made relevant to dealing with inadvertent firings of long-range missiles, especially if they got such upgrades as described here. As such, they would contribute to giving reassurance to the Japanese people as to the defensibility of their country if and when the safety and security of ballistic missiles and nuclear weapons in the former Soviet Union were seriously compromised.

China

Not only are the Chinese expected to keep modernizing their ICBM force, but they may also acquire their first batch of operational SLBMs within several years. China's MRBMs (and IRBMs), many of which can target Japan, will significantly improve in quality, while their quantity may not rise dramatically from the current several dozen. Moreover, the number of SRBMs, especially those on the coast across from Taiwan, is growing rapidly. The People's Liberation Army (PLA) appears to have fielded about 300 such missiles in the area, adding an estimated 50 missile per year. These SRBMs are believed to be nonnuclear but are capable of carrying nuclear warheads.[8]

Despite these trends, China's ballistic missile arsenal will remain small in size compared with the United States, or even the dwindling Russian, arsenal. Beijing, however, may seek to counter territorial defenses of the United States by accelerating the buildup of its ICBM capabilities.[9] Some analysts believe, moreover, that Chinese outlook on nuclear weapons is evolving from adherence to a "minimum deterrence" strategy to a more ambitious "limited deterrence" posture with an emphasis on war fighting and escalation control.[10] If there is indeed such a shift in nuclear thinking, it will have profound implications for ballistic missile developments.

From the standpoint of its military and national strategies, Beijing appears to expect its ballistic missile forces to perform two functions. First, ballistic missiles could enable the PLA to execute better "regional war under high-tech conditions" across the Taiwan Strait, in the South China Sea, and the like, as required by its latter-day military doctrine. Second, the ballistic missile arsenal could serve China in realizing its long-term goal of attaining a position of preeminence in the Asia-Pacific region. The Chinese continue to give the highest priority to the growth and modernization of their economy, for which purpose they value a stable relationship with Japan and the United States. In the quest for regional ascendancy, however, China seeks to diminish U.S. influence in East Asia as well as maintain military superiority over the Japanese, who have consistently restrained themselves on nuclear weapons and ballistic missiles.[11]

As the Chinese see it, to fight and win regional war under high-tech conditions against the Taiwanese, the PLA would need the ability to launch swift strikes to smash critical military assets on the island, while staving off intervention by third parties that are technologically more advanced, namely, the United States and Japan. The SRBMs emplaced in southeastern China near Taiwan would naturally form the core of the forces for a preemptive attack across the strait. Although the MRBMs (and IRBMs) might also be used for such attack in some numbers, they would primarily figure in the deterrence of U.S. and Japanese interference. Beijing could threaten a strike against the Japanese and forward-deployed U.S. forces in an attempt to scare Washington and Tokyo out of giving Japan-based military assistance to Taiwan.[12] Finally, China's ICBMs (and, in the future, possibly SLBMs), which could put the continental United States at risk, might help dissuade the Americans from meddling in the Taiwan question.

Japan's antimissile systems could make limited contribution to defending Taiwan against Chinese preemptive strike, if they were combined with U.S. and Taiwanese BMD capabilities. Interceptors mounted on Aegis destroyers of the SDFs might in theory be employed to shoot down MRBMs flying toward the island. Assuming the absence of lower-tier defenses like the erstwhile Navy Area (NA) defense system of the United States, however, Japanese Aegis ships would have difficulty in engaging the SRBMs that would constitute the mainstay of Chinese offense in the initial stages of the conflict. That task would be left to Aegis vessels of the United States and, if a transfer had been made, to those of Taiwan equipped with lower-tier interceptors, as well as ground-based defenses fielded by Taipei.[13] In any event, the presence of defensive systems, including those possessed by Japan, could complicate the Chinese war plan, especially if Beijing did not have confidence in the accuracy of its ballistic missiles that would be required for prompt destruction of vital military targets.

It should not be so difficult, however, for China to overwhelm any BMD capabilities that might realistically be deployed to protect the island of Taiwan. At the present rate of increase, the Chinese would have fielded 800 or more SRBMs close to the Taiwan Strait by the end of the decade. This number would of itself constitute a formidable threat; apart from the fact that some MRBMs would also be available to strike Taiwan and that fairly sophisticated countermeasures to frustrate defenses might have been administered to those missiles. Taipei would have introduced at most four Aegis vessels, altogether with an ability to engage no more than 200 incoming SRBMs.[14] While some of the remaining several hundred Chinese ballistic missiles might be intercepted by ground-based systems deployed on Taiwan, it would be next to impossible for the United States to dispatch a sufficient number of Aegis ships with the right capability to the conflict zone in time to shoot down the rest.

Japanese BMD could play a major role in countering Beijing's attempt to coerce Tokyo to refrain from assisting U.S. forces operating in the Taiwan area by the threat of an MRBM (and IRBM) strike. Assuming a nuclear balance heavily favoring the United States, it might be presumed that the U.S. "nuclear umbrella" would effectively deter such a strike. Retaliatory threats against an attack on an ally are inherently less credible, however, than those against an attack on the United States itself. There may be a threshold in the level of provocation below which retaliatory threats lose much of their credibility, and China might be able to calibrate its challenge accordingly. Moreover, it is usually easier to deter an adversary than to reassure the allied public that the situation is under control. It is in these senses that Japan's missile defenses could complement U.S. extended nuclear deterrence, even though they might never attain the capacity to repel a full-scale Chinese attack with MRBMs (and IRBMs) loaded with countermeasures. By acquiring defensive systems capable of intercepting a significant portion of relatively small number (i.e., below the "threshold" noted earlier) of Chinese MRBMs (and IRBMs), Tokyo could hope to prevent the onset of panic among the Japanese people and thereby preserve its freedom of action in supporting U.S. troops during a Taiwan crisis.[15]

BMD undertakings by Japan would also stand in the way of Beijing's long-term quest for ascendancy among regional states. Cooperation in missile defense might result in greater vitality of the U.S.–Japan alliance, although this outcome is by no means guaranteed. A closer security tie between Tokyo and Washington would at once help sustain U.S. military presence in the Asia-Pacific and encourage the SDFs to play a wider role in contingencies outside Japan. Moreover, acquisition by Japan of antimissile systems that it had never possessed would by definition mean an enlargement of Japanese military prowess, which would by definition run counter to China's desire to preserve military superiority over Japan. This last point would be valid regardless of the possibility, often underlined by Beijing, that collaboration with the United States in defensive systems might contribute to a Japanese offensive ballistic missile program.

North Korea

North Korea, if it survives, will attain the ability to manufacture ICBMs and IRBMs before long, although the timing of their test launches will depend on the state of its relationship with Washington. The U.S. pursuit of homeland defense may marginally accelerate the pace of development, and possibly deployment, of such missiles. It would be safe to assume that Pyongyang will retain deployed MRBMs and SRBMs at least in current numbers, which some estimates put at roughly 100 and 500, respectively.[16] The light-water reactor project by the Korean Peninsula Energy Development Organization (KEDO) probably will not be completed until the end of this decade; consequently, the question whether the North Koreans have indeed produced nuclear weapons and, if so, how many, will long remain unresolved. On the other hand, it is widely assumed that North Korea maintains a large stock of chemical and biological agents deliverable by ballistic missiles.[17]

In a Korean contingency, Pyongyang could use its SRBMs to launch a preemptive strike against U.S. bases and strategic targets in South

Korea, while at the same time threatening the Japanese with an MRBM attack to dissuade Tokyo from providing support to U.S. troops fighting on the peninsula. Japan's hypothetical BMD systems would have virtually no capacity to engage North Korean SRBMs flying toward the South. Nor is it guaranteed that they could effectively defend the Japanese territory if North Korea mobilized its entire MRBM force for an assault against it. Japanese defenses might, however, help detract from the efficacy of Pyongyang's coercion attempt at Tokyo largely through giving reassurance to the Japanese public, much as they could counter intimidation by Beijing. Small-scale missile attacks by North Korea could be dealt with by defensive systems of the SDFs, while larger-scale strikes would be deterred by the U.S. nuclear guarantee. If anything, the relative weight of missile defense in preventing national paralysis in Japan would be greater in a Korean crisis than in a confrontation with China, for presumably it would be harder for U.S. retaliatory threats to have an impact on the more desperate North Koreans.

Should the regime in Pyongyang collapse, Seoul could suddenly come in possession of more than 100 MRBMs (and, conceivably, IRBMs and ICBMs) as well as a large amount of chemical and biological agents (and, possibly, a few nuclear weapons). The unified Korea would also inherit South Korea's SRBMs, whose range Seoul has recently set itself to lengthen.[18] The meaning of such missiles and WMD materials for the security of Japan would be determined, first, by the quantity of each the Koreas would choose to retain, and, second, by the evolution of Seoul's relations with Tokyo and Washington. High tension between Japan and the unified Korea, against the background of a deteriorating U.S.–Korean alliance, would make Seoul's newly acquired ballistic missile capabilities appear as a threat to the Japanese. In that event, BMD systems fielded by the SDFs could assume the role of deterring and responding to missile threats from the entire Korean Peninsula.

Thus, providing crisis reassurance to the populace would represent arguably the most prominent contribution of antimissile systems that Tokyo might acquire, toward the security of Japan. As the foregoing analysis indicates, however, fulfillment of this function would presuppose a high degree of Japanese confidence in the U.S. nuclear guarantee, which in turn could be maintained only by careful management of the overall alliance relationship. Other things being equal, moreover, reassurance of the public would become increasingly demanding as the people begin to sense the gravity of the ballistic missile and other kinds of military threats posed by regional adversaries.

Threat Reduction

Given Japan's hypothetically adversarial relations with Russia, China, and North Korea, a single-minded pursuit of antimissile capacity by Tokyo might give those states incentives to field greater numbers of more advanced ballistic missiles and otherwise increase military threats to Japan. Not only could such a reaction undermine any missile defense capability that Japan might obtain, but it also might seriously complicate the functioning of U.S. extended nuclear deterrence, with the result that reassurance of the Japanese people during a crisis would become more problematic. The net result might well be lesser, not greater, Japanese security than would be the case if Tokyo had desisted from embarking on defensive undertakings.

As described in the previous section, China seems to recognize that Japanese BMD in collaboration with the United States is most liable to interfere with its military and national strategies, both in relation to Taiwan and long-term regional preeminence. North Korea might also wish to offset Japan's antimissile capabilities, because they could impede the attainment of its wartime objectives. By contrast, possessed of an ability to neutralize, with long-range ballistic missiles, any defensive systems that Tokyo might conceivably acquire, the Russians should have little reason directly to counter missile defense efforts by Japan, unless, of course, Moscow came to take an interest in a limited assault with reintroduced theater missiles.

If the Japanese are to advance toward development and deployment of missile defenses, then, diplomatic initiatives to decrease tension with regional adversaries would have to be taken concurrently. Given its avowed enthusiasm for global approaches to disarmament, Tokyo might attempt to contain ballistic missile threats through revitalization of the multilateral nonproliferation regimes for ballistic missiles and WMD. As a matter of fact, the credibility of these regimes has seriously been in doubt, often with direct negative implications for the security of Japan.

For example, although Russia has joined the Missile Technology Control Regime (MTCR) and China has pledged to observe its rules, both have often been cited as suppliers of ballistic missiles and missile technologies. North Korea, also known as a major source of missile proliferation, is outside the MTCR. Having declared its intention to withdraw from the Nuclear Nonproliferation Treaty (NPT), Pyongyang insists that it is no longer formally bound by its provisions, even though the withdrawal has since been suspended. The Comprehensive Test-ban Treaty (CTBT), which has been rejected by the U.S. Senate as well as denounced by the Bush administration, remains to be ratified by Beijing as well, and it has not even been signed by Pyongyang. The North Koreans have not acceded to the Chemical Weapons Convention (CWC), while the Russians have pushed back the date for the destruction of their chemical weapons required under the accord. The United States has been accused of creating unilateral exemptions to the terms of the CWC and of failing to pay dues in time to the multilateral organization in charge of enforcing the treaty. Despite its membership in the Biological and Toxin Weapons Convention (BWC), North Korea allegedly possesses a large stock of biological agents, as has been mentioned. Finally, the international endeavor to draft an agreement to establish verification measures for the BWC has been blocked by the United States.

There is a remote chance that Tokyo may bring about a change in the North Korean attitude toward multilateral agreements on nonproliferation through creative diplomacy for normalizing bilateral relations.[19] Japan acting alone, however, would probably have little leverage in making Moscow or Beijing (or Pyongyang, in usual circumstances) pay more heed to the international norms against ballistic missile and WMD proliferation. Active support from the United States would be indispensable to any efforts to strengthen the global nonproliferation regimes. The Japanese would accordingly continue to expect Washington to reverse its disapproval of the CTBT as well as to underwrite its commitment to the BWC and the CWC more forcefully.

More importantly, the direct benefits from reinforcement of the nonproliferation regimes might be quite limited in terms of reducing ballistic missile threats to the Japanese archipelago. The MTCR, even if its membership were to include Pyongyang and its regulations tightened, would do nothing to constrain deployments of indigenously developed ballistic missiles by Russia, China, or North Korea. Discussion has been conducted on an international accord to control testing and fielding of ballistic missiles, but so far little headway has apparently been made. Under the NPT, moreover, Moscow and Beijing can legally maintain, and almost legally expand, their nuclear arsenals.

In light of this, Japan and the United States would do well to give priority to arms control and confidence-building measures specifically tailored to regional contexts. Every opportunity for bilateral, minilateral, and region-wide security cooperation should be grasped to persuade regional powers that defensive undertakings by Tokyo should not concern them (unless, of course, those powers were harboring an offensive intent). In order for that effort to succeed, potential adversaries must be given assurance that in the absence of provocation, Japan's defenses would not be coupled with the offensive forces of the United States (and possibly those of Japan, as the Chinese profess to fear) to pose a strategic threat to them.

Tokyo and Washington could capitalize on the Chinese antagonism toward Japanese BMD to draw Beijing into discussions for arms control and confidence-building agreements. Moreover, in such talks, Japan's antimissile capabilities, both potential and actual, could be used as a bargaining chip. A limit to the deployment of sea-based systems might be proposed, for instance, in return for a Chinese promise to curtail SRBMs and MRBMs (and IRBMs) targeted on Taiwan and Japan. Beijing might also be asked to increase transparency on its ballistic missile forces and its nuclear strategy. The Japanese and the Americans, for their part, would have to sustain clarity as to their intention in promoting missile defense. In particular, they should make it explicit that they have no desire to make trouble for Beijing by encouraging Taipei to move toward *de jure* independence.[20]

It is important to note, however that arms control and confidence building vis-à-vis China must be pursued from a long-term perspective. Given fundamental divergences in security interests, Tokyo and Washington should not expect too much too soon out of their contact with Beijing. While Japan and the United States insist on a peaceful resolution of the Taiwan question, the Chinese give sovereignty (as they interpret it) precedence over peace. Beijing's inclination for regional preeminence, when manifested in concrete behavior, would naturally be resisted by Tokyo and Washington. On the other hand, for the enhancement of its economic power, which is still its number one priority, China cannot allow such incompatibilities in security interests to ruin its overall relationship with Japan and the United States for some time to come.

For the time being, therefore, the main aim in making an approach to China should be to initiate a learning process through which Beijing might gradually cast off its essentially zero-sum outlook on its relations with Tokyo and Washington to adopt a more positive-sum thinking. The expectation should be that once lured into a substantive discussion on BMD and related issues, the Chinese might become increasingly receptive to more comprehensive negotiations on tension reduction. As China starts to appreciate, through such negotiations, the strategically defensive motives of Tokyo and Washington in building antimissile systems, then it might begin to tolerate Japanese defenses.

A caveat is in order here. The endeavor to bring Beijing around to acquiesce in U.S.–Japan cooperation in BMD should not be complicated by an endorsement of Chinese nuclear buildup. The Chinese would soften their objection to U.S. territorial defense if, as some in the Bush administration appear to favor,[21] Washington sanctioned their possession of enough ICBM warheads to defeat U.S. defenses. Given that sea-based Japanese systems might one day attain the ability to intercept ballistic missiles flying toward the continental United States, such a policy might also help ease Chinese attitude toward Tokyo's defensive undertakings. After all, China will increase its nuclear forces whether or not the United States approves it, and there may be a point in trying to cap the increase by linking it to the level of U.S. antimissile capabilities.

And yet, legitimation of a larger Chinese nuclear arsenal would run a great risk of aggravating vertical and horizontal proliferation of nuclear weapons (as well as ballistic missiles) in the Asia-Pacific region and hence would be unacceptable to the Japanese. Beijing would be given the green light for further expansion of its nuclear and associated ballistic missile forces, both long range and theater, which would prompt India, and then Pakistan, to strengthen their nuclear and missile capabilities. The United States and China are not enemies in the same sense that the Americans and the Soviets were during the Cold War. Unlike the erstwhile Soviet Union, moreover, China has not attained a clear second-strike capability against the United States. Furthermore, there may be promises of reasonably powerful defenses. In such circumstances, strategic stability should be pursued primarily through restraint on offensive nuclear forces rather than an extension of the logic of mutual assured destruction (MAD), which the Bush administration itself professes to renounce.[22]

Meanwhile, sustained efforts ought to be made to further security cooperation with Russia, and the Koreans should not be left out of the picture either. Greater emphasis in Japanese and U.S. diplomacy should be placed on the safety and security of nuclear weapons and fissile materials that exist in the territory of the former Soviet Union. Tokyo and Washington must also take care that their action on BMD and related matters should never lead Moscow to revive its interest in IRBMs, MRBMs, and nuclear SRBMs as well as employment of those missiles to attack Japan. Pyongyang's willingness to engage in a security dialogue of any substance would essentially depend on the general situation in the Korean Peninsula. As long as North Korea remains hostile to Japanese BMD capability, however, Tokyo (and Washington) might be able to use such capability, potential or actual, as a vehicle to drag Pyongyang into a discussion on tension reduction, perhaps in combination with proposals for normalization of diplomatic relationships.

Finally, active consultation with the South Koreans on regional security would help allay whatever concern they may have about the development of Japanese military capacity. It could also serve as a precaution against the rise of ballistic missile threats when the two Koreas reunite.

Alliance Management

Development and deployment of BMD systems by Tokyo, if at all, must be carried out in ways to preserve, and where possible strengthen, the vitality of its overall alliance relationship with Washington. A Japanese antimissile capability bought at the expense of a decline in the reliability of the U.S. commitment to deter and defend against armed attack on Japan could actually decrease Japanese security. Japanese defenses standing alone would have at best limited capacity to deal with ballistic missile attack, and such an attack would represent only one of the many forms of military threats that might confront Japan. Without a U.S. nuclear guarantee perceived as highly dependable, moreover, attempts to provide reassurance to the Japanese people in the face of serious ballistic missile threats probably would not succeed.

In the present security arrangements, the United States extends a nuclear umbrella over Japan and maintains conventional forces in and around Japan to bolster the credibility of the nuclear deterrent and to help defend Japan in case of a deterrence failure. Aside from providing substantial conventional capabilities for its own defense, Japan critically contributes to the regional and global strategic interests of the United States mainly by giving logistical and financial support to U.S. forces based on its soil, which may come into action not only in East Asia and the Pacific but also in the Indian Ocean and the Middle East.

Japan's BMD effort, if accompanied by proper alliance management measures, could significantly enhance the reliability of the U.S. nuclear guarantee and defense commitment. They could tighten the political bond between Tokyo and Washington by broadening the scope of agreement in security interests. The very pursuit of an antimissile shield by Tokyo might impress the Americans as an indication of the resolve of the Japanese to defend themselves and, as a matter of course, U.S. troops stationed in Japan as well. Japanese defenses, when introduced, would have the capacity to extend protection to U.S. forces in some regional contingencies and thereby facilitate their operation.

Moreover, greater integration of the equipment and operation of the SDFs with those of U.S. forces that is likely to result from bilateral cooperation in BMD would represent a more solid alliance tie. Joint development and production of antimissile systems could also draw the Japanese and U.S. defense industries closer. In the process, the Japanese would have a chance to contribute to U.S. homeland defense, because many of the technologies for defense against theater ballistic missiles could be applied to protection against long-range missiles. Japan's role in the defense of the continental United States would become more evident, should Tokyo allow its defensive capabilities to be incorporated in a more comprehensive U.S. BMD architecture.

Several conditions must be fulfilled, however, for Tokyo's BMD undertakings to actually lead to a stronger, and certainly not weaker, bilateral security relationship. Before going into a discussion of these conditions, it must be presumed that the governments of Japan and the United States would coordinate their policies on missile defense and regional security to pursue such threat reduction initiatives as described in the previous section. If such coordination were absent, and, as a consequence, the Japanese came to see that their missile defense efforts in collaboration with the Americans would do more harm than good to their security, then they would not proceed to introduce defensive systems in the first place.

Assuming that this prerequisite is met, the first condition to be satisfied for a firmer alliance tie would be for Tokyo and Washington to fight the impression, underlined by some concerned observers that the Japanese interest in an antimissile shield may itself imply reduced confidence in the dependability of the U.S. nuclear umbrella.[23] Logically speaking, this task should not be particularly difficult to perform. The promotion of defenses has been a response to the presumed growth of threats that cannot be deterred by the prospect of nuclear retaliation, against the backdrop of substantial progress in missile defense technologies. While these trends may somewhat decrease the relative value of U.S. extended nuclear deterrence to the overall security of Japan, they do not necessarily detract from its credibility in relation to threats that can be deterred.

At the same time, it must be recognized that Tokyo would now have slightly greater grounds to question the reliability of the U.S. deterrence and defense commitments from the viewpoint of both "abandonment" and "entrapment" possibilities. On the one hand, infatuation with missile defense displayed by many Americans appears in part to reflect a growing tendency to tolerate no more than negligible loss of life in military engagements as well as a profound aversion to the use of nuclear weapons in regional contingencies.[24] On the other hand, should an effective antimissile shield over the territory of the United States materialize,

Washington might begin to take a more cavalier attitude to armed conflict in the theater and its nuclear escalation.

Instead of engaging in possibly self-immolating debates over such concerns, however, the Japanese and the Americans should focus their attention on the complementary nature of Japan's BMD capability and U.S. extended deterrence. One feature of that nature has already been illustrated in the discussion of the strategic significance of Japanese defenses: antimissile systems of Japan and the U.S. nuclear guarantee could combine to reassure the Japanese public. Moreover, as long as an invulnerable United States is associated with highly credible retaliatory threats, Japan's defensive undertakings might be said to reinforce the U.S. nuclear guarantee to the degree that they assist in making the territory of the United States less vulnerable to ballistic missile attack.[25]

Second, Washington should furnish Tokyo with sufficient information on its BMD policy to make "real consultation" on the subject, as promised by President Bush, possible. The Japanese would like to have a firsthand knowledge of U.S. thinking, among other things, about the nature of ballistic missile threats, the feasibility of antimissile systems in various configurations, the timetable for their development, and the principles of employment after they are deployed. Exchange of views on such topics would always be instrumental to minimizing concern that Tokyo might have over the possibility of abandonment and entrapment as noted earlier.

Close consultation on missile defense assumes added significance now that the Bush administration has put forward a "new framework" for global security. Even though its details have yet to be worked out, the new framework evidently puts strong emphasis on defense (as well as deterrence by the capability of denial), as opposed to deterrence by the threat of nuclear retaliation. In its pursuit, moreover, Washington seeks to integrate programs for missile defense in the theater with those for U.S. territorial defense against long-range ballistic missiles and to accelerate the development of defensive systems including those for boost-phase intercept.[26] Not only would such a turn in BMD policy have substantial implications for security in Asia-Pacific, but it would also confront official Tokyo with a serious constitutional question.

Third, the Japanese government should revise its long-standing constitutional interpretation on the right of collective self-defense. According to Tokyo, Japan as a sovereign state possesses this right under international law, but the *exercise* of this right, which has been defined as the use of force to protect another state in a situation where Japan itself is not under attack, would exceed the necessary minimum for self-defense and hence be impermissible under Article IX of the Japanese constitution. In such a situation, acts that themselves would fall short of the actual use of force but that might nevertheless be viewed as integral to the use of force by another state would be regarded as unconstitutional.[27]

The official rejection by Tokyo of the exercise of the right to collective self-defense would severely constrain U.S.–Japan cooperation in the employment of BMD systems. Interceptors deployed by the SDFs most certainly could not legally be used to shoot down ballistic missiles flying toward U.S. troops operating outside Japan or U.S. possessions in the Pacific, unless Japan was simultaneously being attacked. The Japanese might in fact hesitate even to transmit to the United States, tactical intelligence on such missiles gathered by their radars. Should that intelligence prove critical to the interception of such missiles by U.S. forces, Tokyo would fear, its transmission might appear to be integral to the use of force by the Americans, making it a putative violation of the constitution.[28]

With the growth in capacity of Japanese BMD, the negative effect of the proscription on collective self-defense upon the alliance tie would become increasingly serious. As has already been mentioned, with improvements in the interceptor, and if supported by advanced sensors and radars, antimissile systems on Aegis vessels would in time acquire the ability to deal with ballistic missile threats against the continental United States. True to its constitutional stand, Tokyo could still turn off its sea-based defenses when it learned that enemy ballistic missiles were headed for the United States and not for Japan, but such an action would doubtless do an irreparable damage to its security relationship with Washington. Finally, when defense in the boost phase became reality, the Japanese government might no longer have the time to ascertain the destination of enemy ballistic missiles before deciding whether or not to launch its interceptors.[29]

Fourth, Tokyo and Washington should prevent Japan's pursuit of BMD capabilities from hindering improvements in other elements of the conventional force balance for the bilateral alliance. Development and deployment of defenses including an upper-tier system might well cost Japan more than a few 100 billion yen annually for over a decade.[30] This would be a substantial burden for the Japanese government, in light of the fact that the yearly expenditure for equipment purchases has never exceeded one trillion yen since FY1994. Barring a significant increase in the overall defense budget, which is quite unlikely for some time given the financial difficulties in Tokyo, procurements for antimissile systems could crowd out other important defense items, such as the new medium surface-to-air missile, the aerial refueling plane, the F-2 fighter aircraft, and intelligence satellites. HNS for U.S. troops, which has been touted as the most generous in the world, might also suffer.

Moreover, assignment of BMD-related roles to the SDFs could make it difficult for them to discharge their more traditional responsibilities. For example, Aegis destroyers that would stay in home waters as platforms for antimissile interceptors would not be able to contribute much to the protection of the sea lines of communication in the northwestern Pacific. The Japanese currently possess the PAC-2, which uses a blast fragmentation warhead, and its replacement with the PAC-3, which relies on hit-to-kill technology, might reduce their capability to engage enemy aircraft. In view of these potential problems for the conventional balance, Tokyo and Washington would be advised to coordinate the timing and manner of introduction of missile defenses and make adjustments as appropriate to the roles and missions of their respective armed forces.

Fifth, Japan and the United States should reach a clear understanding on how much integration between their antimissile systems they should aim for. From the standpoint of military efficiency, incorporation of the C3I (command, control, communication, and intelligence) structure of the SDFs into that of the U.S. military not only involving the sharing of the early-warning information but also extending to the creation of a joint BMD command would have much to recommend it. Only with such a high degree of integration, as well as interoperability of the equipment, could the selection of targets for intercept be optimized and flexibility of employment amid the inevitable "fog of war" be preserved. For that to happen, it would first be necessary to streamline the flow of information across different branches of the Japanese forces. Pressure for bilateral integration would accordingly encourage rationalization of the C3I system within the SDFs as well.

On the other hand, Tokyo would probably want to avoid total dependence on the United States regarding the employment of its defenses. Some degree of independence would serve as a hedge against the eventuality that Washington might suspend cooperation or that Japan might unwillingly be drawn into a conflict by a U.S. decision to use force in the region (e.g., in the Taiwan area). In the absence of a change in the official interpretation of the constitution as suggested earlier, the Japanese would worry that complete incorporation in the U.S. system might deprive them of the chances to avoid actions looked upon as constituting the exercise of the right to collective self-defense.[31] A proper balance must be struck, therefore, between integration and independence and, where independence is retained, a robust mechanism for coordinating antimissile operations would be needed.

Finally, the Japanese and U.S. governments should contain disputes over technology transfer and allotment of contracts in the process of developing and producing antimissile systems and their components. Such disputes could cause a great strain on the bilateral relationship, as was amply demonstrated by the FSX controversy in the 1980s. Washington would have to dispel the Japanese suspicion that an emphasis on integration and interoperability might bring only the defense industry of the United States in a position to profit from bilateral BMD cooperation.

Tokyo for its part would need to reconsider its traditional policy of prohibition on the export of weapons and weapons technologies. While supply of military technologies to the United States has specifically been exempted, the embargo could nevertheless hamper joint development of defensive systems because transfer of weapons prototypes would still be proscribed. Since weapons technologies of Japanese origin could not be provided to any state other than the United States, Tokyo's current policy would also constrain the utilization of such technologies by Washington in BMD development programs that it might engage in with a third country.

Conclusion

By way of summary, Japanese BMD including upper-tier interceptors on several Aegis ships, a capability that Tokyo might begin deploying in 10 to 15 years, would not be without strategic significance. Such defenses might have the capacity reliably to engage at most some tens of enemy theater ballistic missiles and much fewer long-range missiles launched by accident or without authorization. They could not therefore effectively protect the Japanese territory against a full-scale ballistic missile attack by Russia, China, or probably even North Korea. In combination with U.S. extended nuclear deterrence, however, Japan's antimissile systems would help provide reassurance to the Japanese public about deterrence and defense against a Chinese and North Korean strike with theater ballistic missiles. A small-scale assault would be dealt with by the defenses, while a larger-scale salvo would be deterred by U.S. retaliatory threats. The defensive systems would accordingly enable Tokyo to minimize the effect of a Chinese threat of missile strike to dissuade it from giving assistance to U.S. forces during a confrontation over Taiwan or a similar North Korean threat in a Korean contingency. Some reassurance about defense against an accidental and unauthorized launch of Russian long-range ballistic missiles would also be possible. It could make the Japanese better able to cope with further deterioration of the control of ballistic missiles and nuclear weapons in the former Soviet Union.

Potential adversaries could respond to Japan's BMD efforts, however, by significantly intensifying their ballistic missile threats. This might neutralize any increase in Japanese defenses, challenge the reliability of the U.S. nuclear guarantee, and thereby create difficulties in reassuring the Japanese populace in a crisis. Promotion of missile defense, therefore, must be accompanied by diplomatic initiatives to achieve threat reduction. Though endeavors to shore up the global nonproliferation regimes would be valuable, greater emphasis should be placed on regional approaches to arms control and confidence building. Tokyo and Washington could trade on China's aversion to a Japanese antimissile capability to bring Beijing into discussions on regional security. Substantive results probably would be possible only over a long haul, however, as the Chinese might gradually alter their worldview.

BMD undertakings would also damage Japanese security in its deterrence, defense, and reassurance aspects, if in the process they came to weaken the overall security tie with the United States. Parallel to the pursuit of an antimissile shield, then, attention to alliance management would be indispensable. Tokyo and Washington must agree on measures to reduce ballistic missile threats in the region and work together to highlight the complementary nature of missile defense and extended deterrence. The United States should as far as possible allow the Japanese to keep abreast of its BMD policy and the strategic framework that would encompass it. It would be incumbent on Japan to modify its official interpretation of the constitution to permit the exercise of the right to collective self-defense, without which bilateral cooperation in the employment of defensive systems would be placed under severe constraints. Tokyo and Washington ought to coordinate their policies so as to avoid a trade-off between the attainment of missile defense capabilities and upgrades in other elements of conventional forces. The question of how much the command and control of Japanese and U.S. defenses should be integrated must be resolved to the satisfaction of both parties. Finally, steps should be taken to avert frictions concerning the flow of weapons technologies as well as the distribution of work between the defense industries of the two countries.

When it comes to military threats, predictions have constantly been belied by reality, and those in this chapter probably will not fare any better. That North Korea may not survive for more than a decade has been pointed out, together with its implications for the security of Japan. In the meantime, China or Russia may undergo a radical transformation in its political outlook or military capacity. Other states or nonstate actors such as terrorist groups may emerge as a prime source of ballistic missile threat to Japan. Nothing demonstrated the volatility and unpredictability of the international environment in this regard more vividly than did the suicide attacks on the World Trade Center and the Pentagon on September 11, 2001. While the terror strikes cut both ways in the missile defense debate in the United States, political support for antimissile capabilities to protect the U.S. homeland has solidified for the time being. At the same time, the emergence of a common enemy has brought Washington and Moscow, and to some extent Beijing, closer together, brightening the prospects for cooperation on strategic issues. The distinctly moderate Russian and Chinese verbal reaction to the U.S. announcement of withdrawal from the ABM Treaty may signal the beginning of a new trilateral relationship concerning ballistic missiles and nuclear weapons. Even so, it will be some time before these and other tendencies since the September attacks will work themselves out for BMD collaboration between Japan and the United States. The threat situation as symbolized by these incidents seem to underscore, however, the necessity for a robust capacity to reassure the public, which could be attained through proper approaches to missile defense, threat reduction, and alliance management.

Notes

1. According to "Shingata iijisukan wo donyu," *Yomiuri Shinbun*, January 6, 2000, the Defense Agency is planning to field the PAC-3 during the FY2001–05 Mid-term Defense Build-up Plan. However, the Mid-term Defense Build-up Plan, which was approved in December 2000, only pledges to "take necessary measures" on BMD. *Defense of Japan 2001* (Tokyo: Urban Connections, 2001), p. 297.

2. Boeicho, *Dando misairu boei (BMD) ni kansuru kenkyu ni tsuite*, July 28, 2000 (http://www.jda.go.jp/j/library/archives/bmd/bmd.pdf) gives an official account of Japan's participation in the NTW research. For a detailed analysis of various issues related to Japanese involvement in BMD, see Michael Swaine, Rachel Swanger, and Takashi Kawakami, *Japan and Ballistic Missile Defense* (Rand Corporation, June 2001). Patrick M. Cronin, Paul S. Giarra, and Michael J. Green, "The Alliance Implications of Theater Missile Defense," in Green and Cronin, eds., *The U.S.–Japan Alliance: Past, Present, and Future* (New York: Council on Foreign Relations Press, 1999); Satoshi Morimoto, Ken Jimbo, Ken Suzuki, and Yoichiro Koizumi, "Theater Missile Defense (TMD) and Japan's Security," *Plutonium*, No. 20 (Winter 1998) (http://www.cnfc.or.jp/pl20/lecture.e.html); Michael O'Hanlon, "Theater Missile Defense and the U.S.–Japan Alliance," in Mike, M. Mochizuki, ed., *Toward a True Alliance: Restructuring U.S.–Japan Security Relations*

(Washington, DC: Brookings Institution Press, 1997); and Yamashita Masamitsu, Takai Susumu, and Iwata Shuichiro, *TMD: Sen'iki dando misairu boei* (Tokyo: TBS Britannica, 1994), chapters 8–10 are also useful.

3. Possible use of Aegis vessels for U.S. homeland defense is discussed in Prepared Statement of Lieutenant General Ronald T. Kadish, USAF, Director, Ballistic Missile Defense Organization on "The Ballistic Missile Defense Program: Amended Fiscal year 2002 Budget" before the Senate Armed Services Committee, July 12, 2001. See also Ronald O'Rourke, "Sea-Based Boost" and "Sea-Based Midcourse," in *Missile Defense: The Current Debate*, coordinated by Steven A. Hildreth and Amy F. Woolf, Congressional Research Service, January 16, 2002.

4. For an overview of the missile defense issue in East Asia, see Monterey Institute of International Studies, Center for Nonproliferation Studies, *Theater Missile Defense in Northeast Asia: An Annotated Chronology, 1990-present*, June 2001 (http://cns.miis.edu/research/neasia/index.htm); Kenneth W. Allen et al., *Theater Missile Defenses in the Asia-Pacific Region: A Henry L. Stimson Center Working Group Report*, Henry L. Stimson Center, June 2000; Robert D. Shuey, Shirley A. Kan, and Mark Christofferson, *Missile Defense Options for Japan, South Korea, and Taiwan: A Review of the Defense Department Report to Congress*, Congressional Research Service, November 30, 1999; and Stephen A. Cambone, "The United States and Theater Missile Defence in North-east Asia," *Survival*, Vol. 39, No. 3 (Autumn 1997).

5. The ICBM usually denotes a ballistic missile with a range greater than 5,500 kilometers; the IRBM between 3,000 to 5,500 kilometers; the MRBM between 1,000 and 3,000 kilometers; and the SRBM below 1,000 kilometers. In accordance with the INF Treaty, all the United States and former Soviet ballistic missiles with ranges between 500 and 5,500 kilometers were withdrawn. For the purpose of this chapter, theater ballistic missiles are assumed to have ranges of no more than 3,500 kilometers.

6. According to the U.S. intelligence community, Russia in 2015 will most likely have less than 2,000 deployed strategic nuclear weapons, most of which will be mounted on ICBMs. Russia currently maintains nearly 4,000 warheads on its ICBMs and SLBMs. National Intelligence Council, *Foreign Missile Developments and the Ballistic Missile Threat through 2015: Unclassified Summary of a National Intelligence Estimate*, December 2001. Moscow proposes that Washington and Moscow should curtail their strategic nuclear arsenals to about 1,500 to 2,200 warheads each. On the other hand, it is widely expected that the Russians will respond to missile defense undertakings by the United States by retaining some of their multiple-warhead ICBMs, which they have agreed to withdraw as part of the second Strategic Arms Reduction Treaty (START II).

7. For an illustration of the potential capacity of NTW to counter long-range ballistic missiles, see Dean A. Wilkening, *Ballistic-Missile Defence and Strategic Stability* (Adelphi Paper 334), International Institute for Strategic Studies, May 2000, pp. 53–58. A somewhat more cautious assessment is given in U.S. Department of Defense, *Summary of Report to Congress on Utility of Sea-Based Assets to National Missile Defense*, June 1, 1999. In a

report released in March 2001, the Pentagon's Office of Operational Test and Evaluation stressed difficulties in modifying NTW to give it the ability to engage long-range ballistic missiles. Wade Boese, "Pentagon Report Highlights Hurdles for Missile Defenses," *Arms Control Today*, Vol. 31, No. 3 (April 2001).

8. For a comprehensive analysis of the Chinese missile forces, see Shirley A. Kan, *China: Ballistic and Cruise Missiles*, Congressional Research Service, August 2000. According to this source, which classifies the DF-4 as an MRBM, China currently has no IRBMs. Sources such as *The Military Balance, 2001–2002* (Oxford/London: Oxford University Press/International Institute for Strategic Studies, 2001); and *Chugoku soran 2000-nen ban* (Tokyo: Kazankai, 2000) place the DF-4 in the category of IRBM. The Defense Agency of Japan apparently makes no distinction between the MRBM and the IRBM when it says: "China possesses approximately 100 intermediate-range missiles whose ranges cover the Asian region including Japan." *Defense of Japan 2001*, p. 52.

9. The U.S. intelligence community predicts that China's long-range ballistic missiles will increase from the current level of about 20 to the range of 75–100 in 15 years. How much of this increase can be attributed to Beijing's concern over U.S. homeland defense is unspecified (National Intelligence Council, *Foreign Missile Developments*). In August 2000, a classified National Intelligence Estimate reportedly forecast that China could deploy up to 200 warheads on long-range ballistic missiles as a response to U.S. homeland defense. Steven Lee Myers, "Study Said to Find U.S. Missile Shield Might Incite China," *New York Times*, August 10, 2000.

10. Alastair Iain Johnston, "China's New 'Old Thinking': The Concept of Limited Deterrence," *International Security*, Vol. 20, No. 3 (Winter 1995/96) gives a detailed account of changing Chinese nuclear outlook. See also Brad Roberts, Robert A. Manning, and Ronald N. Montaperto, "China: The Forgotten Nuclear Power," *Foreign Affairs*, Vol. 79, No. 4 (July/August 2000).

11. For a concise account of China's military and national strategies, see U.S. Department of Defense, *Annual Report on the Military Power of the People's Republic of China: Report to Congress Pursuant to the FY2000 National Defense Authorization Act*, June 23, 2000; as well as Asano Ryo, "Chugoku no gunji senryaku no hokosei," *Kokusai mondai*, No. 492 (March 2001); and Abe Jun'ichi, "21-seiki no higashi ajia anzen hosho kankyo no naka no chugoku fakuta: chugoku no gun kindaika to TMD wo chushin ni," *Shin boei ronshu*, Vol. 27, No. 4 (March 2000). Most of the Chinese criticism at U.S.–Japan cooperation in BMD may be understood as deriving from such strategies. Kori J. Urayama, "Chinese Perspectives on Theater Missile Defense: Policy Implications for Japan," *Asian Survey*, Vol. 40, No. 4 (July/August 2000) enumerates the concerns expressed by the Chinese.

12. One senior-level researcher at a government think-tank in China reportedly warned Japan not to forget that its role in hosting U.S. troops would make it the first target of Chinese missile attack should a U.S.–China military confrontation break out. Urayama, "Chinese Perspectives on Theater Missile Defense," pp. 602, 608.

13. Washington cancelled the NA project in December 2001 shortly after deciding to pursue it as the Sea-Based Terminal program.

14. Michael O'Hanlon, "Why China Cannot Conquer Taiwan," *International Security*, Vol. 25, No. 2 (Fall 2000), p. 81. In an ideal condition, a properly positioned Aegis destroyer might be able to intercept more than 100 ballistic missiles. Normally, however, Aegis ships must be prepared to deal with aircraft and cruise missiles as well.

15. The role of Japanese BMD in countering threats below the threshold is stressed in Cambone, "The United States and Theater Missile Defence," pp. 72–73. It is further asserted that limited deployments of missile defenses by Japan might discourage the Chinese from developing a limited deterrence strategy.

16. Testimony of General Thomas A. Schwartz, Commander in Chief United Nations Command/Combined Forces Command, and Commander, United States Forces Korea before the House Committee on Armed Services, March 15, 2000. See also "Kitachosen nodon 100-ki wo haibi: kankokushi hodo," *Yomiuri Shinbun*, March 2, 2001 (evening edition); and Department of Defense, *Proliferation: Threat and Response*, January 2001, p. 11.

17. Michishita Narushige, "Chosen hanto ni okeru tairyo hakai heiki mondai," in Naya Masatsugu and Umemoto Tetsuya, eds., *Tairyo hakai heiki fukakusan no kokusai seijigaku* (Tokyo: Yushindo, 2000) gives a concise account of the North Korean ballistic missile and WMD capabilities.

18. In January 2001, South Korea announced its decision to develop ballistic missiles with a range of 300 kilometers. An agreement with Washington had restricted the range of Seoul's missiles to 180 kilometers. Mori Chiharu, "Shatei 300-kiro no misairu, kankoku ga kaihatsu sengen; pyon'yan ni totatsu kano," *Yomiuri Shinbun*, January 18, 2001. Seoul has also reportedly signed a contract for the purchase of 300-kilometer range missiles from the United States by 2004. "Seoul to Get New, Longer-Range U.S. Missiles," *International Herald Tribune*, January 5–6, 2002.

19. Izumi Hajime, "Chosen hanto josei no shin-tenkai to kitachosen no 'tairyo hakai heiki,'" *Shin boei ronshu*, Vol. 28, No. 4 (March 2001) suggests such an approach to normalization.

20. Cronin, Giarra, and Green, "The Alliance Implications"; Abe, "21-seiki no higashi ajia"; and Urayama, "Chinese Perspectives on Theater Missile Defense" all propose utilization of Japanese BMD in arms control and confidence-building negotiations with China.

21. David E. Sanger, "U.S. to Drop Its Opposition to Chinese Nuclear Buildup," *International Herald Tribune*, September 3, 2001.

22. The Nuclear Posture Review of the Bush administration is said to advocate "ending the relationship with Russia that is based on mutual assured destruction." "Special Briefing on the Nuclear Posture Review" by J.D. Crouch, Assistant Secretary of Defense for International Security Policy, January 9, 2002.

23. Such concern is expressed in Cronin, Giarra, and Green, "The Alliance Implications," p. 182; Morimoto Satoshi, *Anzen hosho-ron: 21-seiki no kiki kanri* (Tokyo: PHP Kenkyujo, 2000), p. 435; and Michael J. Green and

Katsuhisa Furukawa, "New Ambitions, Old Obstacles: Japan and Its Search for an Arms Control Strategy," *Arms Control Today*, Vol. 30, No. 6 (July/August 2000), p. 19.

24. Such factors behind the U.S. interest in BMD are noted in John Pike, "Theater Missile Defense Programs: Status and Prospects," *Arms Control Today*, Vol. 24, No. 7 (September 1994), p. 11; and Ogawa Shin'ichi, "Beikoku no sen'iki misairu boei (TMD) keikaku," in Morimoto Satoshi, ed., *Misairu boei: kokusai anzen hosho no atarashii kozu* (Tokyo: Nihon kokusai mondai kenkyujo, 2002), p. 79

25. For an inquiry into the relationship between Japan's pursuit of BMD and the U.S. nuclear umbrella, see Umemoto Tetsuya, "Missile Defense and Extended Deterrence in the Japan–U.S. Alliance," *Korean Journal of Defense Analysis*, Vol. 12, No. 2 (Winter 2000).

26. President Bush propounded the new security framework and pledged real consultations with the allies in his May 2001 speech. "Remarks by the President to Students and Faculty at National Defense University," May 1, 2001. The Nuclear Posture Review also dismisses "reliance on offensive nuclear forces exclusive of other forces" and instead emphasizes "synergy of nuclear/non-nuclear [forces] & offense and defense." "Findings of the Nuclear Posture Review" (slides), January 9, 2002, p. 4.

27. For a concise history of the official construction of the Japanese constitution with regard to the right of collective self-defense, see Sakaguchi Kiyoshi, "Shudanteki jieiken ni kansuru seifu kaishaku no keisei to tenkai: sanfuranshisuko kowa kara wangan senso made," *Gaiko jiho*, No. 1330 (July/August 1996) and No. 1331 (September 1996). Sase Masamori, *Shudanteki jieiken: ronso no tame ni* (Tokyo: PHP Kenkyujo, 2001) offers a pungent criticism on the government's interpretation.

28. The constitutional constraints on the supply of information should not be overstated, however. The Japanese government lists as constitutionally questionable only such action as directing the Americans to shoot their interceptors in specific directions and at specific angles, "with the sole purpose of directly assisting the use of force" by them.

29. For an effective operation of Japanese BMD, Tokyo would have to consider change in other aspects of the legal framework of its defense policy as well. In order to deal with the threat of surprise attack, e.g., the SDFs must be permitted to release their interceptors without the so-called defense operation order (*boei shutsudo meirei*). Appropriate rules of engagement (ROEs) against incoming ballistic missiles, presumably including pre-delegation of the authority to field commanders to shoot interceptors in certain circumstances, would be necessary.

30. In 1994, the Pentagon put the research and development and acquisition costs for a Japanese antimissile capability at $4.5 billion to $16.3 billion (between 500 billion and 2 trillion yen, at the average exchange rate in 2001). Malcolm O'Neill, *Ballistic Missile Defense: Options for Japanese TMD*, U.S. Department of Defense, Ballistic Missile Defense Organization, June 13, 1994. More recent "total cost estimates" (presumably including the expenditures for operations and maintenance as well as

research and development and acquisition) of the Japanese government reportedly vary from $10 billion to $50 billion (roughly from 1.2 to 6 trillion yen). Swaine et al., *Japan and Ballistic Missile Defense*, p. 67.

31. Presumably that kind of constitutional concern made Director General Nakatani of the Defense Agency declare in June 2001 that BMD systems that Japan might acquire should be operated "independently" (*shutai-teki ni*). "TMD 'shutai-teki ni un'yo,'" *Yomiuri Shinbun*, June 23, 2001 (evening edition).

CHAPTER 10

PEACEKEEPING AND THE U.S.–JAPAN ALLIANCE

Stephen John Stedman

Can and should peace operations be an integral part of the U.S.–Japan alliance and Asian security cooperation writ large? On the one hand the answer seems obvious. Between 1990 and 2001, Asia was beset by more civil wars and ethnic conflicts than any other region in the world, including Africa. Prospects for large-scale internal violence are rife in several Asian countries.[1] Peace operations have saved lives and contributed to stability in Asia; against extreme difficulties the UNPKO in Cambodia helped bring to an end a war that had killed millions of people, and the prompt intervention in East Timor, led by Australia and supported by the United States, New Zealand, Philippines, and others, saved tens of thousands of lives.[2] Important American officials, including Admiral Dennis Blair, commander-in-chief of the U.S. PACOM, cite communal violence and humanitarian disasters as threats to Asian security and advocate regional training and participation in UN peacekeeping and humanitarian relief operations as a key step toward an Asian regional security complex.[3] In April–May 2001, combined military exercises between the United States and various Asian nations simulated UNPKO during regional disputes; Japanese SDF officers attended as observers.

The events of September 11, 2001 and the war against terrorism add urgency to this long litany of good reasons to make peace operations central to the U.S.–Japan alliance. The rout of the Taliban laid bare the need for a robust peacekeeping force that could provide basic security for the people of Afghanistan. For the first time, policy analysts could make a direct case for the contribution of peace operations to American national security interests. In the absence of a functioning regime that provides order in Afghanistan, the country could revert again to the anarchic state that proved so beneficial to Al Qaeda. For an American military looking to take the war against terrorism beyond Afghanistan, the need for allies to step forward and take the lead in building peace becomes imperative.

This is not the first time that UN peacekeeping has been suggested as an activity to strengthen U.S.–Japan security relations. In 1994, the Carnegie Endowment for International Peace sponsored a workshop between experts from both countries in the hopes of making peace-keeping a component of the partnership.[4] In 1998, Michael O'Hanlon and Mike Mochizuki argued that the United States and Japan "should develop mechanisms for getting Japan's armed forces more involved in international activities—such as humanitarian relief, peacekeeping, hostage rescue, non-combatant evacuation operations, and counter-piracy and counter-terrorism efforts."[5] Japanese scholars and policy makers have put forth a vision of participation in UN peace operations as a means of establishing Japan's bona fides for international leadership and as an important supplement to its alliance with the United States.[6] And in the aftermath of September 11, Japanese leaders sought ways to lessen the limits on SDF participation in peace operations as a means of showing its support to the antiterrorist coalition.

Alliance cooperation and joint training in peace operations and increased Japanese participation in peacekeeping seem to make good sense. So why then the question whether peace operations can and should be an integral part of the U.S.–Japan alliance?

Current trends in peace operations and doctrine, as well as U.S. foreign policy priorities and Japanese domestic political constraints, limit the likelihood that such operations will gain a prominent place in the alliance. Current assessments of peacekeeping performance warn that if states, either as part of regional coalitions or UN operations, are to continue to accept the task of implementing peace agreements in civil wars—the most fundamental responsibility that peacekeeping shouldered in the 1990s—then missions will have to be willing to use coercion to deter or compel likely spoilers of agreements.[7] If the recommendations are accepted, future peace operations will be configured to provide flexibility to force commanders to change from a confidence-building posture to active protection of noncombatants and peacemakers from attacks by predatory factions and militias.

Such assessments and the policy recommendations that accompany them pose a challenge to the major powers, and the United States in particular. If deployed by the UN, new peacekeeping missions will have to be more robust; member states must be willing to risk casualties to their soldiers; and the peacekeeping headquarters in New York will have to be strengthened to provide better strategic analysis of conflicts and better backstopping of personnel on the ground. If deployed by regional "coalitions of the willing," such missions will probably be better capable of using force and acting strategically. But such regional coalitions are only as effective as the capabilities of regional states and are only as legitimate as the norms of the region allow, and these two factors need not be complimentary. Capabilities can be enhanced through contributions by the United States or other major powers, but to the extent that a regional coalition is seen as doing the bidding of the United States and not the region, its legitimacy may suffer.

Recommendations for more robust peace operations run counter to U.S. and Japanese policies toward peacekeeping. The United States, whose support for peacekeeping during the 1990s under President Clinton was half-hearted at best, will have to more strongly embrace peacekeeping. Before September 11, this seemed unlikely under a Bush administration whose rhetoric was hostile to humanitarian intervention, multilateralism, and the UN. Whether the need to stabilize Afghanistan (and perhaps parts of the Philippines) as a part of the war against terrorism alters Bush administration and broader American antipathy to peacekeeping and nation building remains to be seen. Japan, whose participation in peacekeeping is predicated on a dated evaluation of the wisdom of never veering from traditional peacekeeping doctrine and methods, must now consider participation in more dangerous missions that everyone agrees should be able to deploy and use robust force.

To get at the ought and can of making peacekeeping a key aspect of the U.S.–Japan alliance, I begin by discussing whether Asia, the region most important to the alliance, will see a demand for peace operations in the future. I then turn to the evolution of UN peacekeeping in the 1990s, the changing evaluation of its effectiveness, and recommendations for strengthening the institution. I then ask whether there is the likelihood that United States and Japan will make peacekeeping an integral part of the alliance, and conclude that for the foreseeable future a greater alliance role in peacekeeping is unlikely, but not out of the question. Greater and more robust Japanese participation in peacekeeping must be predicated on assurances that the United States will support such participation by strengthening its own commitment to peacekeeping. For Japan to do more, the United States must make a credible commitment to supporting more aggressive peace operations. While this would seem an unlikely scenario, its possibility has increased since September 11.

Will There be a Demand for Peace Operations in Asia?

Given the numbers of internal violent conflicts within Asia, the answer should be obvious: there is and will be a clear need for peace operations in the region. As mentioned earlier, Asia suffered from more violent conflicts in the 1990s than any other continent.[8] Analysts of Asian security note the potential for ethnic and communal violence in Indonesia, Fiji, and elsewhere to create complex, humanitarian emergencies.[9] If any of the long-standing internal wars end, there could be a role for external implementation of peace agreements. Moreover, the peace operations deployed to Asia in the 1990s helped end violence and created opportunities for stability in Cambodia and East Timor. Further, peacekeeping may become wedded to an antiterrorist agenda, certainly in Afghanistan, but also perhaps in parts of the Philippines, if the war against Abu Sayyaf succeeds.

There is a problem, however. There is a glaring discrepancy between the need for possible peace operations and external intervention in Asia and the fact that there have been comparatively few UN interventions in the region. Research undertaken for the World Bank shows that the UN has a distinct bias against intervention (defined broadly as mediation, consent-based peacekeeping, and enforcement) in Asia.[10] That is, given the amount of civil conflicts in Asia, and given how many times the UN has intervened around the world in the 1990s, one would expect to see much more intervention in Asia than has heretofore taken place.

We are left to speculate about why there have been so few interventions in Asia relative to opportunities and relative to elsewhere in the world, but clearly the answer affects whether there will be a true "demand" for peace operations in the future. One answer perhaps resides in conceptions of sovereignty: that Asian states have been much more reluctant to consent to UN mediation and intervention because of their belief that to do so would be incompatible with their sovereignty. Asian regional organizations are much more fundamentally committed to sovereignty and less committed to norms of internal governance, democracy, and human rights than European, Latin American, and even African regional organizations. Another answer suggests that the states of Asia are relatively stronger than war-torn states elsewhere and better able to resist calls for intervention. Many Southeast Asian states were reluctant to play prominent roles in the Australian-led mission to East Timor, for fear of endangering their relationships with Indonesia, a key power in the region.[11] Finally, the lack of UN intervention in Asia probably reflects the ambivalence and hostility that China and the United States feel toward intervention in the region. Since both are potential vetoers of any UN mission and it is common knowledge that neither Perm-5 member supports others mucking about in Asia, it is likely that demands for intervention are censored before even making it to the Security Council.

Thus, the possibility of increased civil violence in Asia does not imply that there will be greater demand for or supply of intervention. At a minimum, the record of few UN interventions in the region suggests that several major changes will need to occur before more peace operations take place. The major powers, including the United States and China, must be willing to advocate more aggressive deployment of peacekeepers, while states within the region must be more willing to concede to such deployment. Absent a fundamental rethinking of sovereignty in Asia and embedding such rethinking in a regional multilateral framework, states in the region will continue to eschew intervention.

The Evolution of UN Peace Operations in the 1990s

Beyond the issue of whether the region will see a demand for peace operations, there is the issue of whether peacekeeping is changing in ways that make it more or less attractive as a policy tool for the United States and Japan.

The development of peacekeeping should be seen in two stages: before and after 1989. Before 1989 one sees a gradual evolution of peacekeeping concepts, demands, and techniques, as well as a continuity of participating countries that trained their troops in the tasks of peacekeeping. The net result of the evolution, learning, and continuity of participants is that one can speak of an explicit UN joint peacekeeping approach; the major troop-contributing countries before 1989 formed a remarkable consensus about what peacekeeping is and when it should be used.

UN peacekeeping was born of necessity; it was an ad hoc response to international crises, where it was believed that the interposition of a military force could create a buffer between warring parties and lessen the military insecurities of both sides. To reduce conflict and enhance security, the force had to be seen as legitimate, neutral, and impartial. Legitimacy came from the consent of the warring parties; neutrality and impartiality were insured by the multinational composition of the force, the fact that it was lightly armed, and by its rules of engagement that strictly limited the use of force to self-defense.[12]

A fundamental change came in 1989 when the UN was asked to assist in the implementation of a peace agreement to end Namibia's civil war and bring that country to independence. By accepting, UNTAG (United Nations Transition Assistance Group) interjected peacekeeping troops into a civil conflict and took on unprecedented tasks such as the cantonment and demobilization of soldiers, voter registration and education, and election assistance and monitoring. Later that year the UN became involved in the Nicaraguan peace process, when it established ONUCA (UN Observer Group in Central America) to supervise the external supply of weapons to internal factions, help disarm one faction, and observe elections.

Since the establishment of UNTAG and ONUCA, UN peacekeeping has been asked to implement civil war settlements in Angola, Western Sahara, Cambodia, Rwanda, Mozambique, and El Salvador. UN peacekeeping has also been used in the former Yugoslavia, Haiti, and Somalia in humanitarian and peace enforcement operations and in East Timor and Kosovo to provide civilian administration. Between 1948 and 1989 the UN deployed 14 peacekeeping missions. From 1989 to 2001, the UN has deployed 39 missions. In addition to UN-led operations, regional organizations and coalitions of the willing have taken the lead in peace operations ranging from Liberia and Sierra Leone to the Caucases, to the Balkans, to East Timor. Most, but not all, of these regional interventions have had the imprimatur of the UN.

The challenges and risks of these missions differ dramatically from prior ones. Most of the missions in the 1990s and today take place in civil wars, which are much more difficult to resolve than interstate wars, and have multiple unprecedented political, humanitarian, and military components.

Dangers of Peacekeeping in Civil Wars

Civil wars are volatile situations for peacekeepers for two reasons. First, if a civil war is to end with the creation of one integral state, then the parties must overcome a daunting security dilemma.[13] They must disarm, establish a new government and army, and no longer pursue their security unilaterally. But in the short term, the arrangements that lead to an end of hostilities are fraught with risks and dangers. If poorly organized and supervised, the integration of armed forces, the cantonment and disarming of soldiers, and the initiation and maintenance of ceasefires can provide opportunities for one side to take advantage of the settlement and seek complete victory. There are incentives for the parties to cheat during implementation out of fear and out of the hope of gaining an advantage at the end of the settlement.

Second, peacemaking in civil wars face challenges from spoilers: leaders and factions who see a particular peace agreement as hostile to their interests and use violence to oppose it.[14] Spoilers may be signatories to an agreement—leaders whose commitment to peace is tactical and do not intend to live up to their obligations. Or the spoilers may be parties who are excluded from an agreement (or exclude themselves) and attack the peacemakers when they attempt to implement the agreement.

These factors—the intense fear that parties bring to implementation and the opportunities for predation—create multiple dangers and dilemmas for missions that have to implement peace agreements in civil wars.

Nonmilitary Aspects of Post-1989 Missions

Compared to early peacekeeping missions, those after 1989 often have "a substantial or predominantly nonmilitary mandate and composition."[15] The implementation of detailed peace agreements requires a much larger and complex agenda for operations, including such nonmilitary functions as: "verification, supervision, and conduct of elections; supervision of civil administration; promotion and protection of human rights; supervision of law and order and police activities; economic rehabilitation; repatriation of refugees; humanitarian relief, de-mining assistance; public information activities, and training and advice to governmental officials."[16] The growth in such civilian tasks for post-1989 missions created greater problems in staffing, logistics, and coordination among tasks.

Military Aspects of the Post-1989 Missions

Not only have the political requirements of post-1989 missions added to the complexity of peacekeeping, but also the military mandates are often more complicated than earlier peacekeeping missions.[17] Assisting parties to demobilize and disarm, enforcing sanctions and no-fly zones, protecting safe areas, delivering humanitarian aid, are often combined under the umbrella of a single peace operation. Such tasks call for different expertise, therefore multiplying force requirements and placing greater demands on command, control, coordination, and communications.

Many of the post-1989 missions have been marred by ambiguous mandates implying that forceful action can be taken to enforce a settlement, without an explicit command or appropriate troops and materiel to use a forceful approach. As I will describe shortly, this is not a problem that can be willed away by saying, "make mandates explicit."

Rather, the problem is that the UN Security Council has had an incentive to proclaim symbolic commitment to enforcement, usually in conjunction with good things like justice, human rights, and accountability, but none of its members has had the incentive to use aggressive coercive strategies that are necessary to enforce peace and attain all good things.

The Assessment of UN Peacekeeping in the 1990s

The first wave of assessments of UN peacekeeping in the 1990s came in the aftermath of Somalia, where the UN intervened without the consent of the warring parties on the ground, committed itself to an ambitious program of peacemaking and state building, and soon found itself under attack from the armed faction associated with General Farah Aideed. As the UN, with U.S. muscle, pursued Aideed, the mission found itself drawn into urban guerrilla warfare. When 18 American soldiers (and over 600 Somalis) were killed in a firefight in Mogadishu, the United States abandoned the policy of confronting Aideed, and pledged to withdraw from Somalia six months later, a pledge it fulfilled.

After Somalia two arguments were common. One contended that the problem was peacekeeping in civil wars: that civil wars were much more dangerous and unpredictable than interstate wars and that the UN should not deploy to them.[18] Such a sweeping assessment ignored that by 1993 the UN had succeeded in bringing peace to Namibia and Nicaragua; its mission to Cambodia was deemed at least a partial success and its mission to El Salvador was on track to end that country's decade-long war. The other argument acknowledged that the UN had achieved success in some civil wars, but lost its way in Somalia when it veered from its traditional strategy of confidence building, based on the traditional precepts of consent, neutrality, and impartiality.[19] Two recommendations followed: only deploy peacemakers in civil wars when consent is present in the form of a peace agreement and when deployed do not use force in anything more than self-defense as this would inevitably lead to a loss of impartiality, neutrality, and consent. The great fear of the time was "crossing the Mogadishu line," where the use of force inexorably leads to the peacekeepers becoming just another of the warring parties.

There were two problems with the assessment, which were apparent to some at the time, but would not be acknowledged by the UN until 1999–2000. The first problem is that a peace agreement in civil war does not solve the consent problem; while it is a much better marker for consent than the absence of a peace agreement, it is still imperfect. Warring parties in civil wars in the 1990s often signed peace agreements for tactical reasons; if the peace process did not bring them closer to their dream of victory, then they reneged on their commitment and withdrew their consent. This was the Angola problem. Moreover, a peace agreement, even if embodying consent between the main warring parties, implies nothing about other actors to a peace agreement who feel excluded or exclude themselves and attack the peace process. This was the Rwanda problem. And second, if warring parties commit gross atrocities against noncombatants, peacekeepers who follow the traditional doctrine will either be completely compromised by inaction or lack of capability, which was discovered in Srbrenica and Rwanda.

Post-Somalia Judgments and U.S. and
Japanese Views of Peacekeeping

Somalia had differential effects on U.S. and Japanese attitudes toward UN peacekeeping. For the United States, Somalia deterred any presidential advocacy for peacekeeping and the UN in general; indeed, in the aftermath of October 1993, President Clinton scapegoated the UN for the failure in Somalia, which strengthened congressional critics of the UN. The net result was the development of Presidential Decision Directive (PDD) 25, which placed extreme restrictions on U.S. support for and participation in PKO. For Japan, the experience of the UN in Somalia reinforced policy makers' rigid doctrinal distinction between peacekeeping and peace enforcement.

Somalia and U.S. Policy Toward Peacekeeping
The United States has historically harbored a deep ambivalence toward international organizations and their activities.[20] This ambivalence can be seen in the equivocal support the Clinton administration provided to the UN in its first term in office. Although Clinton came to power in 1993 rhetorically supportive of assertive multilateralism and UN peacekeeping, its first major policy priorities were domestic: the economy and healthcare. Clinton's foreign policy advisors espoused a broad and ambitious program of nation building in Somalia and advocated the aggressive strategy of confronting Aideed in the summer of 1993. The deaths of the American soldiers in October brought Clinton and his aides face to face with the costs of enforcing peace in a part of the world outside of America's vital security interest. That the president, faced with the costs, chose to withdraw is not surprising, nor that he chose to assign blame to the UN. What is surprising, however, is that the administration

allowed the forthcoming backlash against the UN to affect its overall assessment of peacekeeping as a foreign policy tool.

A recent study of the politics of PDD 25 shows that original drafts of the document embraced peacekeeping as an important task for providing global order and were supportive of UN efforts to expand operations.[21] As the mission in Somalia got bogged down in the war with Aideed, and congressional opposition to the mission and to the UN increased, drafts of PDD 25 were revised to tone down endorsement of peacekeeping. By the time the contents of the document were shared with the public in May 1994, it had become extremely restrictive of U.S. participation in peacekeeping missions and of U.S. support for authorizing peace operations in the Security Council. In the harsh judgment of one critic: "Rather than being designed to strengthen peacekeeping, PDD 25 was designed to avoid any future confrontations with Congress over U.S. support of a UN mission, or participation in such a mission."[22] That same month the United States stalled in authorizing a strengthening of UNAMIR, the beleaguered PKO in Rwanda, to stop the genocide there.

Somalia and Japanese Attitudes Toward Peacekeeping
The debacle in Somalia came a year after intensive, widespread public and government debate about deploying Japanese troops to UN missions. The debate confronted constitutional limitations on the deployment of Japanese troops and their use of weapons abroad. Despite deep-seated reservations about participation in peacekeeping, the Diet passed the the UN Peace Cooperation Law, which mandated five guiding principles for Japanese participation in peacekeeping missions: that the parties to a conflict have agreed to and will maintain a cease-fire; that the warring parties consent to a mission; that the mission displays impartiality; that the Japanese forces use arms only in strict self-defense; and that any breach of these principles will mean a suspension and termination of Japanese participation.[23] Japanese troops participated in UNTAC, the United Nations Transitional Authority in Cambodia, and were subsequently sent to Mozambique, Angola, Eastern Zaire, and the Golan Heights.[24] It should be emphasized, however, that these deployments were limited in number, mandate, and rules of engagement. As one informed observer wrote in 1995, "the fact remains that at present, Japan is hard put to take on traditional peacekeeping tasks."[25]

Japanese views on Somalia reified the strict distinction between peacekeeping and peace enforcement and criticized the mission for its lack of impartiality. In the words of one Japanese scholar, "Since

Japanese insistence on the prior existence of a domestic cease-fire agreement (and the failure of the 'enforced peace' approach in Somalia), international practice has generally moved closer to Japan's position, and this has made it easier for Japan to participate in peacekeeping operations."[26] This pronouncement was problematic in two regards. First, in the eyes of British and French military planners, Japanese insistence on entry conditions associated with traditional peacekeeping put it out of touch with the hard cases of the 1990s.[27] Second, it could not foresee that the UN would reevaluate its experience with peacekeeping in ways that render Japan's participation in PKO more difficult.

Current Assessments of UN Peace Operations

Recent evaluations of UN peace operations, by scholars and by practitioners alike, produce a much more nuanced portrait of UN success and failure in the 1990s.

A study undertaken by Stanford's Center for International Security and Cooperation and the International Peace Academy shows that peace missions vary wildly in terms of their difficulty and the willingness of international actors to implement them.[28] Mission difficulty is associated with eight variables: having more than two warring parties, lack of a robust peace agreement, the presence of valuable commodities, spoilers, hostile neighbors, secessionist claims, a collapsed state, and more than 50,000 soldiers. Of these factors, spoils, spoilers, and hostile neighbors are most associated with mission failure. International willingness is associated with whether a given case is defined by a major or regional power as in its security interest. The more difficult the case, the more coercive a strategy that is necessary and the more resources that are necessary. A troubling gap exists, however, where the UN intervenes in difficult cases, but where no great or regional power defines the case in its security interest. The net result is failure, sometimes catastrophic, as in the case of Rwanda in 1994 or Angola in 1993.

What jumps out of the data is the fact that the UN's earliest successes in peace implementation occurred in the least difficult cases: Namibia (1989), Nicaragua (1989), and El Salvador (1990–94). Each of these cases scored low in conflict difficulty and moderate to high on international will. Possibly because there was so little variance in peacekeeping context, all the lessons that were learned from these cases tended to emphasize the effectiveness of one universally applicable strategy. As a consequence, peacekeepers emerged with the belief that traditional peacekeeping—impartiality, neutrality, and consent—and its theoretical underpinning of confidence building could be successfully applied to any case or mandates. This overconfidence in the ability of the UN to implement peace agreements led to overcommitment. Between 1991 and 1994, the UN authorized implementation missions to Angola, Cambodia, Guatemala, Mozambique, Rwanda, and Somalia devoting relatively little apparent thought to the extent to which these cases resembled those where the earlier successes took place. In short order, and with the exceptions of Guatemala and Mozambique, the UN found itself in much more dangerous situations using inappropriate strategies, without adequate resources. The ensuing failures were dramatic and costly: in response to the genocide in Rwanda, the UN withdrew its peacekeepers; in response to attacks on safe havens in Bosnia, the UN allowed the Bosnian Serbs to overrun Srebrenica, where they proceeded to kill thousands of unarmed Bosnian men.

As mentioned earlier, in the case of Somalia, where the UN followed a coercive strategy, it interpreted its experience as a failure of strategy—that coercion is incompatible with peace implementation. Just as it ignored context in the case of success, it ignored context in the case of failure. By the end of 1993 the UN updated its selection of strategies based on their relative success, that is, it employed more frequently those strategies that experience had shown to be the most successful. Because the strategy associated with the most difficult case—coercion—had the lowest success rate, the UN found itself applying strategies suited to relatively easy missions in every case, with the effect of reducing the organization's overall success.

Under the leadership of Kofi Annan, the UN looked hard at its weaknesses. At the Millennium Summit of September 2000, a special commission on the future of UN peacekeeping, the so-called Brahimi panel, presented a far-reaching, scathing analysis of UN peacekeeping in the 1990s. Noting that the UN's worst failures, Rwanda in 1994 and Srebrenica in 1995, stemmed from the inappropriate application of the traditional peacekeeping doctrine to situations marked by massive atrocity and genocide against noncombatants, the panel argued forcefully that future UN operations must be configured to allow peacekeepers to stop such atrocities if they arise in the course of the mission. The panel made the issue of spoilers a central challenge that must be confronted head on. The panel recommended that honest assessment of mission difficulty and the commitment of adequate resources by member states need to happen before the Security Council authorizes a peacekeeping mission.

UN peacekeeping is at a crossroads where the member states have to decide whether they will make major changes in how it operates to allow it to be effective. The Brahimi Commission's assessment of peace operations differs radically from previous assessments. It turns the post-Somalia assessment of peacekeeping doctrine on its head. The key question is whether the recommendations of the commission will be implemented and whether the member states are willing in the future to authorize missions with a resolve that if spoilers emerge, the peacekeepers have the resources, personnel, strategy, and commitment to defeat them.

The New Assessment and Current U.S.–Japan Policies Toward Peacekeeping

The new assessment of peacekeeping is unlikely to create the basis for greater U.S. and Japanese support for peacekeeping. Nor is it likely that peacekeeping will become a more integral activity of the alliance. At best peacekeeping and humanitarian relief will provide opportunities for joint training and preparedness exercises, but politicians will balk at the increased deployment of missions.

The United States and Peacekeeping in 2001

Although public opinion data show that American citizens support the UN and peacekeeping, Congress has shown little tolerance for expansive multilateralism, strengthened international organizations, or more frequent peacekeeping. Although such intolerance forms a significant impediment to making the UN an integral aspect of American foreign policy, presidents who are willing to put forward a clear, consistent rationale for American support of international organizations can limit the ability of Congress to obstruct internationalist policies. President Clinton never attempted to articulate such a rationale; indeed, his early scapegoating of the UN gave credence to the more virulent anti-internationalist strains in Congress. The behavior of Clinton and his foreign policy team toward the UN recalls earlier ambivalence of American presidents toward the institution. A common reading of American voters in the past rang true in the 1990s: Americans who support the UN do not reward politicians who support the UN, while Americans who oppose the UN do punish those politicians who support it.[29]

The Bush administration foreign policy began office deeply critical of the UN and unsupportive of intervention abroad. It spoke of strengthening regional capacities to respond to civil violence, but disputes have already emerged over whether the administration will continue to fund regional peacekeeping initiatives in Africa. The rhetoric of key members of the administration, including Secretary of Defense

Rumsfeld and Vice-President Cheney, bolstered those in the military and Pentagon who believe that peacekeeping is an activity that detracts from its ability to do its real job of deterring and preparing to win major wars.

Within this context it is understandable why the Brahimi Report was applauded in Washington. The report's insistence that before any proposed mission is deployed, it must have member-state commitment to the doctrine, strategy, troops, and resources necessary to succeed resonates with Congress's desire to reduce the number of peace operations. If Brahimi is implemented there will likely be fewer peace operations in the future, and these will either be in easier contexts, such as in Ethiopia and Eritrea, or where the mission is led or backstopped by a regional or Great Power that has a security interest in a given country, such as Kosovo. It is unlikely, however, that the Bush administration will increase its financial support of the institution to strengthen the ability of UN headquarters to provide better support for any prospective missions.

The recommendations of the Report also find much support within the U.S. military. Based on its experience in Somalia, it had already decided that its involvement in implementing the Dayton Accords would be based on ample force projection to deter possible spoilers. Based on its present experience in Kosovo, NATO, Great Britain, and the United States are changing their peace operations doctrines to include spoiler management. But the very commitment to ramping up the force requirements for missions is likely to decrease their number. How many Kosovo-size and -type missions can the United States realistically commit to in the future?

It was only in the aftermath of the defeat of the Taliban in Afghanistan that the Bush administration grudgingly perceived the necessity for peace operations and the desirability of UN and allied participation in such operations. In November 2001, Pentagon officials explicitly ruled out American participation in peacekeeping in Afghanistan and limited the early deployment of allied troops to conduct humanitarian missions. In December, it gratefully applauded Britain's initiative in organizing the initial deployment of peacekeepers to Afghanistan, but supported Northern Alliance demands that the mission be small in number and limited to Kabul. By the end of January, Bush officials spoke of a greatly expanded force of up to 25,000 troops, supported by American intelligence and logistics. As the American stake in rebuilding Afghanistan became clear, American commitment to what the Bush administration previously dismissed as nation building grew. Whether this signals a sea change in American support and leadership in peacekeeping writ large remains doubtful.

Japan and Peacekeeping in 2001

For Japan the issue of peacekeeping goes to the heart of its desired identity as a Great Power. Observers in the early 1990s often noted that Japan's choices about participating in peacekeeping would define its identity as either a special type of state with restrictions on what it can do in the military realm (and that will therefore pursue a "niche" foreign policy) or as an evolving Great Power that is moving toward greater military engagement in peacekeeping.[30]

As long as Japan holds to an outdated assessment of peacekeeping, it need not face this choice; it will remain, in Akiki Fukishima's words, "a global civil power."[31] Japan has historically been a key financial contributor to peacekeeping; its monetary outlays to the UN for peacekeeping are second only to the United States. But if it insists that traditional tenets of neutrality, impartiality, and consent are essential for its participation in peacekeeping, it will always lag behind the personnel contributions of other powers and its refusal to put its soldiers at risk will be duly noted by others.

The Brahimi Report raises key issues for Japanese participation in future peace operations. Given the constraints on Japanese policy makers to authorize the participation of Japanese soldiers in traditionally configured peacekeeping missions, will such participation be likely if missions are planned and conceived with the possibility of using lethal force to deter or compel possible spoilers? Will such participation be likely if the UN endorses a much different notion of impartiality than that inferred by traditional peacekeeping? Will the Japanese public accept the deployment of its soldiers to potentially risky and dangerous situations? It is telling that the key issue that Japan has most closely associated itself with in peacekeeping debates concerns strengthening the protection of UN personnel in peacekeeping and humanitarian operations.

Afghanistan may prove a telling case. In the aftermath of September 11, in putting forth special antiterrorist legislation the Cabinet promised to extend humanitarian assistance to Afghanistan and surrounding war-affected countries. Noticeably absent was the mention of possible SDF participation in peacekeeping or peacebuilding operations in what would be a dangerous theater where consent of the parties could prove ephemeral and the need for aggressive enforcement likely.

Asia and Peacekeeping in 2001

A final consideration places the debate on peacekeeping and the alliance into the larger regional context. If domestic restraints on the deployment of Japanese troops into more dangerous peace operations were overcome, would this be greeted by the rest of Asia as a welcome change?

This seems unlikely for historical reasons and for the reasons for which Japan's use of force would be directed. Historical memories of Japanese aggression have dampened the enthusiasm about strengthening Japan's military role in the region, but, as some of our authors have argued, given the desire for a stronger balance against a growing and more powerful China, there are incentives for accepting a redefined Japanese role in the region's security. But to support a greater military role for Japan as an interstate balancer does not easily transfer into support for a stronger, more assertive Japan willing to intervene in civil conflicts in the region. Such a role for Japan is much more likely to aggravate potential concerns over sovereignty and fuel historical grievance.

Some may contend that such resistance can be overcome by embedding a greater Japanese role in peacekeeping within a regional, multilateral framework. But this assumes a region that has gone a far way in embracing changing norms of sovereignty and intervention. Unlike regional frameworks that call for an expanded Japanese military role in traditional interstate balancing, regional regimes for peacekeeping, conflict prevention, and humanitarian intervention require fundamentally different types of norms centered on democracy, good governance, human rights, and domestic conflict prevention. On these scores, not only does ASEAN and the ARF lag behind the EU and the OSCE, but they also trail behind the Organization of American States and the Organization for African Unity.

Conclusion

Arguments that peacekeeping can be an integral part of the U.S.–Japan alliance ignore domestic constraints that render both powers deeply ambivalent toward peacekeeping. Ironically, proposed reforms with regard to how the UN conducts peacekeeping are likely to make peacekeeping a less attractive fulcrum for strengthening the alliance. Policy prescriptions for limiting the number of peacekeeping missions deployed by the UN and for strengthening those missions to be able to overcome the resistance of spoilers may alleviate the concerns of some critics of peacekeeping in the U.S. Congress. By mandating more robust responses to violent challengers on the ground, these prescriptions will increase the fear of casualties that will be suffered by future peacekeepers and strengthen the resistance of Japanese citizens and politicians opposed to military participation in UN peacekeeping.

One could argue that regardless of the authorization and deployment of future operations in Asia or elsewhere, peacekeeping and humanitarian response provides a useful rationale for joint training and preparedness operations for the U.S.–Japan alliance. But at the point of deployment to a real civil war, whether for humanitarian reasons, or to implement a peace agreement, or to rebuild states as part of a war against terrorism, one has to wonder if the American doctrine of how to carry out peace operations, now more closely attuned to UN recommendations, will be acceptable for Japanese participation.

Notes

1. For a survey of potential ethnic problems within Asian states, see Michael E. Brown and Sumit Ganguly, eds., *Government Policies and Ethnic Relations in Asia and the Pacific* (Cambridge: M.I.T. Press, 1997).
2. For a comprehensive evaluations of the UN experience in Cambodia see Trevor Findley, *The United Nations in Cambodia* (New York: Oxford University Press and SIPRI, 1995); Michael Doyle, *UN Peacekeeping in Cambodia: UNTAC's Civil Mandate* (Boulder, CO: Lynne Rienner, 1995) and Steven Ratner, *The New UN Peacekeeping* (New York: St. Martin's Press, 1995). For an overview of the Australian-led mission to East Timor, INTERFET, see Alan Ryan, "Primary Responsibilities and Primary Risks," Land Warfare Study Center, Duntroon, Australia, November 2000.
3. Dennis C. Blair and John T. Hanley, Jr., "From Wheels to Webs: Reconstructing Asia-Pacific Security Arrangements," *The Washington Quarterly*, Vol. 24, No. 1 (Winter 2001), pp. 7–17.
4. The workshop produced an edited book: Selig S. Harrison and Masashi Nishihara, *UN Peacekeeping: Japanese and American Perspectives* (Washington DC: Carnegie Endowment, 1995).
5. Michael E. O'Hanlon and Mike M. Mochizuki, "A Liberal Vision for the U.S.–Japanese Alliance," *Survival* (Summer 1998), pp. 127–134.
6. See Kiyoshi Sugawa, "Time to Pop the Cork: Three Scenarios to Refine Japanese Use of Force," CNAPS Working Paper, Brookings Institution.
7. *Report of the Panel on United Nations Peace Operations*, United Nations Document A/55/305-S/2000/809, August 21, 2000. The Report is known colloquially as the Brahimi Report, named after the Chairman of the Committee, Lakhdar Brahimi. For an analysis of the Report and its critics, see Stephen John Stedman, "Brahimi and Its Discontents: The Future of United Nations Peace Operations," in *A Global Agenda: Issues Before the United Nations, 2001–2002* (Lanham, MD: Rowman and Littlefield and the United Nations Association of the United States; 2001), pp. 1–7.
8. Margareta Sollenberg, *States in Armed Conflict 1998* (Uppsala, Sweden: Department of Peace and Conflict Research, 1999).
9. Blair and Hanley, Jr., "From Wheels to Webs."

10. Michael Gilligan and Stephen John Stedman, "Where Do the Peacekeepers Go? Determinants of UN Intervention in Civil Wars," paper prepared for the World Bank Project on Economics and Civil Wars. This point is also made by James Cotton, "Against the Grain: The East Timor Intervention," *Survival*, Vol. 43, No. 1 (Spring 2001).

11. See Ryan, "Primary Responsibilities," pp. 41–52.

12. Overviews of the genesis of UN peacekeeping can be found in Paul Diehl, *International Peacekeeping* (Baltimore, MD: Johns Hopkins University Press, 1993) and William J. Durch, ed., *The Evolution of UN Peacekeeping* (New York: St. Martin's Press, 1993).

13. Stephen John Stedman, *Peacemaking in Civil War* (Boulder, CO: Lynne Rienner, 1991), p. 15. The fullest exposition of the security dilemma and its implications for civil war termination is Barbara Walter, "The Critical Barrier to Civil War Settlement," International Organization, Vol. 51 (Summer 1997). See also Barbara Walter and Jack Snyder, eds., *Civil War, Insecurity and Intervention* (New York: Columbia University Press, 1999).

14. Stephen John Stedman, "Spoiler Problems in Peace Processes," *International Security*, Vol. 22, No. 2 (Fall 1997).

15. Ratner, The New UN Peacekeeping, pp. 22–23.

16. Ibid, p. 23

17. Donald C.F. Daniel, "Is there a Middle Option in Peace Support Operations?" in *Managing Arms in Peace Processes: The Issues* (Geneva: United Nations Institute for Disarmament Research, 1996).

18. Alan James, "Peacekeeping in the Post Cold War Era," *International Journal*, Vol. 1, No. 2 (1995).

19. The most important statement of this belief is in Boutros Boutros-Ghali, *A Supplement to the Agenda for Peace*.

20. The best work to date on American views of international organizations is Edward C. Luck, *Mixed Messages: American Politics and International Organizations, 1919–1999* (Washington, DC: Brookings Institution, 1999).

21. Michael G. MacKinnon, *The Evolution of U.S. Peacekeeping Policy Under Clinton: A Fairweather Friend?* (London: Frank Cass, 2000).

22. Ibid., p. 106.

23. Ibid., pp. 61–65.

24. For overviews of Japanese participation in peacekeeping, see L. William Heinrich, Jr., Akiko Shibata, and Yoshihide Soeya, *United Nations Peacekeeping Operations: A Guide to Japanese Policies* (Tokyo: United Nations Press, 1999).

25. Aurelia George Mulgan, "International Peacekeeping and Japan's Role: Catalyst or Cautionary Tale?" *Asian Survey*, 1995, p. 1115.

26. Makoto Iokibe, "Japan After the Cold War," April 1997. The article can be found on the internet: http://www.jcie.or.jp/thinknet/insights/iokibe.html.

27. Mulgan, "International Peacekeeping and Japan's Role," p. 1113.

28. Stephen John Stedman, "Implementing Peace Agreements in Civil Wars: Lessons and Recommendations for Policymakers," New York, May 2001, IPA Policy Paper Series on Peace Implementation. The complete findings of

the project will appear as Stephen John Stedman, Donald Rothchild, and Elizabeth Cousens, eds., *Ending Civil Wars: The Implementation of Peace Agreements* (Boulder: Lynne Rienner, 2002).

29. Luck, *Mixed Messages*, pp. 254–279.
30. See, e.g., Takashi Inoguchi, "Japan's United Nations Peacekeeping and Other Operations," *International Journal*, Vol. L, No. 2 (Spring 1995), p. 336.
31. Fukishima, chapter 11 in this volume.

Chapter 11

UN Peacekeeping Operations and Japan's Role in Retrospect and Prospect: A Possible U.S.–Japan Cooperation

Akiko Fukushima

The Cold War divide paralyzed the function of the UN Security Council—the core UN collective security mechanism based on the consensus of the five permanent members. Since the five permanent members of the UN Security Council were divided into two camps of East and West, it was almost impossible to garner consensus on issues of any importance on peace and security.

Meanwhile, the world was not free from armed conflicts during the Cold War. The UN, with its collective security paralyzed, created peacekeeping operations, which were not originally conceived in the UN Charter. This is a measure between Chapter 6 and 7 of the UN Charter, sometimes called the Chapter 6 and half measure. This operation first started by supervising a fragile truce in the first Arab–Israeli war in 1948 and later came to be known as peacekeeping operations (PKO). During the Cold War, peacekeeping missions were sent to different corners of the world, preventing local conflicts from escalating into a major war between the two superpowers. During the first 40 years of the UN, 13 PKO were established.[1]

Immediately after the end of the Cold War, the demise of the East–West divide provided hope that the UN, and above all its Security Council, would finally emerge from its paralysis and function in the manner originally conceived by the drafters of the UN Charter. This hope was reflected in the number of new PKO launched starting in 1988, which amounted to 41 as of September 2002.[2] This initial hope has proven, however, to be short-lived. The UNPKO peaked in 1993, with the total deployment of UN military and civilian personnel reaching more than 80,000 from 77 countries. The number of new UNPKO declined toward the end of the 1990s due to failures in some operations such as the United Nations Operations in Somalia II (UNOSOM II), when its mission was combined with peace enforcement tasks that eventually were not accomplished.

There were several reasons behind the failures. Immediately after the Cold War, member states' hope for the functioning UNPKO, even to the extent of using force to stop gunfire and to expel rebel leaders, rise. As a result peacekeepers in some cases were sent even when there was no peace to keep. Missions with different mandates from its make-up were doomed to fail. In turn member states were disappointed to learn the limit of UNPKO and are now less willing to contribute their troops to it.

The downward trend in peacekeeping missions has reversed itself at the end of the 1990s. New missions like the United Nations Mission in Sierra Leone (UNAMSIL), United Nations Transitional Administration in East Timor (UNTAET), United Nations Organization Mission in the Democratic Republic of Congo (MONUC), and United Nations Mission in Ethiopia and Eritrea (UNMEE) were dispatched in the second half of 1999. In these missions, the UN have included peace-building tasks in addition to traditional peacekeeping missions. In the light of a wider scope of missions beyond peacekeeping, these are called "peace operations" or "peace support operations." In this chapter, cognizant of possible peace enforcement measures required for civil-war type conflicts in the twenty-first century, operations are phrased as peace operations unless it refers specifically to PKO.

Cognizant of new challenges to UN peace operations, the UN Secretary General Kofi Annan created the Panel on United Nations Peace Operations to review the need for new peace operations responding to the need of the post–Cold War world. The Report of the Panel released in 2000 made recommendations for member states, including the United States and Japan, to consider.[3]

Meanwhile during the timeframe of the 1990s, Japan, triggered by its bitter experience of being criticized for not physically participating in the 1990–91 Gulf War despite its significant financial contribution, has decided to contribute to UNPKO more substantially. Domestically, Japan introduced the Law Concerning Cooperation for United Nations Peacekeeping Operations and Other Operations (hereinafter referred to as the International Peace Cooperation Law) in June 1992 in order to make participation in PKO constitutional. With the enactment of this law, Japanese participation in UNPKO in the 1990s started with high hopes in the United Nations Transitional Authority in Cambodia (UNTAC) from 1992 to 1993. Japan has since continued to contribute to various missions including UN Operations in Mozambique (ONUMOZ), and the UN Disengagement Overseer Force (UNDOF) in the Golan Heights. Standing at the dawn of a new decade in the twenty-first century, Japan, however, is sending its forces only to the UNDOF. Its participation in East Timor after its referendum upto summer 2001 was minuscule. Japan has sent three civilian police to the United Nations Mission in East Timor (UNAMET) from July through September, and also sent a contingent of the Air SDFs to Surabaya and Kupang in November to transport aid commodities provided by the UNHCR for East Timorese displaced persons in West Timor, Indonesia.

This chapter begins by reviewing the challenges of UN peace operations in the 1990s and in the twenty-first century. Special attention is paid to Japanese participation or lack thereof in UNPKO in the 1990s and domestic factors behind Japan's decisions. The chapter then delves into what barriers, real and imagined, lay behind Japanese participation in peace operations. Finally the chapter develops an idea for U.S.–Japan collaboration in peace operations in the Asia-Pacific, where a regional security institution, like that found in Europe, is lacking.

Challenges Faced by Peace Operations

The UNPKO were first established in May 1948 when the UN Security Council decided to send a mission to supervise a fragile truce in the first Arab–Israeli war. Over a half century, 54 UNPKO have been established, of which the majority was created after the end of the Cold War. The end of the Cold War released the valve of ethnic confrontations, which were suppressed during the East–West confrontations. As such, many conflicts, mostly intra-state, erupted in different parts of the world, demanding UN dispatches.

In hindsight the UNPKO are the stepchildren of the UN collective security system born during the Cold War, when the collective security mechanism failed to function. Logically, PKO should have ceased to exist after the end of the Cold War when the Security Council's paralysis melted. The evolution of PKO in the post–Cold War era was termed as "the forced development of peacekeeping" by Marrack Goulding.[4] It was a forced development by the sheer need to tackle civil-war type conflicts among different groups by ethnicity, religion, and other factors, sometimes triggered by new national borders drawn as a result of the collapse of the Communist bloc and by a demand for self-determination after the end of the Cold War.

Over the years, the nature of UNPKO has evolved to meet the demands of international peace and security in a changing political landscape. The first generation of PKO is now called "traditional" PKO, involving two types. One is by military observers who are unarmed officers of member states that have been tasked to monitor whether parties observed armistice agreements. The other type of traditional PKO is conducted by troops contributed by member states with the mission to carry out tasks similar to military observers but often in fact to act as a buffer between hostile parties.

Around the end of the Cold War new elements were incorporated into UN peacekeeping missions. First, post-conflict peace building involving civilians have been introduced, ranging from election monitoring, civilian police, return of refugees, disarmament, demobilization, and re-integration (DDR) to civil administration. An early example is the United Nations Transition Assistance Group (UNTAG) in Namibia. A more recent example is UNMEE, which was established in July 2000 to observe the cease-fire agreement between Elitoria and Ethiopia.

Another variation of PKO that emerged in the 1990s was "preventive deployment" to advert potential conflicts from occurring, as exemplified in United Nations Preventive Deployment Force (UNPREDEP) in 1995.

Also attempted in the 1990s were enforcement measures included in peacekeeping missions. This was the case in UNOSOM II in Somalia, which was mandated to act on violations of the cease-fire and disarmament, by force if necessary. Similarly, United Nations Protection Force (UNPROFOR) in Bosnia Herzegovina was tasked to realize the withdrawal of armed forces from a "safe zone." Both UNOSOM and UNPROFOR were unable to achieve their missions. After these failures, multinational forces like Stabilization Force (SFOR) and Implementation Force (IFOR) began conducting operations that involved enforcement measures.

The expansion of PKO to include peace enforcement measures was in response to the change in the nature of conflicts, which are now more civil in nature and cause massive human suffering. Missions in the 1990s had to be dispatched to places where cease-fire agreements were not in place or where cease-fire agreements were ignored. Peacekeepers often faced failed states or collapse of states in conflict-ridden locations and actions by local groups, sometimes irregular forces and militias who ignore or violate humanitarian norms.

Although peace-building operations are on the rise, one should not dismiss the fact that military personnel and the military structure remain the backbone of most of the operations, even though the civil content, like civilian police officers, electoral experts and observers, deminers, human rights monitors, and specialists in civil affairs and communications continues to grow.

In the 1990s and beyond, conflicts are more intra-states rather than interstates. Since parties to conflicts are groups within states, they are harder to identify and thus negotiating lasting agreements is difficult. Causes of conflicts are varied and often are a combination of factors of greed and grievances. The lack of clear organizations has complicated the peace operations required, going beyond conventional PKO. Operations are thus called multifunction peace operations.

The UN Secretary General Kofi Annan has been aware of the changing demands on UNPKO and created the aforementioned Panel on United Nations Peace Operations. He instructed the Panel to make recommendations for change based on world needs. Panel's report on August 17, 2000 cynically noted, "United Nations operations thus did not deploy into post-conflict situations but tried to create them." It has also emphasized the need for preventive action and peace building along with the continued needs for peacekeeping.[5]

The fact that the international community has started to refocus on the benefits of PKO should not be overlooked. The UN has created new missions since 1999, such as the United Nations Interim Administration Mission (UNMIK) in June 1999, United Nations Mission in Sierra Leone (UNAMSIL) in October 1999, United Nations Transitional Administration in East Timor (UNTAET) in October 1999, United Nations Organization Mission in the Democratic Republic of the Congo (MONUC) in December 1999, and United Nations Mission in Ethiopia and Eritrea in July 2000. Accordingly personnel dispatched to missions have started to increase again from the second half of 1999. The UN is planning to send its post-conflict peacekeeping missions to East Timor and Afghanistan. In the light of the security challenges in the twenty-first century, UN peace operations itself ought to evolve further to include a whole spectrum of activities encompassing the entire cycle of disputes and conflicts.

Japanese Participation in Peacekeeping Operations in the 1990s

In the 1990s, as noted in Japan's Ministry of Foreign Affairs Diplomatic Blue Book, Japan has identified UNPKO as one important area of cooperation for international peace and security.[6] The Japan Defense Agency (JDA) and SDF also recognize PKO as important for contributing to international peace as described in their annual white paper, "Defense of Japan."[7]

Since the enactment of the International Peace Cooperation Law in 1992, Japan has contributed to PKO in Angola, Cambodia, Mozambique, El Salvador, the Golan Heights, and East Timor. Japan has also contributed to international humanitarian relief operations for Rwandan refugees and East Timorese as shown in table 11.1.

In fact, Japan's first substantial participation in a UNPKO, though in the civil department, was in 1989 prior to the enactment of the International Peace Cooperation Law. The first mission included 27 electoral observers dispatched to the UNTAG in Namibia.[8] The dispatch of SDF personnel had to wait for the passage of the International Peace Cooperation Law. Immediately after the enactment of the Law, Japan sent 600 SDF personnel and 8 military observers to UNTAC, which was the largest dispatch for Japan since the end of World War II. Naturally Japan's participation in UNTAC in Cambodia attracted a lot of press attention. Based on the International Cooperation Law, Japan participated in PKO in Angola, Cambodia, Mozambique, El Salvador, and East Timor. Despite the upbeat beginning of the 1990s with UNPKO in Cambodia, as of August 2001, Japan is dispatching forces only to United Nations Disengagement Observer Force (UNDOF) in the Golan Heights. In terms of the scale of its participation, Japan's zeal for UNPKO seems to have waned.

Why did it wane? Partially it is in line with the decline of new peacekeeping operations dispatched by the UN toward the end of the 1990s. It is also due to some domestic constraints and debate in Japan, which will be described in the following section.

Constraints on Japanese Participation in UN Peacekeeping Operations

Constraints of the Past

Japan's participation in UNPKO has long suffered from an underlying tension between the country's general support for the UN as reflected in its "UN-centered diplomacy"[9] and its deep-seated reluctance to use military force after World War II. Obviously major barriers still exist for Japanese participation in PKO. The first is Japan's historical legacy, which is reflected in neighboring countries' concerns about Japan's initiatives in the field of security. The second is Japan's pacifist's orientation, which is manifest in the strong public support for Article 9 of the

Table 11.1 Japanese participation in United Nations Peacekeeping Operations under the International Peace Cooperation Law (as of August 2000)

	Area of contribution	Duration	Number of personnel	Primary activities
United Nations Angola Verification Mission II (UNAVEM II)	Electoral observers	September to October 1992	3 persons	*Monitoring to ensure fair conduct of presidential and legislative elections
United Nations Transitional Authority in Cambodia (UNTAC)	Military observers	September 1992 to September 1993	8 persons on two occasions	*Monitoring the storage of collected weapons and cease-fire observance
	Civilian police	October 1992 to July 1993	75 persons	*Advising and supervising police in administrative work
	Troops (engineering units)	September 1992 to September 1993	600 persons on two occasions	*Construction of roads, bridges, etc.; supply of fuel and water to UNTAC division
	Electoral observers	May to June 1993	41 persons	*Monitoring to ensure fair conduct and management of elections for the Constituent Assembly
	Staff officers	May 1993 to January 1995	5 persons on two occasions	*Performing operations planning at ONUMOZ headquarters and coordinating transportation
United Nations Operation in Mozambique (ONUMOZ)	Troops (Movement Control Units)	May 1993 to January 1995	48 persons on three occasions	*Technical coordination and allocation of transportation

Table 11.1 *Continued*

	Area of contribution	Duration	Number of personnel	Primary activities
	Electoral observers	October to November 1994	15 persons	*Monitoring to ensure fair conduct of presidential and legislative elections
United Nations Observer Mission in El Salvador (ONUSAL)	Electoral observers	March to April 1994	15 persons on two occasions	*Monitoring to ensure fair conduct of presidential and legislative elections
Humanitarian Relief Operations for Rwandan Refugees	Troops (Refugee Relief Units)	September to December 1994	283 persons	*Humanitarian assistance in such domains as medical services, sanitation, water purification
	Troops (airlifting units)	September to December 1994	118 persons	*Transport of supplies and personnel for the refugee relief unit and others
	Liaison and coordination personnel	September to December 1994	About 10 persons on several occasions	*Liaison and coordination activities with UNHCR and related organizations
	Staff officers	February 1996 to the present	2 persons on five occasions	*Public relations of UNDOF headquarters; planning and coordination of transport and maintenance work
United Nations Disengagement Observer Force (UNDOF)	Troops (Transport Units)	February 1996 to the present	43 persons on ten occasions	*Transport of food, storage of supplies in storage areas,

Table 11.1 *Continued*

				road repair, and maintenance of heavy equipment, etc.
	Liaison and cordination personnel	February 1996 to the present	4 to 6 persons on several occasions	*Liaison and coordination activities for the SDF unit and staff officers with related organizations
	Polling supervisors	September 1998	25 persons	*Conferring with and advising the cairperson of each polling station; verifications of procedural instructions
International election monitoring activity in Bosnia and Herzegovina	Election observers	September 1998	5 persons	*Monitoring to ensure fair conduct and management of presidency elections, etc. in Bosnia and Herzegovina
	Liaison and coordination personnel	August to September 1998	4 persons	*Liaison and coordination activities for the supervisors and observers from Japan with the OSCE and related organizations
United Nations Mission in East Timor (UNAMET)	Civilian police	July to September 1999	3 persons	*Advising the Indonesia police in discharging their duties
	Liaison and coordination personnel	July to September 1999	3 persons on several occasions	*Liaison and coordination activities for the civilian police officers from

Table 11.1 *Continued*

	Area of contribution	Duration	Number of personnel	Primary activities
				Japan with the Indonesian government and related organizations
Humanitarian Relief Operation for East Timorese Displaced Persons	Troops (airlifting units)	November 1999 to February 2000	113 persons	*Transport of UNHCR humanitarian relief items
	Liaison and coordination personnel	November 1999 to February 2000	6 persons on several occasions	*Liaison and coordination activities with UNHCR and related organizations
International election monitoring activity in Bosnia and Herzegovina	Polling supervisors	March to April 2000	11 persons	*Supervision of several polling stations during the municipal election
	Liaison and coordination personnel	March to April 2000	6 persons	*Liaison and coordination activities for the supervisors from Japan with the OSCE and related organizations

* The Maritime and Air Self-Defense Force contingents provided transport and secondary support operations in Cambodia, Mozambique, and the Golan Heights.

nation's constitution. These two factors combined have complicated the Japanese domestic debate on whether or not Japan should send its forces to UNPKO.

The sensitivity of Japanese dispatch of SDF personnel to overseas missions was reflected in a letter of application for UN membership back in 1952, when then Foreign Minister Okazaki stated, "Japan will accede to the obligations stated in the UN Charter and abide by them by all means at its disposal from the day of its membership." This statement was made on the understanding that due to the constraints of Article 9 of the National Constitution, Japan would not be able to participate in the collective security mechanisms provided for in the UN Charter. Making an explicit reservation to this effect was a possibility considered at the beginning.

Japan's application to the UN coincided with the outbreak of the Korean War setting the scene for intense debate over Japan's role in the deployment of UN forces. In order to conform with Article 9 of the constitution, it was thought that some form of constraint would be imposed upon Japan's membership, and in particular the debate focused on overseas deployment of Japan's SDF.

In the end it was decided that Japan would not be obliged to do, as stated in the application, what was beyond its means. Thus, the application letter did not explicitly mention the reservation to this effect. As a result, some ambiguity was left for the future as to how Japan could participate in UN activities.[10]

After becoming a UN member, the Japanese government was requested to send SDF officers to the UN Observation Group in Lebanon (UNOGIL) in 1958 to assist in monitoring the flow of weapons. The government turned down the request on the grounds that the SDF law did not include UN duties.[11] The question of how far Japan could participate in UN collective security activities was debated frequently in the Diet since the 1950s. The Japanese government's position in such Diet debates was that it did not rule out the possibility of participation in all activities of UN forces, that there were several types of UN forces, and that Japan might be able to participate in UN forces that did not require the use of force.[12]

In December 1982, the UN General Assembly adopted a resolution on "Strengthening UN Peace-keeping Functions," which requested member states to continue their efforts in strengthening the functions of the UN. When appropriate, member states were "to take into account opinions of research institutions and intellectuals" and to report these results to the secretary general. Accordingly, at the request of the Ministry of Foreign Affairs, a group of seven prominent Japanese individuals headed by Ambassador Shizuo Saito was appointed to study this subject. As a result, a recommendation entitled "Strengthening UN Peace-keeping Functions" was completed in 1983. Regarding "the role that Japan should take" Part II of the report stated, "up until today, Japan's participation in PKO has been limited, and prone to be restricted to financial cooperation."[13] The report went further to outline seven steps Japan should take in order to play an increasingly proactive and extensive role in international PKO. These steps included providing financial and equipment support, participating in election monitoring activities, participating in medical activities, participating in communication and transportation activities, participating in civilian police activities, participating in logistical support, and participating in patrol activities. This report, however, was discussed at the Diet and Part II was not supported and not submitted to the UN.[14]

Despite these sensitivities in the Diet, Japan started to explore international contribution commensurate with its economic power, partly because of "free rider" criticisms it received from overseas, as well as due to its own desire to play a significant role not only in global economic affairs but also in international political affairs. The UN was a natural venue for Japan to find its international role. If Japan took its own initiatives in the field of peace and security, neighboring countries would ponder whether Japan is returning to a path for regional military power. If Japan's contribution is within the realm of the UN, it gives a certain comfort to Asian neighbors. Japan continues to pay a high price for its pre- and World War II historical legacy.

After 1988, the Japanese government decided, in order to contribute to the UN peace and stability efforts, to commit civilian personnel resources to UNPKO, and sent one political officer to each of the UN Good Offices Mission in Afghanistan and Pakistan (UNGOMAP) and to the UN Iran–Iraq Military Observer Group (UNIMOG). Japan also sent 31 election monitoring personnel to the UNTAG in Namibia. However these dispatches have been undertaken on the basis of the Establishment Law of the Ministry of Foreign Affairs and the so-called dispatch law (Law on Personal Treatment in Dispatching Administrative Grade Civil Servants), which are normally applied in cases where civil servants are dispatched to work in international organizations. The scale of such participation has been rather limited.[15]

The Battle for Peace in the Diet: Adopting the Law
Concerning Cooperation for United Nations Peacekeeping
Operations and Other Operations
In the wake of the Gulf crisis in 1990, Japan was asked to dispatch personnel to contribute to the UN peace and security efforts. Although Japan contributed financially during the Gulf War, it could not contribute

physically. It became imperative for Japan to establish an appropriate legal framework that would permit Japan to participate in such UN efforts.

The initial "UN Peace Cooperation Law" bill failed to be approved when it was brought before the Diet in the midst of the Gulf War. However, after the Gulf War, the International Peace Cooperation Law did pass and was enacted in June 1992. This law provided a legal framework that enabled Japanese personnel, including SDF units, to participate in UNPKO. Since the enactment of the law in 1992, Japan has sent personnel to six UNPKO and two international humanitarian assistance activities. Japanese personnel still continue to serve in UNDOF as described in the preceding section.

While Japan has made a substantial contribution to UNTAC in the beginning of the 1990s by dispatching 600 SDF personnel, at the end of the decade Japan is participating only in UNDOF. During this decade, the Japanese government was criticized for being slow in responding to the dispatch request for its personnel to UNPKO. Domestic politics seem to have made it difficult to participate in some UN missions in the 1990s. For example, when Yasushi Akashi, the head of UNPROFOR (UN Protection Force in the former Yugoslavia) and UN Secretary General Boutros Ghali appealed to the Japanese government for SDF personnel to be dispatched for preventive deployment on the border between Macedonia and Serbia, the International Peace Cooperation Headquarters (IPCHQ) of the Japanese government felt that it should be able to send SDF. At that time, however, the Japanese government was led by a loose coalition of eight political groups including the Japan Socialist Party, which opposed SDF participation. Since the main goal of the coalition was to push through political reforms, which was more or less electoral reform, it could not afford to consider a proposal that would antagonize its coalition partner; so Japan did not send the SDF to Macedonia.

Japanese participation in UNPKO since 1992, thus, has been made with cautious deliberations. The Japanese government is keen to make sure that SDF personnel, and for that matter civilians, are not involved in combat. If dispatched personnel are injured or killed by gunfire, it hits the headline. If they are injured or killed by other reasons like traffic accidents, it does not hit the headlines. As a result, decision on dispatching the SDF consumes a great deal of time and effort, as officials from the IPCHQ and MOFA labor to convince politicians that the risks to Japanese personnel are minimal. Politicians, particularly Socialist members, subject each proposal to intense scrutiny in order to ensure that the conditions of the International Peace Cooperation Law are met to the letter. Thus, some argue the relative degeneration of the whole matter into Official Development Assistance (ODA) focused operations rather than risking lives for human security and for ending civil strife.

Meanwhile when the International Peace Cooperation Law was enacted, it was stipulated that the Law be reviewed after three years. The Law was amended in June 1998, after a delay. Under the revised Law, Japan is now able, under certain conditions, to take part in election observation activities in post-conflict regions executed outside the framework of UNPKO as well. Thus, the scope of the Law has been widened, and Japan subsequently has dispatched election officers and observers to Bosnia and Herzegovina during the months of August and September of 1998 when it was conducted by the OSCE. Moreover, the Law was revised so that Japan can make material contributions to humanitarian relief activities conducted by international organizations such as UNHCR, even in situations where a cease-fire agreement is not in place. Another important amendment was related to the use of weapons. Under the original law, the use of weapons was left to the discretion of individual officers in the field and the use was not permitted except under unavoidable circumstances where the individual officer's life was in danger. Under the revised law, officers belonging to units of the SDF must follow, in principle, the orders of a senior officer present on the spot. However, the revised law failed to "de-freeze" the so-called core activities normally carried out by infant battalion of peacekeeping forces.

Beyond the International Peace Cooperation Law
In considering Japan's role in PKO in the twenty-first century, the most important task that needs to be addressed is the "de-freezing" of the so-called core activities to be carried out by units of Japan's SDF.[16]

The "core activities" were worded in such a way that the International Peace Cooperation Law would conform to the provisions of Japan's constitution. Therefore, the de-freezing of core activities did not create any constitutional problems. UNPKO normally do not envisage enforcing peace, but are carried out with the consent of states and parties concerned after a cease-fire agreement is in place. Peacekeeping missions are only lightly armed since they are not expected to carry out combat activities. Legally there should be no problem for Japan regarding participation in PKO after the de-freezing of core activities. All that is necessary is political will for participation.

With current constraints, Japan's participation has sometimes been called "passive participation" (Shokyoku Sankashugi).[17] Mere de-freezing will not remove Japanese constraints on participation in UNPKO. Since UNPKO enlarges its scope to wider peace operations, as noted earlier, Japan must eventually revisit the question of its constitution, particularly whether or not it can exercise its right to collective defense or not.

In fact the report released in fall 2000 entitled "The United States and Japan: Advancing Toward a Mature Partnership" by INSS of National Defense University has referred to "Japan's prohibition against collective self-defense [as] a constraint on alliance cooperation. Lifting this prohibition would allow for closer and more efficient security cooperation." The report noted that the decision lies with the Japanese people but it also noted, "Washington must make clear that it welcomes a Japan that is willing to make a greater contribution and to become a more equal alliance partner."

The INSS report further described "the special relationship between the United States and Great Britain as a model for the alliance." Among the elements that are required for this arrangement, the report mentioned "full participation in peacekeeping and humanitarian relief missions. Japan would need to remove its 1992 self-imposed restraints on these activities so as not to burden other troop contributing nations to peacekeeping."

Japan must also take into account that several Third World nations actively seek to provide infantry battalions to PKO as this is an easy way for some of them to earn hard currencies. It can be said that there is no desperate need for Japan to send a large number of infantry battalions. Instead, the trend is for developed nations to look after engineering, telecommunication, and transportation activities of PKO in view of their financial and technical strengths. In order to be considered a major player in PKO however, it would be important for Japan to assume the post of commander or deputy commander of such operations, taking charge of command and control, and intelligence activities. It is often the case that such posts are taken up by countries that have contributed the largest number of infantry battalions. Therefore as long as Japan maintains its freeze on the involvement in core activities, it may be difficult for Japan to assume such posts.

As mentioned earlier, mere de-freezing of core activities will not suffice for future Japanese participation in PKO. Regarding the manner of troop deployments, after de-freezing the core activities, a gap will exists between Japan's five principles on PKO and the UN's principles.

There are three principles guiding UNPKO. They are the consent of the local parties, impartiality, and the use of force only in self-defense as pointed out by the Report of the Panel on United Nations Peace

Operations.[18] Impartiality for UN operations means adherence to the principles of the UN Charter. The Panel report mentioned here also alluded that "in the context of modern peace operations dealing with intra-State/transnational conflicts, consent may be manipulated in many ways by local parties. A party may give its consent to United Nations presence merely to gain time to retool its fighting forces and withdraw consent when the peacekeeping operation no longer serves its interests."

The five principles of PKO as embodied in Japan's International Peace Cooperation Law are somewhat in line with the UN's previous five principles, described in the report of Dag Hammersjold. These are: (1) existence of cease-fire agreement, (2) impartiality and nonintervention (in order to ensure this, the UN requires the prior consent of all states and parties involved in the conflict, (3) noncoercion, (4) the use of weapons only in cases of self-defense and (5) maintenance of the international character of the operation.[19] Japan's five principles are: (1) a cease-fire must be in place between the warring parties, (2) the parties to the conflict and the host country must have given their consent to the operation, and to Japan's participation in it, (3) the operation must be conducted in a strictly impartial manner, (4) Japan's participation may be suspended and personnel or troops withdrawn, if any of the mentioned conditions cease to be met, and (5) the use of weapons shall be limited to the minimum necessary to protect the lives of the personnel. These principles ensured that Japanese personnel would not engage in activities that could be deemed to violate Japan's constitution. Whenever there is danger that Japanese peacekeepers might be obliged to resort to the use of force, the Japanese personnel or troops are withdrawn from the PKO. It was important to ensure that the activities of the Japanese personnel or troops would not be identified with the use of force.

Some of Japan's five principles will have to be reviewed in view of the recent evolution of UNPKO. Also, the discrepancies between Japan's five principles and UN five principles might complicate Japan's future participation in UNPKO.

The condition of a cease-fire agreement as a prerequisite for Japan's participation ensures that Japanese troops are not involved in the use of force. These conditions have been embodied in the International Peace Cooperation Law. With the increase of intra-state conflicts after the end of the Cold War, it is becoming harder to identify the parties to armed conflicts, and thus to have cease-fire agreements in place. One may note that this point was included in Dag Hammersjold's five principles but omitted in the recent UN three principles. For example in the case of United Nations Transitional Administration in East Timor (UNTAET), there was no cease-fire agreement, and consequently Japan was not able to send its SDF units.

Gaining consent for PKO by the parties to a conflict is also not easy though it is one of the conditions for Japan's participation. One may observe that the way Japan interprets this principle is more restrictive than how the UN is actually implementing it. In the case of UNDOF, the UN obtained consent from Israel and Lebanon only, but it was necessary for Japan to independently seek the consent of Syria in order for Japan to dispatch troops. In the case of Cambodia, consent from the Khmer Rouge could not be secured. The consent of the Supreme Council, however, made it possible for Japan to send contingents from the SDF. It is becoming harder to identify such parties in the case of intra-state conflicts because they sometimes include militias and private soldiers. In the future there may be more such cases wherein the identification of the parties to a conflict will be difficult. There is a need for Japan to consider revising the International Peace Cooperation Law so that consent for Japan's participation in a PKO will be the same as the consent the UN obtains for conducting operations.

Above all the argument enrolled around the use of weapons bears a different character compared to the principle of self-defense developed in the three UN principles. The use of weapons, at present, is permitted only to protect the lives of Japanese peacekeepers, the so-called A Type use. Article 24 of the International Peace Cooperation Law provides, ". . . an international peacekeeper may use small arms only under unavoidable circumstances in which one finds his/her life in danger or in a situation wherein another peacekeeper's life is in danger along with one's self, and is believed to be sufficient reason to defend one's life or body, or the life and body of another peacekeeper. Under these circumstances weapons can be used within the limits thought logically necessary to respond to such a situation."

Under the UN practice, the use of weapons for "self-defense" includes the so-called B Type use for the purpose of dealing with situations hindering the execution of missions. The discrepancy between the two types will also have to be adjusted. The UN's concept of self-defense was laid out in the secretary general's memorandum at the time of United Nations Peacekeeping Force in Cyprus (UNFICYP) operation.

When Japanese government officials explained the details of the International Peace Cooperation Law to UN officials, the latter commented that they understood the circumstances under which Japan had to start with Type A use, but pointed out that eventually this would not be allowed to continue. As a matter of fact, during the United

Nations Transitional Authority in Cambodia (UNTAC) operation, the Japanese SDF logistical troops stationed in Takeo were not legally allowed to protect the safety of Japanese election observers in the area. Therefore, they opted to patrol the area under the pretext of information gathering, hoping that they would be able to protect the Japanese election observers with the A Type use of weapons.

Most countries normally have their infantry troops carry out "protection" duties, such as protecting rear-support logistical personnel, which are so-called Type B. The shift from Type A to Type B uses would not be possible simply by amending the International Peace Cooperation Law, but might require the amendment of Japan's constitution, as a result of the governmental "unified view" on the issue submitted to the Special Committee on Peacekeeping Operations of the House of Representatives on September 27, 1991.

The use of force and the right to exercise collective defense must be debated and sorted out in light of the fact that peace operations required in the twenty-first century can be more broad and complex and may need peace enforcement to tackle intra-country conflicts that involve radical groups. Or even short of fighting, an ability to use force may be needed for persuasion during the peacemaking phase.

An early de-freezing of the core activities is desirable, in view of the fact that a basic understanding already exists on this question among the coalition government parties. If de-freezing occurs without constitutional revision, however, the deployment of SDF units will need to be restricted to areas where the probability of a resumption in hostilities is low.

In fact it was reported on August 19, 2001 that the Japanese government, which is reviewing Japanese participation in UNPKO, decided that it would de-freeze and relax the criteria for use of force for Japanese peacekeepers. This change will be prepared as a revision of the International Peace Cooperation Law. This move will be taken in light of the independence of East Timor next year and peace operations to be initiated anew in which Japan wishes to take an active part.[20]

Moreover, aside from the legal adjustments required, the Japanese government also needs some organizational adjustments. Currently, the Japan Defense Agency (JDA) does not regard deployment of its forces in PKO as one of its primary duties. PKO are placed in the same category as the Antarctic Mission and rescue activities in cases of earthquake, volcanic eruptions, and the like, under Article 100 of the Self Defense Forces Act. As such, there is no independent budget specifically allocated for international contributions, such as participation in the UNPKO. At present, such operations fall under the jurisdiction of the International Division of the Bureau of Defense Operation, and the expenses for such operations is looked after by the division's working budget without prejudice toward the implementation of the primary duties of the agency.

Public Opinion on Japanese Participation in Peace Operations

Future Japanese participation in peace operations will also be influenced by public opinion. According to regular opinion surveys conducted by the Prime Minister's Office of the Japanese government, those in favor of Japanese participation in PKO was 45.5 percent in 1991[21] and 48.4 percent in 1994,[22] while 18.8 percent were against it in 1991 and 10.8 percent in 1994. There is a steady increase in those favoring participation and a steady decrease against.

Public opinion polls by Japanese newspapers have reported more significant changes in the participation of SDF in UNPKO. When the Japanese government submitted the aforementioned bill on Japanese cooperation in UNPKO during the Gulf War, which failed to pass the Diet, the majority of the Japanese polled were against the bill. According to the survey of the *Asahi* newspaper, 58 percent were against the bill while only 21 percent were in favor. Immediately after the passage of the International Peace Cooperation Law, the opinion survey of *Asahi* newspaper showed 36 percent in favor and 36 percent against the law, exactly the same percentage of people polled in favor and against. After the Japanese participation in UNTAC, according to the *Yomiuri* newspaper poll, 55 percent were in favor of the law.[23]

The *Yomiuri* newspaper's opinion poll in 1997 revealed that 74 percent of those polled were in favor of dispatching Japanese peacekeepers to UNPKO while 17 percent were against such a move.[24] In a separate set of opinion polls conducted by the *Yomiuri* newspaper in 2001, 69 percent of those who polled responded that the dispatch of the SDF to PKO is in line with the spirit of the Japanese constitution and does not entail any problems, while 19 percent responded that it was problematic. Immediately after the passage of the International Cooperation Law in June 1992, 56 percent had responded that such activities were problematic. After ten years, the Japanese public seems to have come to support Japanese dispatch of SDF in PKO much more than at the time of the enactment of the Law.[25]

U.S.–Japan Cooperation on Peace Operations in the Asia-Pacific

This book on the occasion of the fiftieth anniversary of the U.S.–Japan alliance examines the need to update the U.S.–Japan alliance, including the possible expansion of Japan's regional and global military and peace-keeping role. In fact, Article 1 of the U.S.–Japan Security Treaty alludes to the strengthening of the UN as one of the basic objectives of the Treaty and expressed that the Treaty is based on the framework of the UN's Charter.

On the other hand, during the Cold War, neither Japan nor the United States were very active in the peacekeeping field, but for different reasons. Both have started to engage in UNPKO but lag behind countries like Canada, Sweden, and Norway, who have been top runners in peacekeeping. Since both countries due to different reasons started to be engaged in UNPKO, peacekeeping can be one possible area for U.S.–Japan cooperation, among the conceivable forms of cooperation in the security arena of the twenty-first century.

Why is there need for U.S.–Japan cooperation in the sphere of peace-keeping operations? Do the United States and Japan find their respective interests served in peacekeeping cooperation? If peacekeeping operations are to be conducted in the region, for instance in Myanmar, North Korea, Western China, what will be the feasibility of U.S.–Japan collaboration in peace operations?

There are several motivating factors for the United States and Japan to collaborate on UN peace operations and regional peace operations. First, both are top contributors to the UN budget. It is natural for the two to initiate required missions and collaborate to be cost-effective in the UN peace operations globally.

While the Cold War East–West confrontation recedes in other parts of the world, Asia continues to suffer from the vestiges of the Cold War and from traditional type interstate conflicts but may also face new challenges from post–Cold War intra-state instabilities and conflicts. History has proven that such conflicts, albeit intra-state, in the post–Cold War setting may frequently spill over national boundaries and affect the surrounding region, sometimes the globe. It follows that security in the twenty-first century requires transnational cooperation, inter alia U.S.–Japan cooperation.

The UN Security Council, according to the UN Charter, is the last place for transnational cooperation on international peace and security. The Charter drafters envisaged regional institutions to work on regional issues and if they fail, it was the responsibility of the Security Council to find ways to solve conflicts. The Security Council was initially conceived not to work on conflicts and crisis one after another directly but to work only on major conflicts, letting regional institutions attend to local conflicts.[26] The reality has, however, reversed and regional institutions often involved themselves in conflicts along with the UN, or when they saw a potential or real paralysis of the UN Security Council.

The UN, additionally, has not paid much attention to security issues in East Asia because it has devoted most of its time and energy in Africa, the Middle East, South Asia, and Latin America. It might be because three countries in East Asia are members of the permanent five of the Security Council, which leaves only a little room for the Security Council to deliberate and influence security in this region.

Lacking substantive regional security institutions, Asia has relied upon the UN as the agency of intervention in conflict-ridden areas. The UN, however, has shown its own limitations in engaging in unexpected situations, for instance, a consensus among the P-5 are sometimes hard to get, as in the case of Kosovo. It is also hampered by noninterference in domestic jurisdictions, as articulated in Article 2-7 of the UN Charter, while many of the post–Cold War conflicts have been and will continue to be internal civil-war types.

While Europe has its regional institutions like NATO, OSCE, and EU, Asia does not have a regional framework to rely on for regional peace operations in case there is a need. When the UN, inter alia the Security Council, cannot adopt a resolution to intervene, the region does not have any means to obtain legitimacy for regional intervention in an intra-state conflict. Under those circumstances concrete and effective PKO, when United States and Japan can play its respective as well as cooperative role, may prove to be even more necessary.

Possible U.S.–Japan Cooperation Explored in the 1990s
As a matter of fact, during the 1990s, both the United States and Japan explored a possible peacekeeping collaboration. One such example culminated in a book coedited by Masashi Nishihara and Serig Harrison.[27] The book suggested three types of cooperation. The first case called for the United States to provide rear-area support for Japanese missions. For example, in case Japan participates in the former Yugoslavia, the United States can provide support. A second case called for Japan to provide rear support to U.S. missions. The third case called for Japan and United States to engage in a joint mission.[28]

Regarding peace operations in the 1990s, Japan started the decade with high hopes in Cambodia with the dispatch of 600 SDF personnel, which was Japan's first and to date largest deployment of military personnel since the end of World War II and the decade ended like a small toss stick at East Timor. In between there was an attempt to set up a joint peacekeeping training center in Kuala Lumpur or in Singapore. Masashi Nishihara suggested that Japan be a sponsor of a Joint Peacekeeping Operations Training Center.[29] However the idea did not pan out.

For the United States, the 1990s opened with the triumph of the Gulf War and the dispatch to Somalia for peace enforcement under subsequent assertive multilateralism of President Bill Clinton. However, this surge of interest in UN peace operations degenerated to PDD 25, which was a policy of cautious participation to UNPKO and a zero causality policy of U.S. soldiers at the end of the decade. Program for cooperation in the PKO in Asia, not to mention that with Japan, did not bear fruit.

Another example of yet unrealized U.S.–Japan cooperation is as follows. While the United States is sensitive in placing its forces under UN command, Japan is sensitive in sending its troops to PKO, which may involve use of force. Thus some have argued that the two countries should use high technology and support maritime and air transport. Others are critical of this idea because it seems to suggest that poor countries should provide ground troops, which would face more danger, while rich countries merely offer transport and construction. It is essential for big powers to share risks as well. [30]

Ways Ahead

Standing at the dawn of the twenty-first century, Japan and United States are exploring modes of new cooperation and capitalizing on its bilateral alliance. Amongst many options we can take, cooperation in peace operations is one avenue to pursue.

The ultimate goal might be to build an institutionalized framework of regional governance of peace operations. In the immediate future, East Timor, which plans to move to independence, may provide a testing ground for such cooperation since it continues to require multi-function support for its peace and stability as well as nation building from the international community. Also the simultaneous terrorist attacks in the United States on the World Trade Center in New York and Pentagon in Washington DC on September 11, 2001 signals a new type of threat other than war and demands multilateral cooperation to counter such attack.

U.S.–Japan cooperation does not need to start on a large scale. It can begin in a less institutionalized manner. Cooperation can take several avenues toward the apex of an institutionalized regional governance of peace operations. One is joint training of peacekeepers or future peacekeepers. While peace operation missions will be different for each conflict, there is universal training required for peace operations, particularly PKO (on human rights, international human rights law, theory and practice of PKO, etc.). Joint training will enable the United States and Japan to deploy their peacekeepers swiftly in case of need. The forementioned Report of the Panel on United Nations Peace Operations (the so-called Brahimi report) recommends that "the first 6 to 12 weeks following a ceasefire or peace accord are often the most critical ones for establishing both a stable peace and the credibility of a new operation. Opportunities lost during that period are hard to regain." This holds true for the Asia-Pacific and training will pave the way for prompt deployment. Furthermore when the Japanese constraints mentioned earlier are removed, training can include joint exercise on the ground, at sea, and in the air, including peace enforcement measures.

This bilateral joint exercise can gradually include other countries interested in similar training and can eventually develop as regional peacekeeping training. In fact, the United States has proposed a scheme of multilateral humanitarian assistance and peacekeeping exercise in the Asia-Pacific. This is called the Team Challenge and intends to multilateralize bilateral exercises that the United States has conducted with Thailand, Australia, and Philippines. As a start, the U.S.–Thailand bilateral exercise "Cobra Gold" also involved Singapore. Japan and eight other countries sent their observers to this exercise. This is a sign of hope for future regional training. This will enable countries in the region to have their respective forces ready for quick deployment in case of crisis within a short period of time. Such a mechanism, when built, can provide not only emergency relief but also deter potential conflicts.

This multilateral mechanism could eventually play a role in legitimizing intervention in an intra-state conflict when the UN cannot adopt a resolution. Some sort of multilateral agreement for intervention will allow countries in the region to overcome the question of internal jurisdiction when such operations are warranted. This scheme, however, must create certain criteria for intervention, instead of simply calling them humanitarian.

Peace operations in the twenty-first century will require operations other than peacekeeping and peace enforcement, as mentioned in the preceding section. Another path that Japan and the United States can explore together is civilian police activities in post-conflict areas, to maintain community security and safety. As was evident in the recent peace operations undertaken in Kosovo and East Timor, the rebuilding of a collapsed system of governance, particularly of the security system, is becoming a pressing issue in order to ensure peace and stability among local inhabitants rather than the traditional main tasks of PKO. While it is imperative for troops deployed to cope with these new tasks, it is a fact that the peacekeepers are not trained to carry out policing activities.

Also, it is now being recognized that in most countries there is a lack of civilian police personnel properly trained and available for such international activities. Future deployment of international civilian police will require an increase in the number and quality of skilled personnel. In order to shorten the time gap after a cease-fire and the actual deployment of civilian police as in the case of peacekeeping, advance basic training could be offered for those who are interested through the use of the Internet and other methods. In order to facilitate rapid deployment, trainees would need to receive briefings only on the problems specific to each mission before being sent out.

In the United States, Presidential Decision Directive 71 entitled "Strengthening Criminal Justice Systems in Support of Peace Operations" was issued in March 2000. Prior to this, on February 24, President Clinton stated, "PDD71 will improve America's ability to strengthen police and judicial institutions in countries where peacekeeping forces are deployed." In addition to peacekeepers, in light of the growing importance of the international civilian police in the postmodern PKO, the United States and Japan can cooperate in joint training of civilian police who will be dispatched for peace operations in the future. Also, a minimum level of foreign-language education will be needed. At the same time, civilian police personnel will have to be recruited from local governments and be provided with similar training and education. There is an urgent need to train civilian police personnel who will participate in international peace operations. This can also be extended to other interested countries in the region, to be developed as a regional civilian training mechanism. Since some advance training for future peacekeepers and civilian police would be common, the United States and Japan may find it cost-effective to combine these two trainings.

These two possible paths can be combined as a regional peace operations training center. There are other paths that the United States and Japan can cooperate in, such as preventive deployment, conflict prevention, and peace building. The two paths may lend itself to the creation of some regional governance for peace and stability through U.S.–Japan cooperation.

Notes

1. Fifty years of UNPKO, http://www.un.org/Depts/dpko/dpko/50web/2htm.
2. http://www.mofaj.
3. "Report of the Panel on United Nations Peace Operations," http://www.un.org/peace/reports/peace.operations/docs.
4. Marrack Goulding, "The Evolution of United Nations Peacekeeping," *International Affairs* (London), Vol. 69, No. 3 (July 1993), p. 452.
5. "Report of the Panel on United Nations Peace Operations," http://www.un.org/peace/reports/peace.operations/docs/summary.htm.
6. Gaiko Seisho 2000, pp. 75–82.
7. Nihon no Boei (Defense of Japan 2001), Boeicho, July 2001, p. 203.
8. As for Japanese debate over its participation in UNPKO and its constraints, please refer to Akiko Fukushima, *Japanese Foreign Policy: A Logic of Multilateralism* (Macmillan, 1999).
9. Ibid., pp. 78–89.
10. Ibid., pp. 54–58.
11. Ibid., pp. 58–65.
12. Ibid., pp. 58–65.
13. Shigeru Kosai, *Kokuren no Heiwa Iji Katsudo* (Yuhikaku, 1991), pp. 501–502.
14. Based on the interview with late Ambassador Shizuo Saito in 1996.
15. Takahiro Shinyo, ed., *Kokusai Heiwa Kyoryoku Nyumon* (Yuhikaku Sensho, 1995), pp. 177–178.
16. The so-called core activities include cease-fire monitoring, stationing in buffer zones, collection and disposition of abandoned weapons, monitoring demobilization, etc.
17. Masashi Nishihara and Serig Harrison, eds., *Kokuren PKO to Nichibei Anpo*, (Aki Shobo, Tokyo 1995), p. 153.
18. "Report of the Panel on United Nations Peace Operations," http://www.un.org/peace/reports/peace.operations/docs/summary.htm.
19. Takahiro Shinyo, ed., op. cit., pp. 193–196.
20. "PKF Toketsu Kaijo he," *Yomiuri Shimbun*, August 19, 2001, p. 1.
21. Naikaku Souri Daijin Kanbo Kohoshitsu, "Jieitai Bouei Mondai ni Kansuru Yoron Chosa," January 1991.
22. Naikaku Souri Daijin Kanbo Kohoshitsu, "Jieitai Bouei Mondai ni Kansuru Yoron Chosa," February 1994.
23. Naoto Nonaka, "PKO Kyoroku Hoan wo Meguru Kokunai Seiji Katei to Nihon Gaiko," *Kokuren Kaikaku to Nihon* (Nihonkeizaikyougikai, 1994), p. 50.
24. "Boei Shishin Minaoshi: Yuji Taiou Takamaru Ishiki," *Yomiuri Shimbun*, September 7, 1997, p. 18.
25. "21 seiki nihonjin no ishiki: Kenpo kaisei sansei sedaikoe Shinto," *Yomiuri Shinbun*, April 5, 2001, p. 12.
26. Nishihara and Harrison, op. cit., p. 116.
27. Ibid.

28. Ibid., pp. 204–215.
29. Masashi Nishihara, "Trilateral Country Roles: Challenges and Opportunities," in John Roper et al., *Keeping the Peace in the Post-Cold War Era: Strengthening Multilateral Peacekeeping* (New York, Paris, and Tokyo: The Trilateral Commission, 1993), p. 64.
30. Nishihara and Harrison, op. cit., p. 13.

INDEX